100 THINGS CANADIENS FANS

SHOULD KNOW & DO BEFORE THEY DIE

100 THINGS
CANADIENS FANS
SHOULD KNOW & DO
BEFORE THEY DIE

Pat Hickey

TRIUMPH
B O O K S

Library of Congress Cataloging-in-Publication Data

Hickey, Pat, 1944–
  100 things Canadiens fans should know & do before they die / Pat Hickey.
    pages cm
  Includes webography.
  Includes bibliographical references.
  ISBN 978-1-62937-142-9
1. Montreal Canadiens (Hockey team)—History. 2. Montreal Canadiens (Hockey team)—Miscellanea.   I. Title. II. Title: One hundred things Canadiens fans should know and do before they die.
  GV848.M6H53 2015
  796.962'640971427—dc23

                                        2015019612

This book is available in quantity at special discounts for your group or organization. For further information, contact:
  Triumph Books LLC
  814 North Franklin Street
  Chicago, Illinois 60610
  (312) 337-0747
  www.triumphbooks.com

Printed in U.S.A.
ISBN: 978-1-62937-142-9
Design by Patricia Frey
Photos courtesy of Getty Images unless otherwise indicated

For my long-suffering wife, Joan; my daughters,
Kathleen and Alex; my son, Simon; and my
amazing granddaughters, Aggie and CeCe.
And, of course, to Canadiens fans all over the globe.

Contents

Foreword *by Jacques Demers* xi

1 The Rocket's Red Glare 1

2 Buying Béliveau's League 6

3 The Innovator 8

4 The Richard Riot 11

5 No Respect for Boom Boom 15

6 Who Are the Habs? 18

7 He Couldn't Tell Them How Good They Were 19

8 Harvey Led the Rush 23

9 Cool as a Cucumber 26

10 Spend a Day at the Bell Centre 29

11 King of the One-Liners 32

12 The Rocket's Playmate 34

13 The Elusive Flower 36

14 Dryden's Career: Short and Very Sweet 39

15 Roy Made a Fiery Exit 42

16 The Entrepreneur 46

17 Koivu's Comeback 49

18 The Forum 52

19 The Roadrunner 55

20 Dr. Strangeglove 58

21 Join a Gang 61

22 Rocket's 50 in 50 63

23 A Home Waiting for a Winner 66

24 His Cups Runneth Over 68

25 Buy a Jersey or Two 71

26 The Old Lamplighter 73

27 The Senator. 75

28 The Battle of Quebec 78

29 Big Bird Landed with a Bang 80

30 The Clown Prince. 83

31 The Strongman 85

32 The Pregame Meal 88

33 A Family Business 90

34 The Bob Gainey Trophy. 95

35 The Greatest Game That Wasn't 97

36 Baby, It's Cold Outside. 99

37 Winning Was Everything to Blake 101

38 Jack of All Trades 104

39 Lemaire Was a Two-Way Guy 105

40 The Too Many Men on the Ice Game 107

41 The Farmer. 110

42 Go on a Road Trip 113

43 Pollock Stayed One Step Ahead 116

44 The Quiet Leader 120

45 The Mighty Atom. 123

46 The Scoring Machine 125

47 Giving Back 127

48 Big Jean's 500th 129

49 The Goal-Scorer 132

50 Early Days. 134

51 Who's Next in the Rafters? 137

52 The Ones Who Got Away. 139

53 A Good Bad Man 142

54 Pursuing Howie Morenz. 144

55 The Intimidator 146

56 A Tale of Two Gallys 149

57 Little George's Remarkable Season 151

58 The Semi-Conscious Goal. 154

59 The Defenceman's Defenceman 157

60 O Capitaine, Mon Capitaine, Bon Voyage 159

61 The Rocket Has Left the Building. 162

62 The Cannonball 164

63 Trader Sam 167

64 Play a Game at the Bell Centre. 169

65 Saving His Best for Last 171

66 The First Star 173

67 Too Much, Too Soon. 175

68 Hard Work Paid Off for Reardon. 178

69 Born to Be a Canadien 180

70 Toe Loses It. 184

71 The Torch. 187

72 The Price Is Right 189

73 Wickenheiser and Savard. 191

74 Picking the Wrong Guy 193

75 A Rivalry Like No Other. 195

76 Béliveau Passes the Torch to Dryden. 197

77 Age No Obstacle for Gardiner. 199

78 A Not-So-Good Friday 201

79 The Quotable Guy Lafleur 203

80 He Died of a Broken Heart. 206

81 Perfect Attendance. 209

82 The French Canadian Rule 211

83 The Brothers Mahovlich 212

84 Better Late Than Never. 216

85 Working Overtime 219

86 What If Dryden Had Been a Bruin? 221

87 Gainey's Pain. 222

88 The American 225

89 The Lost Art of Penmanship 228

90 Game Called on Account of Fire. 231

91 Dryden vs. Dryden 233

92 Nicknames 235

93 Danny Boy 238

94 The French Fact 240

95 The Canadien Way 242

96 The Cop on the Beat. 244

97 How Many Cups Have You Won? 247

98 Saving Trent McCleary 249

99 The Depth Player 252

100 Wait 'Til Next Year? 253

A Note on Sources 257

Bibliography 259

Foreword

Long before I dared to dream about coaching the Montreal Canadiens, I was a fan.

I grew up in the Côte-des-Neiges district, no more than 15 minutes from the Forum. I'd go there to watch the Junior Canadiens. I didn't go to Canadiens games because I couldn't afford the tickets but I followed the team on radio and a little bit on TV. My hero—and it's never changed—was Henri Richard, a little guy with a big heart.

To me, the Montreal Canadiens were everything when it came to sport.

I played hockey but I had no chance to play pro hockey, not even junior. I knew I wasn't good enough. Then I started coaching juvenile in St. Leonard and then Junior B with Chateauguay in the Richelieu League. We did well, and when the World Hockey Association came around, I was very fortunate because Marcel Pronovost, the late Hall of Fame defenceman, gave me a chance with the Chicago Cougars and I took full advantage of it. I moved to the Nordiques, and then came the merger. All of a sudden, I was coaching in the NHL in Quebec.

That was my dream, to coach in the NHL, and I moved around, coaching in St. Louis and Detroit. Then I had a chance to coach the Montreal Canadiens. I'm still not sure why it happened but—and this is not a cliché—it was a dream come true.

My parents were Canadiens fans and now their son was coaching the team. I was a French Canadian, raised in poverty, not much education, and here I was coaching this team with so much history.

This was the team of Jean Béliveau, Doug Harvey, and Rocket Richard. I didn't get to see all of them play but I knew them. Then came Guy Lafleur, Larry Robinson, Bob Gainey, all those guys. I felt very fortunate to get that opportunity.

I'm remembered today as the last Canadiens coach to win the Stanley Cup, and I look back to June 9, 1993, and I think of that as a beautiful gift.

But I have mixed feelings about being the last coach to win in Montreal.

It makes me feel good, and my ego is such that I didn't wish them well for the first couple of years after they let me go.

Today, I want the Montreal Canadiens to win again. I'm happy to be a part of the history. Not many coaches have won the Stanley Cup in Montreal. The team has won 24 Stanley Cups but Scotty Bowman and Toe Blake won most of them.

I want them to win for the Molson family. I worked for two of the best owners in the game, Mike Ilitch in Detroit and Geoff Molson's father, Eric, in Montreal.

And the fans deserve to see the team win. They can be critical at times, and the younger fans hear from their parents and their grandparents about the time when the Canadiens won five Stanley Cups in a row. I can see the passion when I travel around Quebec and everywhere I go, there are Canadiens fans. I went to London on Senate business, and when they found out I was a former coach of the Canadiens, people wanted to talk about the team.

People often ask me how it feels to be the last coach to win a Stanley Cup in Montreal and I hope that, in the near future, I won't have to answer that question again.

—Jacques Demers

1 The Rocket's Red Glare

Ask people about their memories of Rocket Richard and they will inevitably mention his eyes.

"When he came flying toward you with the puck on his stick, his eyes were all lit up, flashing and gleaming like a pinball machine," recalled Hall of Fame goaltender Glenn Hall. "It was terrifying."

Maurice Richard was the greatest goal-scorer of his era, a symbol of strength and power. These qualities—and those glaring eyes—appear evident in the stock photos which show Richard barrelling toward the camera, but the reality is that Richard's greatest quality was his determination.

He was not an imposing figure. He was 5-foot-10 and weighed 160 pounds when he made his NHL debut and he never weighed more than 180 pounds during his playing days. He didn't play organized hockey until he was 14, and the Canadiens front office once gave up on him because they thought he was too fragile.

As a 19-year-old, he joined the Montreal Royals, the Canadiens' affiliate in the Quebec Senior Hockey League, but he broke his left ankle in his first game. The following season, he broke his wrist, and his rookie season with the Canadiens in 1942–43 ended after 16 games when he broke his right ankle.

The Canadiens weren't the only ones who had doubts about his health. He tried to enlist in the Canadian military during World War II and was rejected twice for medical reasons. On the second occasion in 1942, X-rays showed that Richard's broken bones had not healed properly and his ankle was deformed, forcing him to change his skating style.

Tommy Gorman, the Canadiens' general manager, was convinced that Richard would never succeed in the NHL and removed his name from the team's reserve list.

Frank Selke, who would be Richard's boss for most of his career, was the interim GM in Toronto at the time and he noted that the Canadiens might have lost the future superstar.

"It was a chance for all the other managers in the NHL to show their acumen by picking Richard for free—as Detroit did some years later when youthful (Gordie) Howe was cut adrift by New York," noted Selke. "None of us were smart enough, however; we all went along with Gorman's analysis."

But Canadiens coach Dick Irvin thought that Richard had potential and convinced Gorman to give him another chance.

Irvin installed the lefty-shooting Richard at right wing on a line with Toe Blake and Elmer Lach and they became known as the Punch Line. The decision to use Richard on the "wrong" wing stemmed from a suggestion by Paul Haynes, a former Canadiens player who was once cut by Irvin because he skipped a team event in New York to attend the opera.

Haynes coached Richard with the Royals and felt he would have more scoring chances if he could move from the wing to the center of the ice. It also allowed Richard to take advantage of what Selke described as the "most devastating backhand" in the game.

The questions about Richard's durability resurfaced when he dislocated his shoulder early in the 1943–44 season. But Richard missed only four games and he led Montreal with 32 goals. He then scored a record 12 playoff goals as the Canadiens won their fifth Stanley Cup.

In the second game of the Stanley Cup semifinal against Toronto, Richard scored five goals against childhood friend Paul Bibeault to tie the NHL playoff record for most goals in a single game.

Maurice (Rocket) Richard was the first player in NHL history to score 50 goals in a season and led the Canadiens to eight Stanley Cups during his 18 seasons in Montreal.

Richard made history again the following season. On December 28, 1944, he had five goals and three assists in a 9–1 win over Detroit to set a single-game record of eight points. That mark would stand for 32 years before Toronto's Darryl Sittler had a 10-point game in 1976.

On February 25, 1945, he scored his 45th goal to break the single-season record of 44 set by the Canadiens' Joe Malone in 1918. He reached 50 goals in the final game of the 50-game season, beating Boston's Harvey Bennett at 17:45 of the third period. His mark of 50 goals in 50 games would not be matched until Mike Bossy of the New York Islanders achieved it in the first 50 games of the 1980–81 season.

Richard's critics would argue that the record was tainted because many players were overseas during World War II. But Richard had established himself as a superstar, a charismatic figure whose passion on the ice was balanced by an easygoing, retiring nature in his personal life.

Failure to Launch

Maurice Richard moved into the Canadiens' front office after he retired as a player but he was never happy with the move because he felt that he wasn't given any responsibility. He announced his resignation in August 1965 in his column in the French-language weekly *Dimanche-Matin*, saying: "It's no fun sitting behind a desk with nothing to do."

Richard had been given the title of vice-president but said it was never more than an honorary position.

"I never had time to do it justice," he wrote. "I would so much like to contribute constructively to the cause of the Canadiens but I was never more than a goodwill ambassador. I was never asked to a meeting behind closed doors, never asked for an opinion. I kept pace with the news the same way you did by reading the sports pages."

He said his main task was opening mail from fans looking for players' pictures.

He scored 45 goals in the 1946–47 season and won the Hart Trophy as the NHL's most valuable player. He was a 14-time All-Star. He was the leading goal-scorer in the league five times. He was the first player to reach 500 career goals and retired with a record 544 goals. He was part of eight Stanley Cup victories.

Richard's one regret was that he never won the Art Ross Trophy, which goes to the leading scorer in the NHL. Richard didn't place much value in assists—a teammate once noted that you would have a hard time getting Richard to pass the salt—and he felt the trophy should go to the player with the most goals. In 1999, the Canadiens presented the NHL with the Maurice (Rocket) Richard Trophy, which is awarded annually to the league's top goal scorer.

Richard did lead the scoring race in the 1954–55 season but his temper proved costly. Richard played with a fierce determination and when opponents attempted to slow him down with rough play, he often retaliated. This led to a running feud with NHL president Clarence Campbell, who fined and suspended Richard on numerous occasions. Richard produced a weekly column in a French-language newspaper and when he accused Campbell of an anti-French bias, he was forced to post a $1,000 good-behaviour bond.

During a March 13, 1955, game against Boston, Hal Laycoe hit Richard in the head with a stick and Richard retaliated with a vicious swing at Laycoe's head. When linesman Cliff Thompson tried to separate the combatants, Richard punched him. Campbell would suspend Richard for the remainder of the season and the playoffs, and that decision touched off what became known as the Richard Riot on St. Patrick's Day. Angry fans pelted Campbell with tomatoes and other objects and the game was abandoned. The riot spilled onto the streets where store windows were broken and fans clashed with police. With Richard on the sidelines, teammate Bernie Geoffrion passed him for the scoring title and Montreal lost to Detroit in a seven-game Stanley Cup final.

Richard went on radio the next morning to plead for calm and promised the fans that he would return the following season and lead the team to the Stanley Cup. He did just that as Richard and the Canadiens began a run which produced a record five consecutive championships. He retired after the last championship in 1960.

2 Buying Béliveau's League

The Canadiens had no difficulty identifying Jean Béliveau as a future superstar. But getting him into a Montreal uniform wasn't as easy.

When the 18-year-old Béliveau left his home in Victoriaville to play for the Quebec Citadelles junior team, he had a deal to play for the Canadiens but only when he turned professional.

As he established himself as a star in Quebec, first with the Citadelles and later with the Quebec Aces of the Quebec Senior Hockey League, Béliveau showed little interest in turning pro.

That's because Frank Byrne, who was a major figure in Quebec's pulp and paper industry, treated Béliveau like the superstar he was and, when he finished playing junior, he spurned an offer from the Canadiens and joined the Aces. Technically, the Aces were an amateur team, although Béliveau was paid $10,000 and enjoyed a number of perks. Businessmen in the city offered steak dinners and suits in return for hat-tricks.

The city's new arena, Le Colisée, was packed to the rafters during the two seasons Béliveau played for the Aces. There were 10,538 seats but the capacity was stretched with standing-room patrons. In Béliveau's first season with the Aces, the team drew 281,000 fans and the next season they drew 386,334 fans for 30 regular-season and six playoff games. One game drew 13,791 fans.

Along the way, Béliveau teased the Canadiens and the fans in Montreal. He had a two-game trial in the 1950–51 season and scored a goal and an assist. He returned in 1952–53 and scored five goals in three games, including a hat-trick against the New York Rangers.

Senator Donat Raymond, the owner of the Canadiens, had seen enough. A year earlier, Béliveau rejected an offer to join the Canadiens in favor of continuing his "amateur" career. But Raymond brought the reluctant Béliveau into the fold by buying the entire Quebec Senior Hockey League and turning it into a professional league. Béliveau had no choice but to turn pro and he signed a five-year contract with the Canadiens on October 3, 1953. He also began a long association with Molson Brewery, joining the company as a $10,000-a-year public relations man.

There was no surprise when Béliveau became an instant success in the NHL. Punch Imlach, who coached the Aces, said his only reservation was that Béliveau "will never reach his potential ability because the National Hockey League isn't good enough to bring it out."

Béliveau offered a counterpoint to the fiery Maurice Richard. The Rocket believed that the shortest distance between himself and the goal was a straight line. Toe Blake, who was Richard's teammate and coach, said the Rocket would do anything to score a goal.

The 6-foot-3 Béliveau was a more graceful player. He would score 507 regular-season goals but he also added 712 assists and is regarded as the best captain in the team's history.

"The thing about Jean is that he could size up a situation so well," Frank Mahovlich told *The Hockey News*. "I remember Jean's 500th goal. We were teamed with a young player named Phil Roberto, and Jean went to the net at just the right time to finish off one of the nicest three-way passing plays you'll ever see. That was Jean Béliveau. He had that vision and he could position everybody and set everybody up."

When Béliveau first broke into the league, he was subjected to some of the rough treatment which frustrated Richard over the years.

"I began to understand what he was going through," said Béliveau, who began to battle back. He collected more than 100 minutes in penalties in his third and fourth NHL seasons and opponents backed off.

Gordie Howe, who was known as a tough but fair competitor, said he had a great deal of respect for Béliveau:

"When I was coming in on him, I'd warn him by saying 'Big Jean, get ready because here I come.'"

The number that counted for Béliveau was the number of Stanley Cups he won. His name is on the Cup 10 times as a player and another seven times as a member of the Canadiens' front office.

Béliveau scored 79 playoff goals, which ranks 10th on the all-time list, and won the Conn Smythe Trophy as the most valuable player in the Stanley Cup playoffs when it was first presented in 1965. He won the Art Ross Trophy as the NHL's scoring leader in 1956 and was a two-time winner of the Hart Trophy as the league's most valuable player.

Béliveau retired after helping the team win the Stanley Cup in 1971. He remained with the team and the brewery in a variety of capacities until his death in 2014.

3 The Innovator

Goaltenders have a reputation for being different, and no goaltender fit that description better than Jacques Plante.

But Plante, who was a dominant goaltender over nearly two decades, was also an innovator who literally changed the face of the game. He was the first goaltender to wear a mask on a regular basis. He was one of the first goaltenders to leave his crease to play the puck. He introduced the practice of raising his arm to alert his teammates when icing was going to be called, and he constantly shouted instructions to his teammates.

Ken Dryden once said, there were great goaltenders but Plante was an *important* goaltender.

Plante's choice of position was dictated by his health. He was diagnosed with asthma when he was a child and he was unable to skate for prolonged periods. He began playing outdoors in his hometown of Shawinigan and his mother taught him to knit toques to protect himself from the cold. Plante continued knitting throughout his life and said it provided a relief from the stress of playing in goal.

Plante began playing for his high school team when he was 12 and two years later he was playing for five different teams, including a local factory team which paid him 50 cents a game. He had offers to move but his mother insisted that he finish high school. After graduating with honours in 1947, he joined the Quebec Citadelles, who paid him $85 a week.

It wasn't long before Plante caught the eye of Canadiens general manager Frank Selke, who signed Plante to play for the Montreal Royals. He received $4,500 and an extra $500 to serve as the Canadiens' practice goaltender. He made his NHL debut in January 1953 when Gerry McNeil was out with a broken jaw and he was immediately involved in a controversy.

Coach Dick Irvin Sr. was a stickler for proper dress on the ice and didn't approve of Plante's handmade toques. The toques disappeared but not before Plante made an impression by allowing only four goals in three starts. Later that season, he shut out the Chicago Blackhawks in his first NHL playoff game. He had a 3–1 record in the playoffs and had his name engraved on the Stanley Cup for the first time.

Plante would spend most of the next two seasons with the Buffalo Bisons of the American Hockey League, where he became a fan favourite. He revolutionized the game—and upset some tradition-bound coaches—by leaving his crease to play loose pucks or by going behind the net to stop pucks and then passing to his defencemen. He paved the way for goaltenders like Martin Brodeur, Tom Barrasso, and Patrick Roy.

While Canadiens coach Toe Blake wasn't entirely comfortable with Plante's happy feet, the two went to the mat over Plante's decision to wear a mask. He initially wore it in practice but he insisted on wearing it in games after he was hit in the face by a shot from the Rangers' Andy Bathgate on November 1, 1959. He did take it off for a game in January but he appeared uncomfortable and Blake reluctantly accepted that the mask was there to stay.

Plante spent nine full seasons with the Canadiens and was part of six Stanley Cup–winning teams, including five in a row from 1956 to 1960. He won the Vézina Trophy as the NHL's top goaltender in each year during the five-season run and added a sixth Vézina in the 1961–62 season. He also won the Hart Trophy that season as the NHL's most valuable player.

Jean Béliveau offered this assessment of Plante in his autobiography: "I rate him and Terry Sawchuk as the best goalies I've ever seen with Ken Dryden, Glenn Hall, Bernie Parent, and Patrick Roy on the next rung down."

Plante was traded to the New York Rangers in 1963 as part of a multiplayer trade which brought Gump Worsley to Montreal. Plante found himself backing up a very bad Rangers team and retired after two seasons of what Béliveau described as "rubber therapy."

Tired of dealing with stress and a worsening asthma condition, Plante retired to Quebec City, where he worked as a salesman for a brewery. But his competitive juices began flowing after he agreed to play for the Junior Canadiens in a game against the Soviet national team at the Forum on December 15, 1965. Plante made 25 saves as the Junior Canadiens upset the Russians 2–1. The junior roster included future NHL general managers Serge Savard and Larry Pleau as well as Carol Vadnais, Robin Burns, Norm Ferguson, Noel Picard, and Jacques Lemaire.

The expansion California Seals offered him a tryout in 1967 but his comeback was blocked by the Rangers. The St. Louis Blues secured his rights the following season and he helped them reach the Stanley Cup final in 1968 and 1969—the Blues lost to the Canadiens on both occasions—and he shared the 1969 Vézina Trophy with teammate Glenn Hall.

Plante would play four more years with stops in Toronto and Boston before a final season with Edmonton in the WHA.

During his second retirement, he worked as an analyst on television and wrote extensively about the game. His 1972 book, *Goaltending*, is still used today as a guide to developing and training goaltenders.

Plante spent the last decade of his life in Switzerland and died in February 1986 after being diagnosed with stomach cancer. He was elected to the Hockey Hall of Fame in 1978 and the Canadiens retired his No. 1 in 1995.

4 The Richard Riot

The darkest day in Canadiens history was March 17, 1955, the night of the Richard Riot.

The immediate cause of the disturbance was NHL president Clarence Campbell's decision to suspend Maurice Richard for the final three games of the regular season and the playoffs following an incident in Boston on March 13. Richard was frequently the target of taunts and rough play from opponents determined to throw him off his game, and the Rocket was just as likely to retaliate. Hal Laycoe, a former Canadien and Richard's frequent tennis partner, high-sticked Richard in the head, opening a five-stitch gash. The play continued on the delayed penalty but, when a whistle stopped the action, Richard hit Laycoe in the face and shoulders with his stick. The linesmen grabbed Richard but he broke free and continued his attack until he broke his stick on Laycoe's body.

Linesman Cliff Thompson grabbed Richard but The Rocket punched Thompson in the face twice, knocking the official unconscious. The Boston police tried to arrest Richard but the Montreal players barred the dressing room door and Bruins officials assured the police that the NHL would deal with Richard.

Richard was summoned to the NHL head office in Montreal on March 16 for a hearing conducted by Campbell.

Richard and Campbell had butted heads on numerous occasions. When Bernie Geoffrion was suspended a year earlier, Richard had used his weekly newspaper column to call Campbell a dictator. The league forced him to retract his criticism and stop writing. Three months before the Laycoe incident, Richard was fined $250 for slapping a linesman.

Richard argued that he was dazed and didn't realize he was hitting the linesman, but Campbell said the attack on Laycoe "was not only deliberate but persisted in the face of all authority" and that he did not believe that Richard struck Thompson as the result of a mistake or an accident. He suspended Richard for the remainder of the season and the playoffs.

The suspension was the longest handed out by Campbell in his 31 years as NHL president and Montreal fans were outraged. The NHL office was deluged with calls from fans and Campbell received death threats. But Campbell said he wouldn't back down and announced his intention to attend the March 17 game against the Detroit Red Wings at the Forum despite Mayor Jean Drapeau's suggestion that it might be more prudent to stay at home.

In the hours leading up to the game, a crowd had assembled in Cabot Square across the street from the arena. They shouted anti-Campbell slogans and offered their support for Richard. The crowd, estimated at 6,000, was well behaved until a small group tried to force its way into the Forum. The mood turned angry when police intervened and fans began breaking windows.

The Canadiens were trailing 2–0 when Campbell arrived with three of his secretaries midway through the first period. He was booed by the crowd and some fans pelted him with eggs, tomatoes, and other debris. One fan eluded security by pretending to be Campbell's friend. When Campbell reached out to shake his hand, the fan slapped him and then threw a punch. Shortly after the attack, a tear-gas canister exploded. Fire chief Armand Paré ordered the evacuation of the building and the Red Wings were given the victory.

Wild in the Streets

While the Richard Riot has been an important part of Canadiens history, it wasn't the only time fans took to the streets.

There were disturbances after Montreal won the Stanley Cup in 1986 and again in 1993. The riot in 1993 followed a Game 5 win over Los Angeles and proved to be the most violent and the costliest. More than 160 people were injured and 110 were arrested as fans streamed down Ste. Catherine Street, burning cars and breaking store windows. Damage was estimated at $2.5 million.

One sign of diminishing expectations was a 2008 disturbance after the Canadiens eliminated Boston in the first round of the playoffs. Sixteen police cars were among the victims and damage was estimated at $500,000. A second-round playoff win over Pittsburgh was the excuse for a disturbance in 2010. A peaceful celebration turned ugly on this occasion, and the police believed that anarchists and common criminals used the victory as cover for mayhem. A Foot Locker store and a liquor outlet were the hardest hit by looters.

Many of the fans leaving the Forum joined the demonstrators as they marched down Ste. Catherine Street, breaking shop windows, overturning cars, setting fire to newsstands, and clashing with police. Twelve policemen and 25 civilians were injured and reports estimate that 100 people were arrested. Damage was estimated at $100,000, more than $870,000 in 2015 dollars.

Richard went on radio the following day and pleaded for calm. He said he would accept his punishment and would return the following season to win the Stanley Cup, a promise he would keep.

There would be no Stanley Cup for Montreal in 1955. The forfeited game on St. Patrick's Day allowed Detroit to finish first and gain home-ice advantage in the playoffs. That would prove decisive in the Montreal-Detroit final. The Red Wings won in seven games and the home team won each game in the series.

The cultural and political significance of the Richard Riot has been the subject of debate over the years. In the days following the riot, journalist André Laurendeau suggested that the riot was a sign of growing nationalism in Quebec, Writing in the French-language daily *Le Devoir*, Laurendeau said the riot "betrayed what lay behind the apparent indifference and long-held passiveness of French Canadians."

The riot has been seen as a precursor of the Quiet Revolution, the cultural and political change which swept through Quebec in the 1960s and 1970s, but Richard was apolitical. In his book *The Rocket: A Cultural History of Maurice Richard*, University of Montreal professor Benoit Melançon argues that the riot solidified the Richard myth by overlooking some of Richard's less admirable character traits.

5 No Respect for Boom Boom

Bernie (Boom Boom) Geoffrion was the Rodney Dangerfield of hockey—he never felt he received enough respect for his achievements on the ice.

Everyone remembers that Maurice (Rocket) Richard was the first NHL player to score 50 goals, but how many people remember that Geoffrion was the second player to reach that magic number?

Geoffrion had the misfortune to be playing in an era with some of hockey's greatest players and he was often overshadowed by Gordie Howe, Andy Bathgate, and teammates Richard and Jean Béliveau.

Geoffrion won the Art Ross Trophy as the NHL's leading scorer in 1955 but was disappointed when Richard was selected as a first-team All-Star right winger and Geoffrion was relegated to the second team.

And the fans in Montreal weren't pleased because of the circumstances surrounding Geoffrion's scoring title. The immensely popular Richard was the leading scorer when he became involved in a battle with Boston's Hal Laycoe in Boston. During the melee, Richard punched an official and NHL president Clarence Campbell suspended the Rocket for the final three games of the regular season and the entire playoffs.

With Richard on the sidelines, Geoffrion scored a goal in the final home game of the season on March 19 to claim the scoring title. The fans booed Geoffrion and continued to jeer him through the playoffs.

"I couldn't deliberately *not* score, that isn't the point of hockey, Montreal," said Geoffrion, who said the boos made him physically sick. "I was feeling the urge to vomit. Even thinking about hockey made me feel ill. Man, did I want to leave."

Geoffrion said that Richard and Béliveau talked him out of quitting but he was disappointed again when he was passed over for the first All-Star team.

"Usually, it's not too much to expect to be on the first team when you have more points than anyone else," said Geoffrion.

Geoffrion did collect a lot of hardware in 1961 when he became the second player to score 50 goals in a season, took the league scoring title, won the Hart Trophy as the league's most valuable player, and finally earned that first-team All-Star recognition.

But the proud Geoffrion felt overlooked a few months later when Béliveau was named captain of the team, replacing defence-man Doug Harvey, who had been traded to the New York Rangers.

A Family Affair

The Geoffrions' association with the game of hockey spanned generations. Bernie Geoffrion's wife, Marlene, was the daughter of Hall of Famer Howie Morenz, whose No. 7 was the first number retired by the Canadiens, on November 2, 1937. When Geoffrion's number was retired in 2006, his son Bob said that when Geoffrion was playing for the Canadiens, he pointed to the Morenz banner in the Montreal Forum and told Marlene that his number would someday hang from the rafters beside her father's banner. Bernie Geoffrion's son, Danny, played for the Canadiens in 1979–80 and Danny's son, Blake, became a fourth-generation Canadien when he was traded from Nashville to Montreal on February 17, 2012. Blake, who decided to honour his great-grandfather and grandfather by wearing No. 57, played only 13 games for Montreal. His career was cut short when he suffered a depressed skull while playing for the Hamilton Bulldogs at the Bell Centre on November 9, 2012. Jean-Philippe Coté sent Geoffrion sprawling with a hip check and Geoffrion's head caught the end of Coteé's skate blade.

Geoffrion said that the snub was a factor in his decision to retire in 1964. He felt that he had demonstrated his leadership by coming back from numerous injuries. His nose was broken six times, he stopped counting the number of stitches he received when he reached 400, and he had Harvey cut a cast off his leg so he could resume playing in the 1961 playoffs.

He also survived a life-threatening injury in 1958. He suffered a ruptured bowel when he was checked by teammate André Pronovost during a practice. He was released from the hospital in mid-February, three weeks after the surgery, and doctors advised him not to play again that season. But he returned for the playoffs and helped the Canadiens win a third consecutive Stanley Cup.

"If I didn't keep suffering all those terrible injuries and yet keep coming back, if I weren't fit to lead, would I have gotten the C and kept playing?" asked Geoffrion after his retirement. "Yes, I think I would. There were times when everybody kept telling me to quit. My doctor even told me I should stop playing but I came back."

Geoffrion came back to the NHL after a two-year hiatus, joining the New York Rangers in 1966, and he became the Rangers' head coach in 1968. He resigned after only 43 games because of stomach ulcers.

In 1972, he became the first coach of the expansion Atlanta Flames and took the team to its first playoff appearance in 1974. But health problems again forced him to quit midway through his third season.

He gave coaching one more shot when he was hired to coach the Canadiens in 1979. When he was hired, he described it as his dream job but the pressure got to him and he resigned midway through the season with a 15–9–6 record.

On October 15, 2005, the Canadiens announced that Geoffrion's No. 5 would be retired on March 11, 2006. Three days before the ceremony, Geoffrion was diagnosed with stomach cancer and he died in an Atlanta hospital 12 hours before his number was raised to the rafters at the Bell Centre.

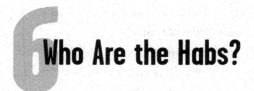

Who Are the Habs?

The nickname Habitants is almost as old as the Canadiens franchise itself.

The first reference to the term in the press occurred on February 9, 1914, when the newspaper *Le Devoir* used the term to describe the players. The paper seemed to take its inspiration from the Canadiens fans of the day who distinguished themselves from the fans of the rival Wanderers by wearing a traditional costume consisting of a wool toque, an arrow sash, and native moccasins.

Over the years, there has been confusion about whether the H in the team's CH logo stood for habitant. But when the term was first used, the Canadiens were known as the Club Athletique Canadien and their sweaters bore the letters CAC. The A was replaced by the H in the 1916–17 season when the full name of the team was changed to the Club de hockey Canadien.

Fans identified with the term habitant, which referred to early French settlers of the 17th and 18th century. Most of the fans at that time were descended from these pioneers, men and women who turned the forests of Quebec into productive farms. Many were anxious to hold on to the romantic notion of a simple rural life even as Quebec was undergoing a change to a less agrarian economy.

7 He Couldn't Tell Them How Good They Were

Mario Tremblay says he was among the many Canadiens who didn't like Scotty Bowman, but he concedes that the legendary coach was the right man at the right time.

"We needed him," said Tremblay. "We had so much talent on that team but we needed somebody to push us. If we had another coach, we might have gotten lazy. You couldn't relax with Scotty. He always pushed the right buttons to make you a better hockey player. You didn't always like it but when you won all those Stanley Cups, you appreciated what he did."

Bowman won the Stanley Cup five times in his eight seasons as coach of the Canadiens. Over that span, he coached 13 players who were elected to the Hockey Hall of Fame but, as good as they were, he pushed them to be better.

Long after his departure from the Canadiens, Bowman would say that his one regret was that "I couldn't tell those guys how good they were."

"To me, Scotty was always about the small details," said Murray Wilson, who was a part of four Stanley Cup teams. "We had simple practices, nothing complicated and everything game-related. If you looked at it, you would think it was a peewee practice. Passes back and forth, tape-to-tape and (assistant coach) Claude Ruel was always around to make sure it was done right. If you didn't do it right, you would do it again and Scotty would be there chewing on his ice and watching every detail.

"(Doug) Risebrough and Tremblay would go down the ice and Mario couldn't pass the puck to save his life. He could slap it good but he'd miss the pass and everyone would stop and start all over.

Canadiens Jack Adams Award Winners
Scotty Bowman   1977
Pat Burns   1989

And when we finally did it right and we thought we were good, Scotty made us do it backhand."

Bowman was an innovator. He pioneered the idea of morning skates on game days and introduced testing and cross-training.

"We'd do things like the long jump and the vertical leap," said Wilson. "One day, he took us to the pool at the YMCA and it was six and a half feet at one end and it was a foot over Henri Richard's head and he didn't know how to swim. He said: 'Where does it say in my contract I have to swim?' He got out and never came back.

"He brought a psychologist in and you heard snoring and Frank Mahovlich is sound asleep. At one point, Henri got up and left, saying: 'I can't understand a word he's saying but I know I can still play hockey.'"

Bowman took a dim view of players breaking the rules. Wilson recalls his first training camp in Halifax.

"Chuck Arnason and I were being sent down to the AHL and on our last night with the Canadiens, we found a house party in Halifax, which is a great college town," said Wilson. "It was late when we left and Arny grabbed a 12-pack of beer and we went back to the hotel. We were on the third floor and we got in the elevator and Scotty gets on at the second floor. We went right to our room, packed our bags, and went right to the airport. We didn't want to face Scotty in the morning."

On one road trip, when he was coaching the St. Louis Blues, Bowman gave the night doorman at the hotel in Detroit a hockey stick and suggested that he get the players to sign it. The next morning, the signatures on the stick provided Bowman with evidence of which players missed curfew.

Scotty Bowman guided the Canadiens to five Stanley Cups in the 1970s. He remains the winningest head coach in NHL history, with 1,244 regular-season victories and 223 more in the Stanley Cup playoffs.

"It cost me $60 but I got six guys for $100 apiece," recalled Bowman. "Doug Harvey was with us, he wasn't drinking then, and he thought I should have fined them $200."

Bowman was a promising forward with the Junior Canadiens but his playing career ended when Trois-Rivieres defenceman Jean-Guy Talbot hit him over the head in a playoff game and fractured his skull. Frank Selke arranged for Bowman to coach a midget team and he quickly rose in the Canadiens organization.

Bowman didn't harbour any ill feelings toward Talbot and he coached the defenceman for three seasons in St. Louis.

In 1958, he won a Memorial Cup title with the Ottawa-Hull Junior Canadiens, who were managed by Sam Pollock. When expansion arrived, Bowman was hired as an assistant coach with the St. Louis Blues and he became the head coach when Lynn Patrick stepped down after only 16 games.

Bowman led the Blues to the Stanley Cup final in three consecutive years and Pollock brought him home to coach the Canadiens in 1971–72.

The Canadiens had won four consecutive Cups when Bowman quit in 1979. Pollock was leaving as general manager and Bowman was unhappy that he was passed over for the GM job, which went to businessman Irving Grundman. Bowman joined the Buffalo Sabres as coach and general manager.

Bowman would win one Stanley Cup in Pittsburgh and three more in Detroit to surpass Toe Blake's record total of eight Cup wins. But Bowman shies away from comparisons with Blake, noting that they coached in different eras.

Harvey Led the Rush

Bobby Orr is generally recognized as the best defenceman in NHL history, but it was Doug Harvey who paved the way for Orr and other offensive-minded defencemen.

Before Orr played a single minute in the NHL, Harvey won the Norris Trophy as the NHL's top defenceman seven times in an eight-year span from 1955 to 1962. Harvey would have made it eight in a row but injuries hampered him in the 1958–59 season and the award went to teammate Tom Johnson. His last Norris Trophy in 1962 came when he was a player-coach with the New York Rangers.

"He changed the game," said teammate Bernie Geoffrion.

Harvey revolutionized the game by refining the role of the puck-moving defenceman, using his skating and passing skills to produce offence. He was at his best as the quarterback on a power play that was so effective the NHL had to change its rules.

Prior to 1956, a player receiving a minor penalty had to stay in the box for the entire two minutes, even if a goal was scored. It wasn't unusual for the Canadiens to score twice during a power play but, on November 5, 1955, the power play, with Harvey and Johnson at the points, and Jean Béliveau, Bert Olmstead, and Maurice Richard up front, produced three goals while enjoying a 5-on-3 advantage. Béliveau scored all three goals in a 44-second span, which stands as the fastest hat-trick in Canadiens history.

At the end of the season, the NHL revised its rules, allowing a player to return to the ice after a goal was scored. The vote was 5–1 with the Canadiens voting against the change.

Veteran sportswriter Red Fisher said it was difficult not to like Harvey's performance on the ice and said the Montreal native "was

Montreal's Norris Trophy Winners

Doug Harvey	1955, 1956, 1957, 1958, 1960, 1961
Tom Johnson	1959
Jacques Laperriere	1966
Larry Robinson	1977, 1980
Chris Chelios	1989
P.K. Subban	2013

the NHL's best defenceman of his time and ranks all-time behind only Bobby Orr. Harvey was an integral part of six Stanley Cup–winning Canadiens teams, blessed as he was with the uncanny talent of either speeding up a game or putting the brakes on it. He controlled its pace more than any of the great stars who were part of the record five consecutive Cups the Canadiens won in the second half of the '50s."

Fisher recalled a night in New York when the team was down to two healthy defencemen and pressed forward Murray Balfour into service on the blueline. Harvey was among the ailing players but he would be on the ice for 51 minutes and the Canadiens went home with a 3–1 win. X-rays later revealed that he had a cracked bone in his ankle.

But Harvey was a source of frustration for general manager Frank Selke. In an era when players didn't question contract offers, Harvey was a tough negotiator. He would often wait until the last minute before signing, usually upping the ante before doing so.

Harvey incurred Selke's wrath when he became involved in the first attempts to form a players association. He and Detroit's Ted Lindsay were among those who were upset that the NHL hadn't lived up to its promise to match the players' contributions to a pension plan. The league fought the association and many of the players involved with the new group were traded or sent to the minors. Lindsay, who was the association's president, went from Detroit to Chicago in 1957 but the Canadiens held on to

Harvey until 1961, when they traded him to the Rangers for Lou Fontinato.

The Canadiens insisted that Harvey's involvement with the association was not a factor in the trade. Selke pointed to Harvey's declining play and age—he was 36—but Harvey was convinced that the trade was in retribution for his union activities.

"I was a first-team All-Star and I won the Norris that year," Harvey said. "You don't give away a player like that."

Harvey joined the Rangers as player-coach and proved that he was still a force by winning the Norris Trophy a seventh time. He was uncomfortable in the coaching role, though, and gave it up after one season.

In 1967, he was hired as a playing coach with the St. Louis Blues' farm team in Kansas City, and the Blues called him up to face the Canadiens in the Stanley Cup final.

He finished his playing career with the Blues in 1968–69, scoring two goals and 20 assists in 70 games as a 45-year-old.

He was inducted into the Hockey Hall of Fame in 1973 but, ever the free spirit, Harvey skipped the ceremony to go fishing.

Harvey battled alcoholism in his later years and lived in a converted railway car at Connaught Park racetrack, which was owned by Joe Gorman, the son of former Canadiens general manager Tommy Gorman.

The Canadiens retired his jersey in 1985 and gave him a job as a part-time scout, He was diagnosed with liver disease in 1988 and died on December 26, 1989, a week after his 65th birthday.

Cool as a Cucumber

Joe Cattarinich was the Canadiens' first goaltender but he scouted himself out of a job.

On February 17, 1910, the Canadiens travelled to Chicoutimi, a remote town 130 miles from Quebec City, to play a game against a local amateur team. The Montrealers were heavy favourites but they were unable to score against the local goaltender, Georges Vézina. Two months earlier, Vézina had shut out the Grand'Mere Seniors, who were preparing for the Allen Cup.

As Douglas Hunter points out in his history of goaltending, *A Breed Apart*, shutouts were rare in those days, akin to a no-hitter in baseball. There was only one shutout in the National Hockey Association's inaugural season in 1910–11 and when Vézina moved to the NHA, he didn't register a shutout until his third season.

Cattarinich was so impressed that he returned to Montreal and urged the team's management to offer Vézina a tryout even though it put his own job in jeopardy.

The Canadiens agreed but there was one problem—Vézina didn't want to leave Chicoutimi. He rejected the Canadiens' initial offer. The Canadiens returned to Chicoutimi in December and this time they convinced Vézina to come to Montreal along with his brother Pierre.

Pierre failed to make the team but Georges, who put on his first pair of skates when he was 16, signed a contract which paid him $800 a year. He made his debut with the Canadiens on December 31, 1910, and he would be the team's only goaltender until he collapsed during a game on November 28, 1925.

Hockey had been introduced to Chicoutimi by some McGill University graduates who were managers at Price Brothers, the pulp and paper company that was the major employer in the area. The company built the town rink and Vézina first played in boots, like many of his friends.

His father, an immigrant from France who was the town baker, bought the rink and Georges donned skates so that he could play for the local team. There weren't any nearby towns and no league for the team so they barnstormed through Quebec playing games where they could be found.

Joining the Canadiens provided Vézina with a structure that was missing in Chicoutimi and he flourished even when the Canadiens didn't share in his success. He had the lowest goals-against average in the National Hockey Association in his first two seasons but his heroics couldn't prevent Montreal from finishing in last place in the 1911–12 season.

Things came together for Vézina and the Canadiens in the 1915–16 season. Vézina had the second-best goals-against average behind Clint Benedict and Didier Pitre and Newsy Lalonde provided the offence as Montreal won its first Stanley Cup. The Canadiens defeated the Portland Rosebuds of the Pacific Coast League 3–2 in the challenge series for the Cup.

The day after winning the Cup, the Canadiens headed to Chicoutimi to play an exhibition game and Vézina had an added incentive to go home. On the night the Canadiens won the Cup,

A Family Man

One of the enduring myths surrounding Georges Vézina was that he fathered 22 children, including two or three sets of triplets. The story began when Leo Dandurand, one of the team's owners, told reporters that Vézina "speaks no English and has 22 children, including three sets of triplets, and they were all born in the space of nine years." The truth is that Vézina and his wife, Marie-Adélaide-Stella, had two sons. Jean-Jules was born in 1912 and Marcel Stanley was born the night the Canadiens won their first Stanley Cup in 1916.

his wife gave birth to their second son. He commemorated the occasion by naming the youngster Marcel Stanley.

Vézina was a quiet man on and off the ice and his calm demeanor earned him the nickname the Chicoutimi Cucumber.

Hall of Famer Frank Boucher recalled facing Vézina in the 1924 Stanley Cup final.

"I remember him as the coolest man I ever saw, absolutely imperturbable," said Boucher. "He stood upright in his net and scarcely left his feet; he simply played all his shots in a standing position. Vézina was a pale, narrow-featured fellow, almost frail-looking, yet remarkably good with his stick. He picked off more shots with it than with his glove."

Vézina's frail appearance may have been due to the fact he was already suffering from tuberculosis.

Vézina played 15 seasons with the Canadiens and appeared in 328 consecutive games and 39 playoff games before his life came to a tragic end.

The Canadiens opened the 1925–26 season on November 25 against the Pittsburgh Pirates. After a scoreless first period, Vézina returned to the dressing room where he began coughing up blood and briefly lost consciousness. He returned for the second period but minutes later he collapsed and had to be carried from the ice. He had a temperature of 102 degrees and was experiencing chest pains. The original diagnosis was that he was on the verge of pneumonia. The following day, doctors told him he had tuberculosis.

He would return to the dressing room on December 3 and there were tears rolling down his face as he looked at the skates and other equipment which trainer Eddie Dufour had placed in his corner. Vézina asked owner Leo Dandurand if he could keep the sweater he wore when he won his second Stanley Cup in 1924. He tucked the sweater under his arm and left the Forum.

He returned to Chicoutimi and, on March 27, 1926, Vézina died at age 39.

His name lives on with the annual presentation of the Vézina Trophy, which recognizes the top goaltender in the league. Dandurand and Cattarinich donated the award, which was presented for the first time in 1927 to Vézina's successor in Montreal, George Hainsworth.

10 Spend a Day at the Bell Centre

Attending a game at the Bell Centre is always a special event but fans can enhance the experience by visiting the Canadiens Hall of Fame and by taking a tour of the Bell Centre.

There aren't many teams in any sport which can match the history of the Canadiens franchise and that history is reflected in the 10,000-square-foot hall, which showcases many unique items as well as interactive displays.

Up until expansion in the 1960s, most travel was done by train, and you can see a replica of the cars used to transport the team. There are tributes to the many Canadiens elected to the Hockey Hall of Fame, a display outlining the evolution of the team's uniform, and a life-size reproduction of the Canadiens dressing room.

The interactive displays include an opportunity to play reporter and interview the late Jean Béliveau.

You can visit the Hall of Fame as a separate experience or you can combine it with attendance at a game. The Hall of Fame is open every day except Monday and admission is $11 for adults, $8 for seniors, and $6 for youngsters age six to 16. A family of four costs $34. There are some special rates: if you have a ticket for the

The Bell Centre has been home to the Canadiens since the team moved there from the Montreal Forum in 1996.

game, admission to the Hall is $6, and the museum is reserved for ticket holders during the 90 minutes preceding the game.

There are also two specials tied to the club's history. On the ninth of each month, the team celebrates Maurice (Rocket) Richard's legacy and adult tickets are $9 and include an 8x10 photo of Richard.

On the 24th of each month, the Hall offers family tickets for $24, a $10 discount, and throws in a photo of Patrick Roy.

Fans can also add a guided tour of the Bell Centre for an additional $6.

There will be occasions when tours are not available because of security around concerts and other events in the arena and it's advisable to call ahead. You should also be aware that backpacks and bags are not permitted in the Bell Centre at any time and there are no checking facilities.

If you're looking for tickets to a game, the best advice is to plan ahead. Single-game tickets go on sale on the first of the month and the key is to get online as soon as they are available.

The Canadiens have followed the lead of other teams and have established a resale site for season-ticket holders who don't plan to use their seats. There is one difference between the Canadiens site and those maintained by most other teams. Occasionally, you can find a bargain on other sites but the Canadiens don't allow sellers to offer seats at below the face value. That might explain why the site is called The Vault.

There are usually tickets available on StubHub or Craigslist and you can find scalpers outside the arena. If there isn't a huge demand for a game, there is the possibility that a scalper will reduce his price close to game time rather than get stuck with the tickets. This strategy is not in play when the Canadiens are playing teams such as the Bruins, Maple Leafs, or Penguins.

If you're looking for a cheap thrill, Canadiens practices are open to the public at the Bell Sports Complex, which is located in Brossard, about a 10-minute drive from downtown Montreal unless there's congestion on the Champlain Bridge.

11 King of the One-Liners

Gump Worsley was once asked how he was elected to the Hockey Hall of Fame after a career in which he lost more games than he won.

"Do you know how good you have to be to lose 352 games?" he replied.

Worsley's NHL career ran from the 1952–53 season, when he won the Calder Trophy as the outstanding rookie in the NHL with the New York Rangers to 1974, when he announced his retirement after finishing his career with the expansion Minnesota North Stars.

The Montreal native had only two winning seasons in New York before he was traded to the Canadiens in 1963. He was alternately loved and hated by the fans at Madison Square Garden who ignored his given name of Lorne in favor of Gump. It was the name a high school friend gave him because of his resemblance to the comic-strip character Andy Gump.

Worsley looked like a comical figure on the ice. He was only 5-foot-7 and his bulky pads gave him a roly-poly appearance. When Rangers coach Phil Watson suggested he had a beer belly, Worsley said, "Just to show you what he knows—I only drink Johnnie Walker Red."

When he was down on the ice, he would often lie across the crease with his pads stacked, leading to the expression "stacking the Gumpers."

The Rangers weren't very good for most of Worsley's nine-season tenure in New York and he often faced 40 to 50 shots a night. They made the playoffs four times and lost in the first round on every occasion. When a New York reporter once asked him which team gave him the most trouble, he replied: "The Rangers."

In his book *Open Net*, George Plimpton noted that objects thrown at Worsley during his career included "eggs, beer, soup cans, marbles, an octopus, rotten fish, light bulbs, ink bottles, a dead turkey, a persimmon, a folding chair, and a dead rabbit."

"The only job worse than being a goalie is being the javelin catcher on a track team," said Worsley.

But when he was asked about the dangers in his profession, he would answer, "It beats carrying a lunchbox."

Worsley's career took a turn for the better when he was traded to the Canadiens on June 4, 1963. The Rangers were unhappy with Worsley's involvement in attempts to form a players' union. He spent most of his first two seasons with the Quebec Aces but he was called up by the Canadiens for the 1964–65 season and won the first of four Stanley Cups.

He shared the Vézina Trophy with Charlie Hodge in 1966 and with Rogie Vachon in 1968 when Worsley led the NHL with a 1.98 goals-against average.

But it was the playoff performances in Montreal which earned Worsley his spot in the Hall of Fame. He posted a 29–7 record with a 1.91 goals-against average.

Worsley and the Canadiens parted midway through the 1969–70 season. He was upset because Vachon was getting most of the starts and he quit when general manager Sam Pollock wanted to send him to the minors. He returned later in the season with the Minnesota North Stars.

Worsley was known for his eccentricities.

He was one of the last goaltenders to play without a mask and that led to an exchange with Jacques Plante, who pioneered the use of a mask.

"My face is my mask," said Worsley. "If goaltenders were afraid of being hit, they wouldn't be out there at all."

To which Plante responded: "If you jumped out of a plane without a parachute, would that make you brave?"

He'll Have the Usual

Lorne (Gump) Worsley was often kidded about his beer belly but when it came to alcoholic beverages, the Gumper had a preference for John Walker Red Scotch or Canadian Club rye whiskey.

Of course, getting on a plane was terrifying to Worsley and a parachute wouldn't have eased his fears. He suffered a nervous breakdown in 1968 after a bumpy flight to Los Angeles. When the plane touched down in Chicago, Worsley got off and took a train back to Montreal.

The Canadiens arranged for him to take time off and see a psychiatrist but Worsley returned to the team after he was told that the only cure was a change of professions.

12 The Rocket's Playmate

Maurice (Rocket) Richard became the first player in the NHL to score 50 goals in 50 games in the 1944–45 season, but he wasn't the league's most valuable player that season.

The honour went to Richard's linemate Elmer Lach, who led the league in scoring. He put up 80 points that season, including 54 assists, which was an NHL record. He assisted on 27 of Richard's goals, including the 50th on March 18, 1945.

While the details of that historic goal are sketchy—there's no videotape to consult—Lach may have done more than pass the puck to Richard. There's at least one report which suggests Lach created an opening for Richard by bumping into Boston goaltender Harvey Bennett.

Lach was the center on the legendary Punch Line with Richard and Toe Blake on his wings. In the four and a half seasons the line was together, it amassed more than 700 points, While he had an accurate shot and scored 215 goals in 664 games, Lach used his great vision to become the era's ultimate playmaker. He collected 408 assists and when he retired in 1954, he was the NHL's all-time assist leader (he had been the all-time points leader until Richard passed him that season).

Lach was also a strong defensive player. When *The Hockey News* rated the top 100 players of all time, it described Lach as the "defensive conscience" of the Punch Line.

He often sacrificed his body and his offensive numbers to help out on defence. He suffered a fractured skull but returned to win a second scoring title in 1947–48. A fractured leg prompted him to retire and the list of injuries he suffered is staggering. He broke his arm, he played through two broken jaws and hundreds of stitches, and his nose was broken seven times. The last broken nose was the result of a collision with Richard as the Canadiens celebrated their Stanley Cup victory in 1953.

Lach played only one game in his second season in 1941–42 because of the broken arm and the following season he rebounded with 58 points, one behind team leader Blake. He began that season on a line with Richard and Tony Demers, which was nicknamed the Broken Bone Line because all three had been injured the previous season. A healthy Richard joined Lach and Blake for the 1943–44 season.

"As a group, we were very good; individually we were just average hockey players," Lach told Dave Stubbs of the *Montreal Gazette* on the occasion of his 92nd birthday in 2010.

Lach, who grew up in Saskatchewan, once joked hockey was the worst job of his life. He was playing senior hockey in Moose Jaw when the team owner, Cliff Henderson, recommended him to Canadiens scout Paul Haynes. When he reported to the Canadiens' training camp, Lach thought his chances of making the team were slim and he arrived in camp with an overnight bag.

After his retirement, Lach coached the Montreal Junior Canadiens for one season and then spent two seasons coaching the Montreal Royals senior team. He left coaching to launch a successful business career. He also played golf into his nineties and often shot his age in his eighties.

Lach was inducted into the Hockey Hall of Fame in 1966. He was honoured on December 4, 2009, when the Canadiens raised his No. 16 to the rafters at the Bell Centre. The number had previously been retired in 1975 to honour Henri Richard. He passed away in 2015 at the age of 97.

13 The Elusive Flower

Guy Lafleur's longtime linemate Steve Shutt once remarked on the Flower's creativity by noting: "He's all over the ice and he has no idea what he's going to do, so how can I know?"

Opponents also had difficulty figuring out what Lafleur was going to do. In a six-season period from 1974–75 to 1979–80, Lafleur was the most dynamic offensive player in the NHL, averaging 55 goals and 128 points a season.

He was the first player to have six consecutive 50-goal seasons and six consecutive 100-point seasons. He was the youngest player to reach 400 goals and 1,000 points. He won three scoring titles and was a two-time winner of the Hart Trophy as the NHL's most valuable player.

Lafleur first burst on the scene as a peewee at the Quebec International Tournament and was a scoring star with the Quebec Remparts.

Canadiens general manager Sam Pollock made a couple of trades to ensure that Montreal would be able to select Lafleur with the No. 1 overall draft pick in 1971.

Lafleur had three decent seasons to start his NHL career but fans wondered whether he would ever live up to his predraft hype. The Canadiens traditionally brought even their star players along slowly and he watched some games from the press box. In 1974–75, he had a breakthrough with 53 goals and while he was given more playing time and some quality linemates—Steve Shutt and Peter Mahovlich—former Bruins coach Don Cherry is among those who believe that his transformation coincided with a decision to take off his helmet.

Lafleur was transformed into Le Démon Blond—the blond demon—with his locks flying in the breeze created by a rush up the ice.

"Guy has all the talent in the world," said Scotty Bowman, who coached Lafleur on five Stanley Cup teams. "He skates like a genius, he's puck-hungry in the best sense, and he'll go into the corners when he has to. But he's best in front of the net. I think the real secret of his success is his physical condition. It's amazing. We had the team tested two years back and Lafleur was in better shape than anyone else."

It was doubly amazing because Lafleur partied as hard as he played. He was a regular at Montreal's hottest clubs and teammates talked about Lafleur puffing on a cigarette in the minutes before a game.

The Canadiens dynasty ended with the 1979 Stanley Cup. Ken Dryden, Jacques Lemaire, and Yvan Cournoyer retired, and Bowman left to become coach and general manager of the Buffalo Sabres. Lafleur kept his streak alive in 1979–80 with 50 goals and

125 points but his numbers declined the following season when a knee injury limited him to 51 games.

On March 24, 1981, Lafleur was returning from a night on the town when he fell asleep at the wheel of his Cadillac and crashed into a highway fence. A metal post came through his windshield. It missed his head by inches, nicking off part of his ear.

The next three seasons were marked by a growing frustration. Lafleur's numbers were good but not up to his standards and the team wasn't winning Cups.

There was a run to the Eastern Conference final in 1984 when the Canadiens ran into the tail end of the New York Islanders dynasty but things changed drastically the following season. Lemaire was in his first full season as coach and installed a defence-first system. Lefleur was unhappy with his role and asked for a trade. General manager Serge Savard didn't want to be known as the man who traded a legend and refused the request. On November 24, 1984, Lafleur retired.

Lafleur was elected to the Hockey Hall of Fame in 1988 but a few days later he announced he was making a comeback with the New York Rangers. He explained that he never felt comfortable with the decision to leave the Canadiens and that it had been forced on him. He played one season with the Rangers and then came home to play two seasons with the Quebec Nordiques.

The skills were greatly diminished but Lafleur seemed happy to be playing and, when he retired after the 1990–91 season, he said, "I know it sounds strange but I made this comeback so I can have a nice retirement."

Lafleur, whose No. 10 was retired on February 16, 1985, is the Canadiens' all-time leading scorer with 1,246 points.

14 Dryden's Career: Short and Very Sweet

Ken Dryden's career as the Canadiens' goaltender began and ended with hockey's ultimate prize—the Stanley Cup.

Dryden joined the Canadiens after winning a remarkable 76 of 81 starts at Cornell University. He played one season for Canada's national team but joined the Canadiens organization in 1970 after they agreed to let him pursue a law degree at McGill University while he played for the Montreal Voyageurs, the Canadiens' American Hockey League farm team. The Canadiens decided to take a look at him late in the season and his performance changed the history of the franchise.

Rogie Vachon, who had led the Canadiens to the Stanley Cup in 1969, was the No. 1 goaltender but the untested Dryden got the call in the playoffs after going 6–0 in the regular season with a 1.65 goals-against average. The Boston Bruins were the defending champions and were favoured to repeat but the Canadiens prevailed in seven games. They went on to eliminate Minnesota in six games and defeat Chicago in a seven-game final. Dryden won the Conn Smythe Trophy as the playoff MVP, a full year before he collected the Calder Trophy as the rookie of the year. It's a feat which is unlikely to be duplicated.

You won't find Dryden's name on the list of goaltenders with the most wins or shutouts because his career was relatively short. But he put together an impressive resume in seven-plus seasons. He won the Stanley Cup six times, won the Vézina Trophy as the top goaltender five times, and was named to the first All-Star team five times and the second All-Star team once.

Dryden played 397 regular-season games and had a .790 winning percentage with 258 wins, 57 losses, and 74 ties. He had a

2.24 goals-against average. He added 80 wins and 32 losses in the playoffs with a 2.40 GAA.

But Dryden viewed hockey as only a temporary part of his life and he walked away from the game twice. After leading the leading the Canadiens to a second Stanley Cup in 1973, he became embroiled in a contract dispute with general manager Sam Pollock, who wasn't accustomed to having to fight players over money.

Ken Dryden made the most of his relatively short eight-year hockey career, winning six Stanley Cups and five Vézina Trophies.

Always Saving Something

Ken Dryden was known for his thriftiness and *Montreal Star* sports columnist Red Fisher witnessed it one night when Dryden offered him a ride home after a road trip. Dryden's wife, Lynda, picked them up at the airport and informed Dryden that they were low on gas.

"Dryden went to the gas station on the way out of the airport and asked the attendant for $2 worth," recalled Fisher. "I offered to give him some money if he was short but he explained that would be enough to get home and that gas was cheaper in the city."

Dryden held out for an entire season but he kept busy. He completed the requirements for his law degree by working as an articling student at a law firm.

The Canadiens had a decent season with Wayne Thomas as the No. 1 goaltender but lost in the first round of the playoffs. Pollock and Dryden were able to reach an agreement for the following season and Dryden was a key member of the team which won four consecutive Stanley Cups from 1976 to 1979.

Dryden walked away from the game a second time after the 1979 win.

In his book *The Game*, Dryden said he realized that it was time to move on with his life. He told Pollock before the 1978–79 season that he planned to retire and he resisted the team's efforts to change his mind.

"I have not enjoyed this year very much but it has been a necessary year," wrote Dryden. "If I had retired a year ago, I would have left with doubts. I have none now."

At 31, at the top of his game, Dryden walked away the same way he entered the game—on his own terms.

Dryden's post-hockey career reflects his varied interests. He wrote books, including *The Game*, an insightful look at the Canadiens' dynasty of the late 1970s which is considered a classic of sports literature. He produced another book after going back

Canadiens Calder Trophy Winners	
John Quilty	1941
Bernie Geoffrion	1952
Ralph Backstrom	1959
Bobby Rousseau	1962
Jacques Laperriere	1964
Ken Dryden	1972

to high school for a year and collaborated on a history of hockey which served as a companion for a documentary TV series.

He was elected to the Canadian Parliament and ran for the leadership of the Liberal Party. He was the president of the Toronto Maple Leafs, a return to hockey which was far less successful than his career as a player.

He was elected to the Hockey Hall of Fame in his first year of eligibility in 1983 and the Canadiens retired his No. 29 on January 29, 2007.

15 Roy Made a Fiery Exit

The night of December 2, 1995, marked a turning point in Canadiens history.

A very good Detroit team rolled into the Montreal Forum that night and lit up Patrick Roy, the team's franchise goaltender. The Red Wings scored five goals on 17 shots in the first period. It was obvious that this wasn't Roy's night but coach Mario Tremblay kept Roy in the game until the 11:57 mark of the second period. By that time Roy had given up four more goals and the Canadiens

Patrick Roy was arguably the greatest goaltender of his generation and a two-time Stanley Cup winner with the Canadiens before he was traded to Colorado in 1995.

were well on their way to an 11–1 drubbing, the worst loss in the franchise's history.

The crowd jeered the hero who had led the team to the Stanley Cup in 1986 and again in 1993 and Roy responded by throwing his arms into the air in mock celebration after making an easy save.

Here's the way Red Fisher described Roy's departure from the game in the *Montreal Gazette*:

"He walked into the small hallway leading to the Canadiens' room, rested his goalie stick among others already there, removed his gloves slowly, shrugged his shoulders, ran his hand through his hair, then walked leisurely toward the empty stool behind the bench. He got no more than one stride beyond a jut-jawed, tight-lipped, arms-folded Tremblay when it appeared a word or two was exchanged between the two. Roy then stopped suddenly, walked back several steps, and snapped off a couple of words to president Ronald Corey, who was sitting in his seat behind the bench. Then Roy turned again and clomped back to his stool."

Roy's message to Corey was simple.

"It's my last game in Montreal," he said.

Roy wasn't available after the game but two days later he held his own press conference in suburban Laval and said he felt that Tremblay left him in the game to humiliate him.

Four days after the incident, the Canadiens traded Roy and captain Mike Keane to the Colorado Avalanche for goaltender Jocelyn Thibault, Martin Rucinsky, and Andrei Kovalenko in what many regard as the worst trade in franchise history, particularly after Roy won two more Stanley Cups in Colorado.

Réjean Houle, who had been hired as general manager only 40 days earlier, was criticized for not doing more to mend the rift between Tremblay and Roy, but in an interview for this book, he said the trade was inevitable. Houle also confirmed that his predecessor, Serge Savard, had discussed trading Roy to the Avalanche during the off-season. The team had moved to Colorado from

A Star in Goal

Patrick Roy led the Canadiens to Stanley Cup victories in 1986 and 1993, winning the Conn Smythe Trophy as the MVP in the playoffs on both occasions. He had an undistinguished junior career with the Granby Bisons but the Canadiens spotted him while scouting his teammate Stéphane Richer and drafted him in the third round in 1984. He benefitted from the coaching of François Allaire, who schooled him in the butterfly technique. Roy was the master of the butterfly and served as a model for the next generation of goaltenders from Quebec.

Quebec City and its general manager was Pierre Lacroix, who had been Roy's agent.

Corey decided to make wholesale changes after the Canadiens began the season with five consecutive losses. Savard and coach Jacques Demers were fired and Houle and Tremblay were cast in unfamiliar roles.

Houle was working in promotions for the Molson Brewery and Tremblay was doing commentary on radio.

"We did the best we could but we learned on the job," said Houle.

There were reports that Tremblay and Roy had an uneasy relationship going back to their days as teammates but Tremblay said they weren't true.

"We were roommates, we got along," said Tremblay. "We could have salvaged the situation but you know Patrick, he was very stubborn. And I think he was unhappy in Montreal and wanted to move on."

But Tremblay's radio commentaries were often critical of Roy and the two had a heated argument on Long Island the day before Tremblay was introduced as the coach.

Roy laughed when he heard that Tremblay was the new coach and later tried to explain that he was laughing because having a former teammate as a coach made him feel old.

Tremblay wasted no time exercising his authority, telling Roy, "You stop the pucks, I'll coach."

This did little to heal the rift between the two because Roy had been spoiled when Demers was the coach. Demers knew that Roy was the key to success on a mediocre team. He allowed the goaltender to decide when and where he wanted to play and also involved Roy in other team decisions.

"That made my job more difficult, for sure," said Tremblay.

Roy was proud to the point of being arrogant and he wasn't happy when he met his match in Tremblay.

16 The Entrepreneur

It's nearly impossible to walk past a construction site in Montreal, Ottawa, or Toronto without seeing Dickie Moore's name on a trailer or a piece of heavy machinery.

Moore, who grew up in the working-class neighbourhood of Park Extension in Montreal, said he used the lessons he learned in hockey to turn a small tool-rental business located behind a Dairy Queen franchise he owned in the suburb of Lachine into a multi-million-dollar business.

"Toe Blake was the greatest coach ever and the secret of our success was that we were a team, we were a family, and that's the way we approached our business," said Moore. "I wanted the people who worked for us and our customers to feel that we were all working together."

Moore came from a family of nine boys and one girl and he credits his sister, Dolly, for helping him and his brother Jimmy land tryouts with the Montreal Royals junior team. At a time when

A Moore by Any Other Name

From 1952 to 1960, Richard (Dickie) Moore appeared in nine Stanley Cup finals and his name was etched on the Cup six times, though there was some confusion about his name, which appears five different ways: D. Moore, Richard Moore, R. Moore, Dickie Moore, and Rich Moore.

sports opportunities for women were limited, Dolly played softball and hockey and was a champion sprinter who barely missed qualifying for the Olympics.

Moore played a variety of sports as a youngster despite a series of injuries. He was hit by a car when he was 10, was bit on the lip by a dog, and broke both legs. He had knee problems that threatened his NHL career before it began.

Moore grew up as a Toronto Maple Leafs fan after listening to their games on radio and he idolized Leafs scoring star Gordie Drillon. He led the Montreal Royals junior team to the Memorial Cup in 1949 and a year later, he won a second Memorial Cup with the Junior Canadiens.

"Jo Jo Graboski, who was scouting for the Leafs, asked me if I was interested in joining them, and I said 'Sure,'" recalled Moore. Word of the Leafs' interest reached Canadiens general manager Frank Selke, and he registered Moore as Canadiens property. Moore signed his first contract in 1951 for $7,500 but the key to the deal was a promise that the Canadiens would call him up from the Royals senior team by Christmas.

"I joined the team in '51 and I had some great linemates, Rocket Richard and Elmer Lach," Moore said in a 2005 interview with Kevin Shea of the Hockey Hall of Fame. "I stayed for a while and when Elmer retired, Jackie Leclair was our center and then the Pocket (Henri Richard) came along and I played nine seasons with the Pocket and the Rocket."

Moore was an immediate success. He had 18 goals and 15 assists in his first half season but the next two seasons weren't as memorable. He didn't get along with head coach Dick Irvin Sr. and when he wasn't in the minors, he was often a healthy scratch. But he did play all 12 games in the playoffs in 1953 and won his first Stanley Cup.

His fortunes changed when Toe Blake was named head coach in 1955.

"When Toe became the coach, I was elated," said Moore. "He kept me on the team. I was lucky to have a guy who believed in me. You're only as good as how somebody can lift you up to the heights where he thinks you can play. Toe Blake had that in him. When he joined the team we went on to win five consecutive Stanley Cups and I was fortunate to win two scoring titles. I attribute that to the coach."

Moore won back-to-back scoring titles in 1958 and 1959. On March 22, 1959, Moore scored a goal and added an assist in a 4–2 win over the New York Rangers. That allowed him to set a single-season scoring record of 96 points, breaking the mark of 95 established by Gordie Howe in the 1952–53 season.

If Moore loved Blake, he wasn't as enamored of general manager Frank Selke. In the 1962–63 season, Moore had 24 goals and was the team's No. 3 scorer behind Henri Richard and Jean Béliveau. But Selke decided he was going to trade Moore after the Canadiens were eliminated by Toronto in the first round of the playoffs.

Moore, who had started his rental business two years earlier, retired rather than accept a trade.

"Nobody trades me," said Moore. "I can make a living where I am."

It was the first of three retirements for Moore.

In 1965, Punch Imlach was looking for some veteran leadership in Toronto and Moore supplied it. Injuries limited him to 38 games and he retired again after the Canadiens eliminated the Leafs in the playoffs.

Moore was playing once a week with the Montreal Oldtimers when he received another opportunity to revive his career. Scotty Bowman and Cliff Fletcher lured him to the expansion St. Louis Blues in December 1967. He had five goals and three assists in 27 games but he bowed out with a strong playoff performance. The 37-year-old Moore had seven goals and seven assists in 18 games as the Blues went to the Stanley Cup final, where they were swept by the Canadiens.

He was inducted into the Hockey Hall of Fame in 1974 and the Canadiens retired the No. 12 worn by Moore and Yvan Cournoyer on November 12, 2005.

17 Koivu's Comeback

The Canadiens' annual golf tournament is a time for optimism and the 2001 event was no exception. While businessmen donated thousands of dollars to charity for the privilege of joining an NHL player for an afternoon on the links, general manager André Savard and coach Michel Therrien talked about the bright prospects for the coming season.

They had no idea they were about to embark on an emotional roller coaster.

Shortly before the shotgun start, the team announced that captain Saku Koivu would not be on hand but there was no cause for alarm.

"He wasn't feeling well on the flight," said teammate Brian Savage, who had accompanied Koivu on a flight from Europe. "It's just the flu."

Two days later, the Canadiens announced that it was not "just the flu." Team doctor David Mulder ordered a series of tests which revealed that the pain in Koivu's stomach was caused by non-Hodgkin's lymphoma, a life-threatening cancer.

Mulder had some good news. The cancer had been detected early; it was treatable; and while the survival rate was 50 percent, it was higher for a young person who was in good physical condition. Treatment would begin immediately.

Over the next four months, Koivu underwent chemotherapy and radiotherapy. Between treatments, he would make regular visits to the Bell Centre, where he would talk with teammates and watch practice from a cordoned-off area behind the Canadiens bench.

"Those days that I was able to spend with the guys, I kind of felt like I was living a normal life," said Koivu. "I didn't think about the cancer or my days at the hospital. I had something else to think about and it made my life easier."

That something else was a comeback. In October, he had difficulty climbing a flight of stairs. In late March, he was told the cancer was in remission and he was able to take a few tentative steps on the ice.

Koivu was encouraged by Mario Lemieux, who returned from a year-long battle with cancer and won the NHL scoring championship in 1995–96 with 161 points.

"I talked to Mario Lemieux when this all happened, then I talked to him maybe a month or five weeks ago after I found out I was in remission," Koivu said after he returned to the ice. "It helps when you can talk to people who know what it's like. It's tough when you don't know how you're going to feel or how you're going to react. Mario said the most important thing was to stay positive. There are going to be some tough days but you try to smile and take the best things out of your days."

While the cancer was in remission, there was still work to be done. Koivu had to regain the weight and strength that he had lost and he had to pass a test to show that his blood levels were normal.

Koivu joined his teammates on April 1 when they traveled to Pittsburgh and Philadelphia but he didn't play. He said hoped to play the final two games of the regular season and it was a surprise when that schedule was pushed up by a game. After receiving positive results from a blood test in the morning, Koivu returned to the lineup on April 9 for a crucial game against the Ottawa Senators. The opening faceoff was delayed after Koivu was introduced and the crowd burst into a cheer. The ovation would continue for eight minutes.

Koivu's ice time that night was only slightly longer. He played 8:22 as the Canadiens advanced to the playoffs after a three-year absence.

Montreal would go on to upset Boston in the first round of the playoffs before losing to Carolina in the Eastern Conference semifinal. Koivu scored 10 points, tied for the team lead.

His performance amazed Dr. Mulder, who had witnessed Koivu's determination through the recovery process.

"The miracle isn't that Saku is alive, it's that he's already back playing," said Mulder.

After his recovery, Koivu said he wanted to do something to thank the doctors and other personnel who had saved his life. During his treatment, he had to drive two hours to Sherbrooke to undergo a PET/CT scan. He asked Blair Whittemore, one of his doctors, why there wasn't a similar machine in Montreal and he was told it was a matter of money. The result was the establishment of the Saku Koivu Foundation, which raised $3.5 million toward the purchase of a PET/CT machine for the Montreal General Hospital.

Koivu's career in Montreal came to a close after the 2008–09 season, when general manager Bob Gainey decided to remake the team. The captain wasn't offered a contract and he signed as a free agent with Anaheim. He played five seasons in California and retired in 2014 after 18 seasons in the NHL.

But there was at least one more Montreal ovation in the works for Koivu.

On December 18, 2014, the Canadiens played the Ducks and Koivu was honoured in a pregame ceremony.

The carefully timed program was thrown off when the Bell Centre erupted into cheers which continued for five minutes.

"I always felt that I was respected as a player and for the way I played the game but what makes me feel humble was the way I was loved by the fans," said Koivu, who was joined on the ice by his wife, Hanna; daughter, Ilona; son, Aatos; and parents.

"Sometimes you think about why it happened, why they took me as their own," said Koivu. "You can't explain it but there was a real bond between the fans in Montreal and myself. They've shown their passion and love and support throughout the years and it's been amazing."

As Koivu choked back the emotion, there was one more roar as he said: "Montreal is truly the most exciting place to play hockey. I will always be a Hab in my heart."

18 The Forum

The Montreal Forum conjures images of the Canadiens' greatest moments but the arena, which was home to 22 of the team's 24 Stanley Cups, was originally built as the home of their NHL rivals, the Montreal Maroons.

The city's English-speaking population had been without a team since the Wanderers folded six games into the 1917–18

Drawing a Crowd

The Canadiens don't hold the record for the largest hockey crowd at the Montreal Forum. The two largest crowds were for junior games between the Junior Canadiens and the Toronto Marlboros in the 1969–70 season. Both teams were loaded with future NHL players including Hall of Famers Gilbert Perreault for Montreal and Steve Shutt for Toronto. But the main attraction for the crowd was the prospect of a fight between Montreal's Allen Globensky and Toronto's Steve Durbano.

inaugural season in the NHL. The team had been playing in the Montreal Arena but that building was destroyed by fire on January 2, 1918.

William Northey, who was involved in the construction of the Montreal Arena and Arena Gardens in Toronto, felt there was a market for a team catering to the English-speaking population and he found an unlikely ally in Donat Raymond, a French Canadian Catholic who had found success in the Montreal financial world dominated by English Protestants.

Once they agreed on the need for a new team and an arena, Northey and Raymond needed money and they turned to Edward Beatty, the well-connected chairman of the Canadian Pacific Railway. Beatty put the arm on his fellow millionaires and, by the summer, he had raised more than $400,000 and the newly formed Canadian Arena Company Ltd. was in business.

After heated discussions over the site and size of the new arena, the Atlas Construction Company began work in late spring and needed only 159 days to complete the building which, with standing room, could accommodate 10,000 fans.

While the Canadiens and Maroons were rivals, they discovered they could help each other. Leo Dandurand, the Canadiens owner, fast-tracked the new team's entry into the NHL for the 1925–26 season. The Canadiens were originally opposed to a second team

The Canadiens called the Montreal Forum home from 1926 to 1996. In its final game in the Forum, Montreal beat Dallas 4–1.

but relented when they received $10,000 of the $15,000 expansion fee. And when the Canadiens became frustrated over arena owner Tom Duggan's reluctance to install an ice-making plant at the Montreal Arena, the Canadiens moved to the Forum in 1926.

The teams enjoyed a spirited rivalry and some success on the ice. The Maroons won the Stanley Cup in 1926 and 1935 and the Canadiens won in 1930 and 1931 but both teams felt the effects of the Great Depression. The Canadiens fared better than their rivals because they had a larger fan base but both teams struggled at the gate. There were reports that a group was interested in buying the team and moving it to Cleveland but the Canadian Arena

Company, the owners of the Maroons, invested in the Canadiens and it was the Maroons who suspended operations prior to the 1938–39 season. Raymond and Northey assumed control of the Canadiens in 1940.

As interest in the team grew in the postwar era, the capacity of the building was increased to 13,551 seats in 1949. There was a more ambitious renovation prior to the 1968–69 season when the roof was literally raised and the seating capacity was boosted to 18,200.

By the early 1990s, it had become apparent that the iconic building had outlived its usefulness. Team president Ronald Corey announced plans to build a new arena which would not only increase the seating capacity but also added luxury boxes and other modern amenities.

The final game at the Forum was played on March 11, 1996, and Andrei Kovalenko scored the final goal in the building as the Canadiens defeated the Dallas Stars 4–1.

The building has been converted into a retail space with a multiscreen movie complex but nostalgic fans can sit in a block of seats from the Forum and watch the world go by.

19 The Roadrunner

While Dickie Moore thought his career took off when Toe Blake became coach of the Canadiens, Yvan Cournoyer feels his career received a lift when Blake retired.

In his early days with the Canadiens, Cournoyer was used primarily on the power play. Blake was reluctant to use him on a regular shift because he felt the 5-foot-7 Cournoyer was a defensive liability.

In his second season in 1965–66, Cournoyer scored 16 of his 18 goals on the power play and the following season he scored 20 of his 25 goals with the extra man. His speed and playmaking ability made him a fan favourite but Blake became upset when fans chanted, "We want Cournoyer."

Blake said the fans were hurting Cournoyer by putting undue pressure on him.

Claude Ruel gave Cournoyer a chance to play a regular shift when he replaced Blake in 1968 and Cournoyer responded with the most productive season of his career. He scored 43 goals and added 36 assists to lead the Canadiens in scoring. He scored 40 or more goals four times in his career and he scored at least 25 goals in 11 consecutive seasons. He had a career-high 47 goals in 1971–72. The following year, he guided the Canadiens to their 18th Stanley Cup. He set a modern-day playoff record with 15 goals and won the Conn Smythe Trophy as the most valuable player in the postseason. He was part of eight Stanley Cup winners. When a back problem forced him to retire at the end of the 1978–79 season, he was fourth on the Canadiens' all-time scoring list.

Cournoyer was part of Team Canada in the 1972 Summit Series against the Soviet Union and loves to talk about the New Year's Eve game in 1975 when the Canadiens tied the Red Army 3–3. Cournoyer scored a goal and added an assist in that game. On his goal, he sped past a Soviet defenceman and joked later that he was going so fast the defenceman caught a cold from the breeze.

Cournoyer said he dreamed of playing in the NHL as a youngster but most of the people around him thought he was too small. His development took off when his family moved from Drummondville to Montreal. At 15, he was the only francophone playing for the Lachine Maroons junior team, and when he was injured, the only way he could communicate was to point to the area where it hurt.

His English and his hockey improved rapidly and he moved on to the Junior Canadiens, scoring 63 goals in 53 games in his final season.

Cournoyer said Jean Béliveau helped him with the transition to the NHL.

"I roomed with Jean a lot," Cournoyer told Dave Stubbs of the *Montreal Gazette* after Béliveau's death in 2014. "I was the youngest on the team and he'd call me 'son': 'C'mon, son, it's time for bed. It's late enough.' He was very happy when I arrived because I had good legs."

"Good" hardly describes the power in Cournoyer's lower limbs. The man ran on rocket fuel.

"Jean always said to me, 'Come from behind, Yvan, come from behind,'" Cournoyer recalled not long ago. "Sometimes after warmup I'd tell him, 'Jean, I think tonight to come from behind, I'm going to need a parachute. I feel very good, I have my tailwind tonight.'

"I just had to put my stick on the ice and the puck arrived right on it from Jean. It was very easy for me."

In Dick Irvin's oral history of the Canadiens titled *The Habs*, legendary Bruins defenceman Bobby Orr recalled the frustration of trying to catch the player they called the Roadrunner.

"We're playing them in an afternoon game in Boston and Yvan is flying," recalled Orr. "I mean, I can't catch him. Nobody can catch him.... There was a faceoff in front of our bench. Gerry Cheevers was the backup goalie that day and he says to Cournoyer, 'Hey, Yvan, take it easy. Slow down.'

"Yvan turns to Cheevers and says, 'No, Gerry, I can't do dat. I got the big tailwind today.'"

After his playing career ended, Cournoyer owned a brasserie in Lachine. He coached a roller hockey team, appropriately named the

Montreal Roadrunners, and spent one season as an assistant coach with the Canadiens. He was inducted into the Hockey Hall of Fame in 1982 and the Canadiens honoured Cournoyer and Dickie Moore when they retired their No. 12 on November 12, 2005.

20 Dr. Strangeglove

When it came to negotiating contracts, Canadiens general manager Tommy Gorman was known as a shrewd operator but he met his match in goaltender Bill Durnan.

Durnan vowed that he would never play pro hockey after the Toronto Maple Leafs released him when he suffered a knee injury as a teenager. He was content to play senior hockey with a number of teams in Northern Ontario and helped the Kirkland Lake Blue Devils win the Allan Cup in 1940.

The next season he found himself playing for the Montreal Royals, who helped him find work in the accounting department at Canadian Car and Foundry. Between his full-time job and the extra money from the Royals, he was content. But his boss at the foundry, Len Peto, was a director of the Canadiens, and he pressured Durnan to give the NHL another shot. Montreal wasn't happy with Paul Bibeault, who had allowed nearly four goals a game in the 1942–43 season, and Gorman was ready for a change.

But when Gorman committed to using Durnan, there was one problem. The 28-year-old hadn't signed a contract.

"Somehow I managed to hold out until the day of the opening game and got the Canadiens' management to give in to my wishes," Durnan recalled. "I signed for $4,200 and found myself on a hockey team just beginning to gel."

In his first season, Durnan provided the defence to support the Punch Line of Toe Blake, Elmer Lach, and Rocket Richard, and the Canadiens won the Stanley Cup. Durnan won the Vézina Trophy with a 2.18 goals-against average. It was the first of four consecutive Vézina Trophy wins for Durnan, who would go on to become the first six-time winner of the award.

In 1949, he earned a spot in the record book with a shutout streak of 309 minutes, 21 seconds, the longest in the NHL's modern era that began when forward passes were allowed in the attacking zone in the 1929–30 season. He had four consecutive shutouts in a string that ran from February 26 to March 6. Chicago's Gaye Stewart ended the shutout streak on March 9. The record stood until 2004 when Brian Boucher of the Phoenix Coyotes had five consecutive shutouts and a scoreless string of 332 minutes and one second.

Durnan had an unusual style. He was a natural right-hander but he learned to be ambidextrous and would switch the stick from one side to the other. He didn't use a blocker and he wore custom-made gloves that were a hybrid of a trapper and a stick glove. He was an outstanding baseball and softball player in the off-season and the reflexes he developed on the diamond allowed him to make glove saves. His unusual ability earned him the nickname Dr. Strangeglove.

He told *Inside Sports* in 1967 that being ambidextrous gave him an advantage.

"It was a tremendous asset and I owe that gift to Steve Faulkner, one of my coaches in a church league in Toronto when I was just a youngster. Steve showed me how to switch the stick from one hand to the other. It wasn't easy at first because I was so young and the stick seemed heavy, but Steve kept after me and eventually the stick got lighter and I could switch automatically. I noticed the opposition was unaware I was switching hands and, later on when

I was in the NHL, it often took years before the other guys knew I was ambidextrous."

He and Blake shared the C as the Canadiens captains in the 1947–48 season. Opposing teams complained that Durnan would give the Canadiens an opportunity to rest by leaving his crease to ask the referee for an explanation of a call. The following season, the NHL adopted what became known as the Durnan Rule, which prohibited goalies from wearing the C.

Durnan won his sixth Vézina Trophy in seven seasons in 1949–50 but he pulled himself out of the playoffs after the underdog New York Rangers took a 3–1 series lead.

"I was afraid I was blowing things," said Durnan. "I felt I wasn't playing as well as I did in the past. The nerves and all the accompanying crap were built up. It was the culmination of things and I realized, 'What the hell. I'm quitting and this is as good a time as any.'"

When asked about his decision years later, Durnan said, "Hockey started getting rough for me at the end of the 1940s. I had broken my hand and after it mended it felt like my arm was falling off whenever I'd catch the puck. My reflexes had gotten a little slow, and besides, the money wasn't really that good. I'll admit that if they were paying the kind of money goaltenders get today, they'd have had to shoot me to get me out of the game (but) at the end of any given season, I never seemed to have more than $2,000 in the bank so I wasn't getting anywhere that way."

Durnan believed that the workload for a goaltender was too much for one man and lobbied the NHL to expand its rosters so that each team was required to dress two goaltenders. That change wasn't adopted until the 1965–66 season.

Durnan was inducted into the Hockey Hall of Fame in 1964. He suffered from diabetes in his later years and died of kidney failure in 1972 at the age of 56.

21 Join a Gang

In 2006, the *Montreal Gazette* launched Habs Inside/Out, a website devoted to news about the Canadiens. It offered game reports, daily coverage of practices, video interviews, and a forum for fans to discuss their favourite team.

Shortly after the site began—and before the threat of a lawsuit from the Canadiens forced the paper to rename the site Hockey Inside/Out—some of the more active posters on the site decided they wanted to match some faces to the names they were seeing on the Internet, and the Hockey Inside Out Summit was born.

Each year, the Hockey Inside Out gang converges on Montreal for a weekend of activities built around a Canadiens Saturday night home game.

"It gets bigger every year," said Ian Cobb, a lifelong Canadiens fan who has been a principal organizer of the event since its inception. Each July, he begins working with the HIO posters and the team to line up tickets, hotel accommodations, and restaurants with room for a large gathering.

Cobb, a lifetime Canadiens fan who grew up in the Montreal suburb of St. Lambert and now lives in Belleville, Ontario, said that the HIO Summit attracts "people from all different walks of life, so it's always fun."

"One guy comes from France every year," Cobb told *Gazette* sports editor Stu Cowan in a 2014 interview. "There's a couple coming from Northern California and we've had people attending from Alaska and the Yukon. So it's pretty much the whole North American continent."

The weekend activities include an opening dinner on Friday, an informal breakfast on Saturday followed by a tour of the Bell

Centre and the Canadiens Hall of Fame, a pregame meal, and the game itself. There's a final gathering after the game at Hurley's Irish Pub where the mood depends on the outcome of the game.

One of the highlights of the pregame meal is an auction of Canadiens memorabilia with the proceeds going to the Montreal Canadiens Children's Foundation.

Cobb says his favourite part of the annual Summit is "just meeting the people. I'm a people guy. I had five families (from the HIO group) drop by here (at his home) this summer on vacation. It's kind of neat."

Organizing the Summit is a lot of work for Cobb but he says it's payback for the days when other HIO members helped teach him to read and write.

Cobb said he never completed elementary school because he was unable to read or write; it wasn't until he was in his fifties that he discovered that he was dyslexic. But hard work trumped his illiteracy and Cobb went from doing odd jobs around the Forum as a teenager—"I used to start Boom Boom Geoffrion's station wagon when it was cold," he recalled in a 2008 interview with Mike Boone of the *Gazette*—to running several successful businesses.

Here's how Cobb describes himself in his HIO profile: "Born in Montreal…Worked many different jobs around Mtl. as a kid, later went working pipeline construction as a labourer, equipment operator and scuba diver for oil & gas co's…owned and operated two corporations in three provinces, illiterate until my late 50s. Raised three children, retired 10 years ago as just your average millionaire, drive school bus and read and write on Inside/Out, learning here every day with friends!!!"

"I'd go with the flow," Cobb said. "My first trip out west was riding the freight cars." The constant was Cobb's ability to live by his wits. He didn't have to be literate to run a ranch in New Brunswick, where Cobb had 2,000 silver foxes and 36,000 minks, breeding animals to supply furriers in Montreal and developing a feed formula he sold to Ralston Purina.

He says he managed to hide his illiteracy throughout his business career, only revealing his secret after former Canadiens coach Jacques Demers announced he battled illiteracy in 2005 in a biography titled *Jacques Demers: En Toutes Lettres.*

"After Jacques came out of the closet, I figured, what the hell," said Cobb.

Rocket's 50 in 50

The world of sports is filled with magic numbers and the legendary athletes associated with those numbers.

There's Babe Ruth with his 60 home runs in a single season and 714 homers in his career.

Roger Bannister, the first man to run a mile in under four minutes.

Ted Williams, whose .406 batting average marks the last time a baseball player topped .400.

Wilt Chamberlain and his NBA record of 100 points in a single game.

And there's Maurice (Rocket) Richard, who was the first NHL player to score 50 goals in 50 games and then went on to establish the NHL career record of 544 goals.

The last number is significant because it answers the critics who disparaged Richard's 50-goal output in the 1944–45 season, claiming the talent pool in the NHL was depleted because many players were serving in the armed forces during World War II.

This debate was an extension of a wider discussion in Canada over conscription. Many French Quebecers opposed a universal draft, arguing that they didn't support what they saw as a British war. The Canadiens benefitted from this debate because many players stayed at home, working in defence plants while moonlighting as hockey players.

Richard tried to enlist on at least three occasions. He was rejected twice because he had suffered a number of injuries playing hockey and had weak bones. On his second attempt, X-rays showed that a broken ankle hadn't healed properly.

He made a third attempt in 1944, hoping to be selected as a machinist, but was rejected because he didn't have the necessary qualifications. He had attended the Montreal Technical School as a teenager but dropped out before graduating to concentrate on hockey.

Richard's critics point out that several of the top goaltenders were missing that season because of military service. Boston's Frank Brimsek, who was nicknamed Mr. Zero, was gone and so were Turk Broda of Toronto and Chuck Raynor of the New York Rangers.

But Richard scored 14 of his 50 goals—including five in one game—against Detroit's Harry Lumley, who survived the onslaught to earn a place in the Hockey Hall of Fame.

But Richard would build on that season. While he never reached 50 goals in a season again—no NHL player matched that number until the Canadiens' Bernie Greoffrion did it in 1961 and no player scored 50 goals in 50 games until Mike Bossy hit that mark in 1981—Richard was a prolific goal-scorer. Today, the Maurice Richard Trophy is awarded to the NHL player with the most goals in a season. If it had existed in Richard's day, he would have been a five-time winner.

When the Rocket retired, his 544 goals were an NHL record. He would be passed first by Gordie Howe and then by all-time leader Wayne Gretzky. On the current list, there are 26 other players with more career goals. But Howe had the advantage of longevity while Gretzky and the others benefitted from longer seasons and careers in an era in which the talent pool was diluted by expansion.

It's interesting to note that Richard was playing his 863rd game when he became the first player with 500 goals; Howe needed 1,045 games to reach that mark.

New York Rangers coach Frank Boucher was among those who dismissed Richard as a "wartime wonder" but he would revise his opinion a few years later when he called Richard "the most spectacular player I've ever seen and that includes Howie Morenz."

Another unlikely fan was Conn Smythe, the owner of the Toronto Maple Leafs. While Smythe was serving in the Canadian Army in Europe, he received regular reports from his deputy, Frank Selke, who commented on the poor quality of wartime hockey. On his return to Canada, one of the first games Smythe saw featured Richard and he told Selke that the game looked pretty good to him.

Selke would move from Toronto to manage the Canadiens and, in their book *Maurice Richard: Reluctant Hero*, Chrys Goyens and Frank Orr recount Smythe's attempts to acquire Richard:

"Conn Smythe was quick to appreciate the Rocket's potential as a hockey star," Selke said. "One night in the director's room during the intermission period of a hockey game, Conn—who earlier that week had been quoted as saying that Richard was a top scorer but couldn't backcheck—offered Senator Donat Raymond, the president of the Canadiens, $75,000 for Richard's playing contract.

"The senator, who loved to beat Toronto more than anything else in life, answered: 'I have read that you say Richard won't backcheck. You say he is only a great player when he is advancing. Does this mean if I get him to play coming and going you would offer me $150,000?'"

Two years later, the Leafs did offer $135,000 for Richard and Selke rejected the offer without consulting Raymond. In a reply to Toronto coach Happy Day, Selke said if he sold Richard, the entire team would be run out of town by their angry fans.

Selke would later say: "In all of his years of playing, there was never any money that could buy the Rocket."

23 A Home Waiting for a Winner

The Canadiens have won a record 24 Stanley Cups but they haven't won a title since the team moved out of the Forum and took up residence in a new building which began its life as the Molson Centre on March 16, 1996.

The building was the brainchild of team president Ronald Corey. He said a new arena was necessary to accommodate the thousands of fans whose names were on the waiting list for season tickets at the Forum.

But accommodating fans wasn't the only factor in the decision to find a new home. The economics surrounding the game were changing. Salaries were rising and the sagging Canadian dollar played a part in the Jets and Nordiques being sold and moved to the United States. New arenas were popping up throughout North America and the new buzzword was premium seating—luxury boxes and club seats which offered a higher level of comfort and higher-priced tickets.

Corey promised fans larger washrooms, particularly for women, as well as improved access to concessions. There would be a state-of-the-art sound system and new technologies would allow for ideal ice conditions while also allowing fans to sit in comfort without heavy winter clothing.

The site, behind the Canadian Pacific Railway's Windsor Station, was a nod to history. CPR chairman Edward Beatty had joined with two Molson cousins to raise the funds to build the Forum and now a new generation of Molsons joined with the railway on the new arena project.

It took three years and $230 million to build the new facility. When it was finished, it didn't quite live up to Corey's prediction that "Montrealers will love this place."

The new building was too new, too big. Some fans in the steeply pitched upper deck complained of vertigo. Longtime season-ticket holders complained that their sightlines had changed. There wasn't an expected rush for the additional seats, particularly in the club level.

The biggest problem? It wasn't the Forum.

It took fans a while to warm to the new building but the Canadiens gave the building some character by gradually adding displays that celebrate the team's history. Bell obtained the naming rights to the arena after the Molson Brewery sold the team and the building to George Gillett for a bargain basement $275 million.

The original capacity for hockey was 21,271 but 16 seats were added for the 2014–15 season after the penalty box was made smaller and the goal judges were moved to the press box.

While the Bell Centre will never achieve the magical status of the Forum, players have come to regard it as a prime destination because of the intense fans. It has a reputation for being one of the noisiest buildings in the NHL; levels reached as high as 135 decibels on May 10, 2010, when the Canadiens scored during Game 6 of their Eastern Conference semifinal against the Pittsburgh Penguins.

The Bell Centre also serves as a venue for major concerts, boxing, the Cirque du Soleil, and UFC competitions. It ranks as one of the top five arenas in North America in terms of revenue produced.

The only thing missing is a Stanley Cup banner to call its own.

24 His Cups Runneth Over

When asked about his success, Henri Richard always said he was lucky—lucky to have played his entire career in Montreal and lucky to have played with a great cast of players that included his older brother, Maurice.

But Richard needed more than luck to play 20 seasons in the NHL and win a record 11 Stanley Cups.

When legendary general manager Frank Selke was asked to comment on Henri Richard, he said, "I have been blessed with some of the greatest players in NHL history but game in, game out, Henri Richard may have been the most valuable player I've ever had."

That's quite a statement when you consider that the Canadiens featured a parade of Hall of Fame players under Selke's watch.

Henri Richard grew up idolizing Maurice, who was 15 years older. He dreamed of playing in the NHL but he was only 5-foot-7 and his junior coach, the Rocket's former linemate Elmer Lach, told him he would never make it.

"I remembered that when I made it ahead of a lot of very good hockey players," Richard said.

Montreal Gazette columnist Red Fisher recalled Henri Richard's first training camp prior to the 1955–56 season. Some observers viewed his arrival as a publicity stunt, and Fisher noted that

Richard wasn't expected to stick because few players made the jump from junior hockey to the Canadiens.

"He was too young, too small," Fisher wrote. "Furthermore, the mere idea of carrying the Richard name would be too heavy a cross to bear for the kid. So, invite him to training camp, let him play with the big boys for a little while—then ship him out."

It didn't work out that way. As coach Toe Blake told Fisher, "He'd be out on the ice controlling the puck...I wouldn't start

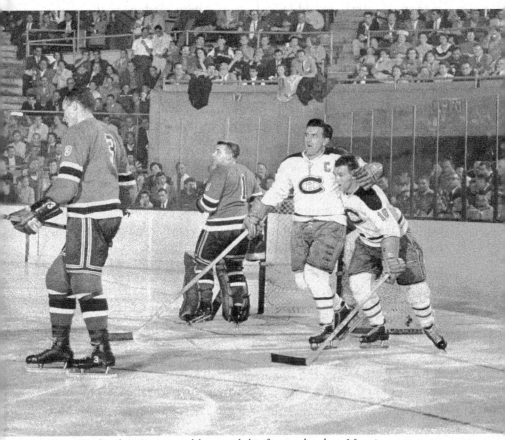

Henri Richard (16), pictured here with his famous brother, Maurice, was a Hall of Fame player in his own right. He won 11 Stanley Cups during his Canadiens career, still the most by any player in NHL history.

comparing him to somebody like Béliveau but I know this—when Richard was on the ice, nobody else had the puck."

Blake said his only reservation was Henri's ability to handle the rough play in the NHL. He didn't want Maurice Richard to be riding shotgun for his kid brother.

That concern was eased early in the season when a bench-clearing brawl erupted in Boston. Richard took on four Bruins in succession, winning the first three fights before battling Fern Flaman to a draw. Flaman, who was one of the toughest defence-men in the NHL, would often be tasked with shadowing the player who was dubbed the Pocket Rocket. Flaman would later say, "In all the years I played in the league, there was only one player I hated—Henri Richard."

Henri Richard never approached his brother in terms of scoring goals but he became a more complete player. He would score 358 goals—the Rocket scored 544—and added 688 assists for a total of 1,046 points. That's 81 points more than his brother, and Henri is third on the Canadiens' all-time scoring list behind Guy Lafleur and Jean Béliveau.

Henri once explained the difference between himself and his brother: "My brother's biggest thrills came when he scored many goals. I am most satisfied when I play in a close game and do not have any goals scored against me. Sometimes people have asked whether it helped or hurt to have Maurice as an older brother. It was not easy because many people expected me to be as spectacular as Maurice. But I believe it helped me as well as hurt me. Don't forget, Maurice was a great scorer and he could get goals many other players could not get. That helped me with my passing because I knew he would always be near the net waiting for a shot. But Maurice never gave me any advice. I never asked him for it and he never really offered it."

While the Richard brothers had different styles on the ice, they shared a fierce pride and a temper which occasionally landed them in trouble.

Midway through his career, Henri was injured and was replaced in the lineup by a young Jacques Lemaire, who played so well that Blake kept him in the lineup even after Richard was healthy.

Richard was steamed at the idea of sitting on the bench and briefly left the team, saying, "I'd rather pick garbage than sit on the bench."

Blake and Richard resolved their differences, with Henri saying, "I'll wait for my chance to play. I still have a lot of years left."

Richard was involved in a similar situation during the 1971 playoffs. He was benched by coach Al MacNeil during the final series against Chicago and he called the coach incompetent. Richard was in the lineup for Game 7 in that series and he scored the tying and winning goals as Montreal rallied from a 2–0 deficit to win 3–2.

25 Buy a Jersey or Two

Go to any Canadiens game and you will find fans proudly announcing their allegiance by wearing team jerseys.

Paul Anroniadis, a longtime season-ticket holder, has three jerseys but you won't find him wearing them to a game.

"I'm not really into wearing jerseys but I enjoy collecting them," said Antoniadis, whose collection includes game-worn jerseys by Carey Price, P.K. Subban, and Brandon Prust.

The Canadiens sell game-worn jerseys on their website and the prices and availability offer a classic case of the laws of supply and demand. The club goes through three sets of home jerseys each season, which means that if you want a Carey Price sweater, you have to be quick off the mark and be willing to pay top dollar.

"I wanted a Price from the last segment of the (2013–14) season, after he had been in the Olympics," said Antioniadis, who paid $2,750, plus tax. He also spent a similar amount to land a Subban jersey and then picked up one of the jerseys Prust wore in the 2014 playoffs for $750.

"I also had my eye on a Price jersey from the playoffs but, by the time I made up my mind, it was gone," said Antioniadis.

Antioniadis figures he made a good deal with the sweaters because the Canadiens are asking $1,000 more for the Price and Subban sweaters worn in the 2014–15 season.

If you have your eye on a particular player, the best course of action is to reserve the jersey in advance, a move which requires a 100 percent deposit. Even then, there's no guarantee you'll get your sweater. For example, if a player were to score his 50th goal in the sweater, the Canadiens retain the right to keep it for their Hall of Fame. The club also reserves the right to add a surcharge for any sweater deemed to have been involved in a milestone.

The pricing of the sweaters is often based on popularity. A Brendan Gallagher sweater from the 2013–14 season was priced at $1,750, while a Tomas Plekanec jersey from the same season was $750. A Max Pacioretty sweater could be had for $1,500, while a sweater worn by linemate David Desharnais cost $825. A Jaroslav Spacek jersey from the 2011–12 season is a bargain at $250.

Each jersey is accompanied by a letter of authenticity signed by equipment manager Pierre Gervais and contains a security chip to ensure it's the real deal.

While the jerseys are a new addition to his collection, Antioniadis has been collecting sports memorabilia for more than a quarter of a century.

"I used to go to flea markets where guys were selling stuff out of the trunks of their cars," said Antoniadis. "Some of those same guys are the rock stars of the business today."

Antoiniadis has unused Canadiens tickets from 1944 and 1955, and his prize possession is an Elmer Lach stick signed by the members of the 1950–51 team.

If you just want a jersey to wear to the game, expect to pay between $150 and $200 for a licensed NHL-quality jersey depending on whether you want a name and number. Licensed replica jerseys can be found at Costco for as little as $50.

26 The Old Lamplighter

Toe Blake is best remembered as the most successful coach in Canadiens history, guiding the team to eight Stanley Cup victories in 13 years.

But it was Blake's performance as a player which earned him a spot in the Hockey Hall of Fame in 1966. During the 1940s, he was part of the Punch Line, one of the most feared lines in hockey, with fellow Hall of Famers Elmer Lach and Maurice (Rocket) Richard.

Blake had already established himself as an elite player when Lach and Richard arrived on the scene. He led the NHL in scoring with 47 points in 1938–39 and was awarded the Hart Trophy as the most valuable player. His knack for scoring goals earned him the nickname the Old Lamplighter.

Legend has it that language played a part in coach Dick Irvin's decision to put the line together in 1943. Blake grew up in the Sudbury area in Northern Ontario and learned to speak French and English. Irvin thought the bilingual Blake could bridge the communication gap between the English-speaking Lach and the French-speaking Richard.

Communication wasn't a problem on the ice as the line helped the Canadiens win the Stanley Cup in 1944. The Canadiens beat the Toronto Maple Leafs in five games in the semifinals and then swept Chicago in the final. Blake scored the winning goal in overtime as Montreal beat Chicago 5–4 to clinch the Cup. Blake was the leading scorer in the playoffs with seven goals and 18 points, and his playoff average of two points a game was an NHL record which wasn't broken until Wayne Gretzky arrived on the scene in the 1980s.

Blake had his most productive season in 1944–45 when he collected 67 points in 50 games. Lach would lead the NHL in scoring that year with 80 points, including a record 54 assists, but he and Blake would be overshadowed by Richard, who became the first player to score 50 goals in 50 games. Lach collected assists on 27 of the Rocket's goals, while Blake would get assists on 25 of them.

Blake helped the Canadiens win another Stanley Cup in 1946 when he had a playoff-best seven goals in nine games. He had only two penalty minutes in the regular season and won the Lady Byng Trophy as the most gentlemanly player in the league.

His career ended on January 10, 1948, when a check by Bill Juzda of the New York Rangers sent Blake crashing into the boards at the Forum. He suffered a double fracture of his ankle and retired at the end of the season.

The Punch Line produced 350 goals in five seasons and Blake retired with 235 goals and 292 assists in 569 games.

All of those points were scored in a Canadiens uniform, although Blake began his NHL career with the rival Montreal Maroons. He had a successful junior career, helping the Sudbury Cub Wolves to the Memorial Cup in 1932, and played for the Hamilton Tigers of the Ontario Hockey Association before Tommy Gorman signed him for the Maroons in 1934. Blake would fail to score a point in the eight games he played and he watched from the sidelines as the Maroons won the Stanley Cup. While he only appeared in one playoff game, Blake's name was inscribed on the Cup for the first time.

He started the following season with the Providence Reds but in February 1936 he was traded to the Canadiens for goaltender Lorne Chabot in what proved to be a one-sided deal. While Chabot had won a Vézina Trophy and had been a first-team All-Star, he was nearing the end of his career and would play only 22 more games before retiring.

27 The Senator

Education was always important to Serge Savard but when the Canadiens offered him a contract in 1966, he put his formal schooling on hold.

Savard had planned to join Canada's national team which was based in Winnipeg in preparation for the 1968 Winter Olympics. He had been accepted at St. Boniface College, a French-speaking branch of the University of Manitoba, and had a plane ticket to Winnipeg.

"The Canadiens got wind of it and the same day they signed me to a contract and sent me to play for the Houston Apollos in the Central League," said Savard. The 20-year-old Savard was the rookie of the year and the following season he became the first of Montreal's "Big Three" defencemen to arrive in the NHL.

On two occasions, injuries threatened to end Savard's career but he played 14-plus seasons for the Canadiens and was a part of eight Stanley Cup teams.

It didn't take long for Savard to establish his dominance. In his second season with the Canadiens, he collected 10 points in 14 playoff games and became the first defenceman to win the Conn Smythe Trophy as the most valuable player in the playoffs.

Savard played in an era when the goalposts were securely anchored in the ice and he crashed into the net in a game in March 1970. His leg was broken in three places.

"I was scared when the doctor took off the cast for the first time because the break was moving inside," said Savard.

Savard broke the same leg 11 months later when he was checked by Toronto's Bobby Baun. He missed almost a year and played a different style of hockey when he returned.

"When I was younger, I was more of a basher, but after the two bad leg injuries, I didn't have the same speed, so I became more of a defensive defenceman," said Savard, who became known for his shot-blocking.

The injuries didn't prevent Savard from perfecting a spin move to avoid a check and announcer Danny Gallivan added to the lexicon of hockey when he described the move as a "Savardian spinarama."

Savard was selected to play for Team Canada in the 1972 Summit Series against the Soviet Union and Canada had a 4–0–1 record in the games he played. He didn't dress for Game 1 in

Canadiens Conn Smythe Trophy Winners

Jean Béliveau	1965
Serge Savard	1968
Ken Dryden	1971
Yvan Cournoyer	1973
Guy Lafleur	1977
Larry Robinson	1978
Bob Gainey	1979
Patrick Roy	1986, 1993

Montreal and missed Games 4 and 5 after he suffered a hairline fracture in his leg when he stopped a shot by Red Berenson in practice.

He joined Larry Robinson and Guy Lapointe to form the Big Three, and all three players were subsequently elected to the Hockey Hall of Fame and had their numbers retired by the Canadiens.

A tired Savard announced his retirement in 1981 but it proved to be a short-lived decision. John Ferguson, who been Savard's teammate and a partner in the ownership of some race horses, was the general manager of the Winnipeg Jets and claimed Savard on waivers.

Savard resisted Ferguson's original overtures but eventually joined the Jets and provided leadership to a young club.

"I felt wanted," said Savard.

In 1983, the Canadiens wanted Savard. On April 28, Savard was introduced as the team's managing director. He had already established himself as a solid businessman. He had one of the first lottery licenses in Quebec and he became involved in real estate, buying old apartment buildings and renovating them. He owned several hotels, including the Marriott Chateau Champlain, which is located one block from the Bell Centre.

His interest in politics earned him the nickname Senator. On several occasions, he was asked to run for public office but declined.

The Canadiens won two Stanley Cups under Savard's watch but he was replaced by Réjean Houle as part of a wholesale house-cleaning at the start of the 1995–96 season. But Savard would return briefly after Geoff Molson bought the team. The new owner needed counsel and Savard led the search which led to the hiring of Marc Bergevin as general manager.

28 The Battle of Quebec

For history buffs, the Battle of Quebec was fought on September 13, 1759. The British beat the French and both commanding officers, General James Wolfe and Joseph-Louis, the Marquis de Montcalm, were fatally wounded.

For hockey fans, the Battle of Quebec was the bitter rivalry between the Canadiens and the Quebec Nordiques.

"It was a crazy time," said Réjean Houle, who played for both teams. "Everyone had to take sides. It was about hockey but it was also about politics and beer."

The Nordiques started life in the World Hockey Association and there were some ruffled feathers when defenceman J.C. Tremblay defected to the new league, followed by Houle and Marc Tardif a year later.

But the battle didn't reach fever pitch until 1979, when the WHA ceased operations and four teams were merged into the NHL. The Canadiens were opposed to the Nordiques making the move because the team was owned by Molson Breweries. The Nordiques would not only be battling the Canadiens for the hearts and minds of Quebec fans; they also had strong promotional ties with Carling O'Keefe, a rival brewery.

Montreal reluctantly supported the merger because they feared a boycott of Molson beer, not only in Quebec but also in western Canada, where there were WHA franchises in Winnipeg and Edmonton.

It was the rivalry between the big city and a small town, which Montrealers derisively called the village. While the Canadiens were founded to benefit French-speaking players and fans, the team was now seen as a symbol of the English-dominated business community in Montreal. There were still fans in Quebec City who resented the Canadiens for spiriting away Jean Béliveau nearly three decades earlier.

Then, there was the political tenor of the time. The nationalist Parti-Québecois came to power in 1976 and was preparing a referendum on whether the province of Quebec should separate from Canada. Marcel Aubut, the lawyer who ran the Nordiques, was opposed to separation, but the team sweaters sported the fleur-de-lis and the team was viewed as an expression of Quebec's nationalist yearnings.

But Michel Goulet, who polished his Hall of Fame credentials with the Nordiques, said the bottom line for the players was the hockey.

"You can talk about the rivalries with Montreal-Ottawa and Montreal-Toronto but there was never a rivalry like the one we had with the Canadiens," said Goulet. "We met them in the playoffs five times and each series was a battle."

The Canadiens won three of those series, including a six-game clash en route to the Stanley Cup in 1993. Three of the series went seven games.

The playoff rivalry extended to the pregame meals for the media. Aubut, who was a master promoter, brought in chefs from

American Imports

Former Canadiens enforcer Donald Brashear was raised in Quebec but he was born in Indiana to a francophone mother and an American father. He represented the United States at the world championships in 1997 and 1998. Brashear's uncle, Carl Brashear, was the first African American to qualify as a U.S. Navy master diver and his life story was told in the movie *Men of Honor* starring Cuba Gooding Jr. Another Quebecer with a U.S. connection was defenceman Francis Bouillon, who was born in New York. He has also represented the United States at the world championships.

some of Quebec's top restaurants to prepare salmon, prime steaks, and other delicacies.

The rivalry ended when the Nordiques were sold and moved to Denver in 1995. Aubut had tried everything to maximize revenues at Le Colisée—the Nordiques were the first team to sell advertising on the steps—but rising salaries, a weak Canadian dollar, and the absence of luxury boxes in Le Colisée proved too great an obstacle to success.

But as Quebec builds a new arena and prepares for a return to the NHL, the memories linger.

"Those games took so much out of you," former Canadiens captain Guy Carbonneau told *Montreal Gazette* columnist Michael Farber. "In one way, I won't miss it because what went on detracted from the game. But in another way, it was fun. The pressure was incredible and it made everyone better. The fights in the stands, the fights at home, the feeling in the air. It was unbelievable."

29 Big Bird Landed with a Bang

When the Canadiens played the Philadelphia Flyers in the second round of the playoffs in 1973, Larry Robinson started the series sitting on the bench.

The Canadiens had a tradition of bringing young players along slowly and Robinson, a second-year pro, played one shift in Game 1 of the series. He spent most of Game 2 as a spectator until Jacques Laperriere suffered an injury. He came off the bench to score an overtime winner and never again worried about playing time.

But it was three years later, in the 1976 playoffs, that Robinson made an impression on the Canadiens—and the Flyers' Gary Dornhoefer.

Here's how Robinson described the incident in his book *Robinson on Defence*:

"Dorny and I had hammered each other at will. It seems as if we had an unspoken agreement; whenever we met on the ice, it would be a collision. There was no animosity, just two pros acknowledging that the other had a job to do.

"We were leading 2–1 midway through the third when Dorny led a rush up Philadelphia's right side. I was playing left defence and angled toward him, trying to get a hip into him. He was just inside the blueline when I got my hip into him. Bang into the boards he went and down he went. When he got up, he was looking at the boards curiously; we had broken the boards, as it turned out. There was a big dent near the top. Players on both teams skated by the area, sneaking looks and shaking their heads."

Dornhoefer told reporters after the game that Robinson hit like a pussycat but 30 years later, he told *Montreal Gazette* sports editor Stu Cowan, "It's the hardest I've ever been hit. I finished the game but I was spitting blood for about two or three days afterward."

Canadiens coach Scotty Bowman described Robinson as the "total package."

Said Bowman: "Offensive, defensive, toughness, and leadership. He and Serge (Savard) were the best tandem I ever saw in the NHL. He could really skate for a big man and he never backed off a challenge."

Robinson was one of four players drafted by the Canadiens among the first 20 picks of the 1971 draft. The prize that year was Guy Lafleur, who was the No. 1 overall pick. Montreal added Chuck Arnason at No. 7 and Murray Wilson at No. 11 before making Robinson the 20th pick overall.

As was the case in those days, he served an apprenticeship, playing a season and a half with the Nova Scotia Voyageurs before landing in Montreal in January 1973. He played 17 seasons in Montreal and became one of the greatest defencemen of all time.

He still holds the Canadiens' career record for points by a defenceman with 197 goals and 686 assists for 883 points. He was a part of six Stanley Cup–winning teams. He won the Norris Trophy as the NHL's top defenceman twice and took the Conn Smythe Trophy as the most valuable player in the playoffs in 1978.

He won his first Norris Trophy in 1977 when he scored 19 goals and 66 assists for 85 points. He also had a plus/minus rating of plus-120 that season.

Robinson played his final three seasons with the Los Angeles Kings, and there are conflicting stories about his departure from Montreal. The Los Angeles Kings offered Robinson a two-year contract with an option for a third season. Savard, his former defence partner who became the Canadiens' general manager, insists that he offered to match the Kings' deal but Robinson said the Canadiens' offer was for one season and Savard wasn't willing to guarantee that his number would be retired.

Robinson served as head coach of the Los Angeles Kings and led the New Jersey Devils to the Stanley Cup in 2000 and to the Cup final a year later. But he was uncomfortable in the role of head coach and has spent most of his post-playing career as an assistant coach.

He was inducted into the Hockey Hall of Fame in 2000 and the Canadiens finally retired his No. 19 on November 19, 2007.

30 The Clown Prince

Guy Lapointe was an outstanding defenceman with the Canadiens for 14 seasons. He was part of the Canadiens' Big Three with Larry Robinson and Serge Savard and he helped the team win six Stanley Cups between 1968 and 1982.

He was the runner-up to Boston's Bobby Orr in the 1973 balloting for the Norris Trophy presented to the NHL's top defenceman. He was elected to the Hockey Hall of Fame in 1993 and the Canadiens retired his No. 5 in 2014.

But when former teammates discuss Lapointe's legacy, his considerable achievements on the ice often take a back seat to his Hall of Fame career as a prankster.

"Guy Lapointe made a lot of things fun for a lot of people," goaltender Ken Dryden told Dave Stubbs of the *Montreal Gazette* before Lapointe's number was retired. "The importance of that can't be underestimated on a team."

Dryden's introduction to Lapointe's wild and wacky sense of humor came when he was a rookie. The Canadiens were playing an exhibition game in Halifax and the team meal included ice cream with chocolate sauce as a dessert. Lapointe said he was too full and asked Dryden if he wanted his ice cream. Dryden, who said ice cream was one of his favourite foods, eagerly grabbed Lapointe's dish and found himself digging into a bowl of sour cream under the chocolate sauce.

Canadian prime minister Pierre Trudeau once visited the Canadiens dressing room to congratulate the players after a big win and fell victim to one of Lapointe's favourite gags. He coated his hand with Vaseline and when Trudeau reached Lapointe's stall, the defenceman engaged Trudeau with a firm but slimy grip.

"He was kind of surprised," said Lapointe. "He laughed. I mean what are you going to do? Then I gave him a towel."

The one player who was immune to Lapointe's jokes was team captain Jean Béliveau, who was Lapointe's idol when he was growing up. But Lapointe wasn't above pranking coach Scotty Bowman, who is not known for his sense of humor.

During a practice at the Verdun Auditorium, Lapointe tucked a whistle into his glove and secretly blew it to cut short skating drills. A baffled Bowman spent most of the practice scanning the stands for a troublemaking fan who didn't exist.

At the 1976 Canada Cup tournament, players were told to wear black shoes for a formal team picture. Lapointe showed up with brown socks and brown shoes.

"I make sure I walk in the room with everyone already there," recalled Lapointe. "I'm wearing my brown shoes and brown socks and immediately everyone picks on me. What are you doing, Pointu? Were you drinking last night? Are you hung over? So now it's time to practice and I make sure I'm the last one going on the ice."

Before joining his teammates, Lapointe gathered everyone's shoes and socks and dumped them in a large laundry barrel.

"After practice, everyone's pissed," recalled Lapointe. "I dump the barrel on the floor and say, 'Holy gosh, I'm glad I wore brown shoes and socks. And I found them right away while everyone is sorting through the mess looking for their stuff."

Lapointe engaged in such pedestrian pranks as cutting skate laces and lining jockstraps with analgesic heat rubs. And he once nailed Dryden's shoes to a bench.

Lapointe recalled the day when he shredded the laces of defenceman Terry Harper, who had a habit of arriving for practice at the last minute.

"I remember one day Terry running out on the ice and wobbling onto his ankles with the cut laces. Happily with Terry Harper, one could hardly tell the difference in his skating," said Lapointe.

But Lapointe's all-time favourite prank was also his most elaborate.

When Mario Tremblay was a rookie in the 1974–75 season, he celebrated his arrival in the NHL by buying a Pontiac Grand Prix. He was so proud of the purchase that he invited his teammates to view the car, parked in the Alexis Nihon Plaza garage across the street from the Forum.

Lapointe was off the ice before Tremblay and he grabbed the keys to the car, hustled across the street, and moved the car to another level.

When Tremblay and his teammates went across the street, they discovered an empty space where the car should have been.

"You should have seen his face," Lapointe told the *Montreal Gazette*. "'My car's been stolen!' he's screaming, and I'm just saying, 'What are you talking about Mario? Did you really buy one?'"

The police were searching for the car and Tremblay was in negotiations with his insurance company and the car dealership over a replacement when he found a note in his locker three days later informing him that his car could be found one level up from where he parked it.

31 The Strongman

Emile (Butch) Bouchard surprised coach Dick Irvin when he arrived at his first NHL training camp in 1941 because he was in peak condition at a time when players used the camp to work off the excesses of the off-season.

"He appeared to be chiseled out of stone," teammate Dickie Moore said of Bouchard, who was one of the first players to recognize the value of weight training. At a time when the average NHL player was 5-foot-8 and 165 pounds, Bouchard was considered a giant at 6-foot-2 and 205 pounds. He developed a reputation for hard checks and his stay-at-home style would later provide the perfect complement for the offensive-minded Doug Harvey.

Bouchard had a late start in hockey. Money was scarce during the depression and he was 16 when he borrowed $35 from his brother to buy a set of hockey equipment that included his first pair of skates. He proved to be a quick learner and played for the Verdun Maple Leafs and the Junior Canadiens before joining the Providence Reds. He showed his financial acumen when he picked the Reds over a career in banking. Hockey paid him $75 a week, while the bank offered $7.

Bouchard's hard-hitting style proved popular at a time when the Canadiens were struggling at the gate. Within a few seasons, the Canadiens would be contenders with the Punch Line of Elmer Lach, Toe Blake, and Maurice Richard along with goaltender Bill Durnan. They won the Stanley Cup in 1944 and again in 1946. Bouchard was a second-team NHL All-Star in 1944 and was named to the first team in each of the next three seasons. He would serve as captain of the team for eight seasons, the longest tenure until Jean Béliveau came along.

On February 28, 1953, the Canadiens honoured Bouchard with a night at the Forum presided over by Montreal mayor Camillien Houde. As Canadians watched the ceremony on CBC, Bouchard was presented with a new Buick during the second intermission of a game between the Canadiens and the Red Wings. The plan was for him to drive off the ice in his new car but the keys were missing. They had been pilfered by Detroit captain Ted Lindsay, who skated to the car, gave Bouchard the keys, and congratulated him on behalf of the Red Wings.

Later that year, Bouchard won his third Stanley Cup, and there would be a fourth three years later. Injuries had slowed Bouchard

No Substitutions

Emile Bouchard's wife, Marie-Claire, said her husband could be tough off the ice. She told Ronald King of *La Presse* that the local mob wanted her husband to hire their people for his restaurant, Chez Butch Bouchard. She said Bouchard invited the head man to dinner at the restaurant and told him, "Over my dead body. Je n'embaucheme jamais un de tes hommes." That translates to "I will never hire one of your men."

and he planned to retire after the 1953–54 season, but coach Toe Blake convinced him to stay on so that he could help with the younger players. He played 36 games in 1955–56 but missed the last half of the season and the playoffs because of injuries. But Blake dressed him for the final game against Detroit and sent him on the ice late in the game to provide him with his fourth Stanley Cup.

Bouchard didn't have many fights, at least partially because few players were up to challenging him. But one prolonged and one-sided fight against Boston's Terry Reardon in the 1946–47 season led to a change in the referee's role. After the fight, NHL president Clarence Campbell made the referee responsible for breaking up fights.

In the 1970s, Bouchard's son Pierre, also a defenceman and also nicknamed Butch, played for the Canadiens. Pierre didn't enjoy the same individual success as his father but he was part of five Stanley Cup victories. Bobby and Brett Hull are the only other father-son duo to win the Cup.

After he retired, Bouchard ran a successful restaurant in Montreal and was involved in several other businesses. He was inducted into the Hockey Hall of Fame in 1966 and the Canadiens retired his No. 3 in 2009 after a grassroots campaign, one which had the support of the Quebec National Assembly.

Bouchard was also honoured for his work off the ice. In 2008, he received the Order of Quebec and, a year later, he was made a Member of the Order of Canada "for his contribution to sports, particularly professional hockey, and for his commitment to his community."

He died in 2012 at the age of 92.

32 The Pregame Meal

Montreal has long been known for its restaurants and there is plenty of variety within a few blocks of the Bell Centre.

If you want to be in the heart of the action, there are four restaurants in close proximity to the arena, including one which is inside the arena itself. They are all chain restaurants but they offer tasty fare at reasonable prices. The biggest drawback is they start filling up two hours before the game and there are often lineups.

La Cage aux Sports is located in the Bell Centre with an entrance on Avenue des Canadiens. Chicken and ribs are the specialty but you have also salads and seafood items like a shrimp brochette. If the Canadiens score five goals, you can come back for a nightcap and exchange your ticket stub for an order of chicken wings.

Rotisserie chicken is on the limited menu at St. Hubert Bar-B-Q, which is located at the adjacent Windsor Station. The chicken is accompanied by cole slaw, crisp fries, a bun, and a tangy sauce for dipping.

Baton Rouge (1050 Rue de la Montagne) offers more chicken and ribs prepared with a Southern touch.

The most recent addition to the neighbourhood is Madison's (1065 Drummond St.) which bills itself as a New York bar and grill. The food is upscale from its neighbours with an emphasis on steaks and designer cocktails like the Madison's Bloody Caesar, which has a jumbo shrimp clinging to the rim of the glass.

A block away from the Bell Centre is the Marriott Chateau Champlain Hotel, which offers pregame specials in Le Bar Senateur. The watering hole is named for former Canadiens defenceman Serge Savard, who was once part of the hotel's ownership group.

Head north of Boulevard Rene Levesque and you'll find more variety and a little more room to spread out.

The Sir Winston Churchill Pub (1459 Crescent St.) is a longtime Montreal favourite, and visitors from the United States get some relief from the sticker shock of alcohol prices during happy hour, when the drinks are 2-for-1.

One block over at 1234 Bishop St. is the Irish Embassy. You can't renew your Irish passport there but you can get a perfect pint of Guinness and, if you're there on a Saturday, you can listen to the TSN-690 radio crew broadcast its pregame show on location. If you wear a sweater from a team other than the Habs, be prepared for some good-natured razzing from host Abe Hefter.

Hurley's Irish Pub (1425 Crescent St.) started the Irish pub renaissance in the midtown area and is the place to go after the game where you're likely to run into journalists, agents, on-ice officials, and the occasional player. There's live music on two floors; The Clubhouse on the second floor is a sports bar within Hurley's.

McLean's (1210 Peel St.) caters to a younger crowd and is a favourite with the *Hockey Night in Canada* broadcasters. It's crowded before and after games and the kitchen is open late.

Fast food? There's a McDonald's across the street from the Bell Centre on Rue de la Montagne and the second floor features a Canadiens-themed decor.

If you're looking for a blowout dinner, there are two recommendations within walking distance.

Da Vinci (1180 Bishop St.) offers some of the finest Italian food in the city and is a popular stop for players on their off nights. The restaurant has an interesting history. It was once located on Ste. Catherine St. near the Montreal Forum and the sign over the door read KING OF THE PIZZA. It was a tiny storefront that was known for good food and the clientele included hockey players and Los Angeles Dodgers manager Tommy Lasorda, who declared that it was his favourite Italian restaurant. When the Canadiens moved from the Forum to the Bell Centre, the restaurant followed. The new digs in a converted brownstone were more spacious, the menu and the wine list reflected the new neighbourhood, and the place was an instant success.

La Queue de Cheval (a polite translation would be the horse's tail) offers prime steaks and gigantic lobsters at its new location at 1181 Rue de la Montagne. This is a steakhouse in the New York tradition, which means that you select your cut of beef and then start paying for the extras like an oversized, overstuffed baked potato and fresh asparagus dripping with hollandaise.

Finally, here's a recommendation for out-of-town visitors who want a dining experience the night before a game: Gibby's (298 Place d'Youville) is a steakhouse located in the former D'Youville stables in Old Montreal. The quality of the food matches the historic backdrop of the centuries-old building and the potato, asparagus, and soup or salad are in included in the price of the steak. Reservations are a must late in the week.

33 A Family Business

Geoff Molson grew up with a family tradition based on beer and hockey.

He's a direct descendant of John Molson, who founded Canada's first brewery in 1786. The family's association with hockey goes back to its investment in the Montreal Forum in 1924.

Geoff Molson *returned ownership of the Canadiens to his family in 2009. The Molsons' involvement in the team dates back to the 1920s.*

"I grew up with the idea of the team being owned by the family indirectly," said Molson, who bought the team from American businessman George Gillett Jr. in 2009. "In the 1970s, the family owned it for a period of time, then was sold to the Bronfmans for a short period."

Molson Brewery bought the team in 1978. It was a public company but Geoff's father, Eric, and his uncle, Steven, were heavily involved in the brewery and the hockey operation.

The brewery sold a majority interest in the team to Gillett in 2001 as part of a corporate restructuring. "It was a very difficult decision to sell to George Gillett," said Geoff Molson. "The core of our family business has been beer for over 230 years and the strategy in the public company was to concentrate on our core business. The slogan at the time was, 'Get back to beer.'"

Canadiens Sale Timeline

1909: Team founded by Ambrose O'Brien. No information available on startup costs but he reportedly made a 50 percent profit the next year when he sold the team to pro wrestler George Kennedy.

1921: Kennedy died in 1921 as the result of the Spanish flu epidemic two years earlier. Kennedy's estate sold the team to Leo Dandurand, Joe Cattarinich, and Louis A. Letourneau for $11,500.

1935: Letourneau left the ownership group in 1931 and Cattarinich and Dandurand sold the team to the Canadian Arena Company for $165,000.

1940: Senator Donat Raymond and William Northey of the Canadian Arena Company—the owners of the Montreal Forum—take control of the financially strapped Canadiens.

1957: Senator Hartland de Montarville Molson and his brother Thomas buy controlling interest in the Canadian Arena Company (the Forum and the Canadiens). The brothers pay an estimated $4.5 million for a 60 percent share of the company.

1968: Hartland and Thomas Molson sell team to cousins J. David, William A., and Peter B. Molson for $5 million.

1971: The Molson cousins sell to brothers Edward and Peter Bronfman for $13 million and company reorganized as Carena Bancorp.

1978: Molson Breweries buys team for $20 million and signs long-term lease for Forum.

2001: Molson sells 81.1 percent of the team to George Gillett in deal valued at $275 million. Gillett puts up $185 million and absorbs some debt. The brewery also throws in the five-year-old Molson Center, which would be renamed the Bell Centre a year later.

2009: Gillett sells to brothers Geoff, Andrew, and Justin Molson for a reported $550 million.

The company owned two hardware chains in Canada, a number of chemical companies in the United States, and 80.1 percent of the hockey team.

"It was a hard moment for the family," said Geoff, whose grandfather, Tom, and great-uncle, Hartland, owned the team from 1957 until 1964 when they sold it to their cousins, David, Peter, and Bill Molson.

"It was a business decision," explained Geoff. "Hockey wasn't that profitable a business. It depended on making the playoffs. The public company recommended selling to George Gillett, keeping 20 percent, just in case, and to stay close to the culture of hockey."

Geoff Molson had been working in the United States but he returned to Canada to work for Molson and served as the brewery's representative on the Canadiens board.

Molson said he never dreamed that he would own the team but that opportunity presented itself when the heavily leveraged Gillett ran into financial difficulties after buying the Liverpool soccer team.

"When we first sold, I wished we still had it," said Molson. "When George called me to say he was selling, the wheels started turning. I never would have dreamt it before."

There were no other serious bidders when Gillett bought the team for a reported $275 million. Molson, who was joined by his brothers, Andrew and Justin, faced a few rival bidders, including Pierre-Karl Peladeau, who was looking for content for his proposed all-sports TV network. The bidding pushed the price over $500 million.

"The price came up in my interview with the NHL Board of Governors," said Molson. "It was the first question they asked. They knew what I was paying and they said, your grandfather and uncle bought it for $10 million, and they asked me why they sold it.

"Back then, it was probably worth $10 million and now it's worth what I paid for it. Times have changed. Back in the Forum, there was no advertising in the rinks, there was no big TV money, no sponsorships, and the players weren't making the money they're making now. And we have the concert business which we've expanded from what George started."

The franchise may be worth even more than Molson paid for it. In its annual evaluation of NHL franchises, *Forbes* magazine estimated the value of the franchise at $1 billion.

"It might be worth that if it was for sale, but it's not," said Molson.

Molson is a hands-on owner who also serves as the team president. He says he has to find the fine line between being a fan and an owner.

"I'll always be a fan," he said. "But as an owner, you have that sense of responsibility to the community. The expectations are very high. You almost have to force yourself to be less of a passionate fan and more of a responsible owner. That means trying to make every right move to put the best team on the ice. I wake up every morning with that responsibility."

Molson said he reads newspapers, listens to talk radio, and gets feedback from fans when he watches his three sons play hockey.

"I love the passion, I like the feedback, but I put it in a compartment," said Molson. "I rely on general manager Marc Bergevin and the team he's assembled. We take all the information we have, then we make what we hope will be the right decisions."

34 The Bob Gainey Trophy

Bob Gainey didn't invent the role of defensive forward, but he was so good at it that the National Hockey League felt it had to create an award to recognize his achievements.

In 1978, the league instituted the Frank J. Selke Trophy to honour a forward who excelled in the defensive aspects of the game.

Defence was Gainey's calling card. He was a defenceman when he was introduced to the game as a six-year-old and it was his defensive play as a forward with the Peterborough Petes which prompted Canadiens general manager Sam Pollock to draft him eighth overall in 1973.

The selection was considered a surprise. When Canadiens goaltender Ken Dryden first heard the news, he thought Montreal had selected highly touted Peterborough defenceman Bob Neely, who was the 10th overall pick by Toronto.

The Canadiens were a team built on offence, but Pollock realized that good teams needed a balance and Gainey had received a solid grounding in two-way hockey under legendary coach Roger Neilson in Peterborough.

If there was any doubt about the selection, it was erased in Gainey's first NHL exhibition game against the Boston Bruins.

Here's the way *Montreal Gazette* columnist Red Fisher described Gainey's debut:

"Bobby Orr was on the ice to start the game. So was Peterborough alumnus Gainey. Orr jumped on a loose puck in his zone and then, in classic Orr skating style, slipped behind one man and yet another. On the opposite side of the ice, rookie Gainey gathered his legs beneath him, gathering speed with each stride, and crashed into hockey's best player. Orr went down in a

Canadiens Selke Trophy Winners

Bob Gainey	1978, 1979, 1980, 1981
Guy Cabonneau	1988, 1989, 1992

heap, blinking into the lights at Gainey's back. In his seat, no more than 20 feet away from the collision of the rookie and the legend, Pollock thinly smiled. Sam knew."

Gainey brought his skills and a strong work ethic for 16 seasons, including eight as the team captain. He never scored more than 23 goals in a season and he finished his career with 239, a decent number but not the number you would expect from a player who was selected to the Hall of Fame. But it was his play at the other end of the ice and the intangibles which led to his election in 1992.

Teammate Larry Robinson offered this testimonial: "You watched the way Gainey worked and you had to go out there and try to work the way he did. There was no other way."

Red Fisher described Gainey as the "poster boy for players who played with and through injuries." Canadiens coach Jacques Lemaire made it clear that he didn't expect Gainey to play in Game 6 of the 1984 Eastern Conference final because he had a serious shoulder injury, but Fisher noted that Gainey played "the Gainey way" in a losing cause.

"His confrontations with the Islanders' Bryan Trottier and Vancouver's Stan Smyl have become part of hockey lore," Fisher wrote a decade after Gainey had retired as a player. "He rarely gave an inch, but if he had to, he made certain it was only an inch. It's what made him a member of five Stanley Cup teams and a Conn Smythe winner in 1979."

Dryden joked about Gainey's inability to score during a 1983 roast in Peterborough but quickly added: "But that didn't matter. I played with Bob Gainey for five years. In that time we played on four Stanley Cup teams and each year he played a larger role on the team. By the end of my time there he was really the driving force on the Canadiens. We put through a very difficult last season (1978–79) and in many ways it was Bob who held things together. He was a goalie's best friend in all senses. He made me look good in practice and even better in the games."

The Canadiens retired Gainey's No. 23 on February 23, 2008.

35 The Greatest Game That Wasn't

Many people believe that the 1975 New Year's Eve game between the Canadiens and the Red Army was the greatest hockey game ever played.

It's safe to say Canadiens goaltending great Ken Dryden isn't in that group.

The game ended in a 3–3 tie because Russian goaltender Vladislav Tretiak played a great game and Dryden didn't.

In his classic book *The Game*, Dryden said he made a mistake in the day leading up to the showdown.

"The night before a New Year's Eve game with the Soviet Central Army Team in 1975, I got away from the bustle of visitors who were arriving at our house and went to a downtown hotel," he wrote. "There, alone with myself for 24 hours, I built slowly for the game and kept on building until the game and it became a fixation. I thought and worried and filled up with doubts, I could never get mentally free enough just to play, and while the great Soviet goaltender Tretiak stopped 35 shots, I stopped 10 in a 3–3 tie."

The goaltending was the story of this game and Dryden's performance is the one thing that separates this game from greatness.

When legendary sportswriter Red Fisher looked back at the highlights of his five decades of covering hockey, he told *Montreal Gazette* readers that the game was No. 5 on his list.

"Almost 29 years after The Game, people are still calling it the greatest ever played," wrote Fisher. "It had all the ingredients: the Stanley Cup Canadiens playing at their best against the Central Red Army with all of its great stars from the 1972 Summit Series. Who could ask for more, eh?

"Question: does it even come close to that accolade? When the Canadiens outshot the Soviets 38–13 in a 3–3 skirmish, holding them to four shots in the first period, three in the second, and six in the third, they were as near perfect as any team can be. Call it a highlight-reel game for the Canadiens, but when the most important position on any hockey team springs leaks, 'greatest' is hardly the word for it."

If Dryden had played up to his usual standard, this game would have resulted in a Montreal win. The Canadiens showed they could shut down the skilled Soviets and they answered any questions about the relative conditioning of the teams.

In the Summit Series, Team Canada was ambushed because the players were coming out of the off-season and had difficulty keeping up with the Soviets in the opening games. That was not the case in 1975. The Canadiens knew what to expect and were in midseason form.

So how did the 1975 game come to be regarded as the greatest?

It's probably because people wanted it to be the greatest. There was a hunger for international hockey after the Summit Series and the Canadiens–Red Army game was the only Canadian stop on the Super Series tour.

The Cold War was still on and this game represented a clash of systems ranging from hockey styles to political debate over the relative merits of democracy and communism. Toronto Maple Leafs owner Harold Ballard was so opposed to the Soviet system that he refused to play the Soviets and he said he was rooting for the Canadiens for the first time in his life.

The game attracted media from across Canada and from major markets in the United States, and the Canadiens had to find room in the stands for 60 of the 200 accredited reporters.

Dinner reservations were pushed back until 10:00 PM or later to accommodate fans who wanted to watch the game. The Forum was filled to capacity and scalpers were getting $100 for tickets with a face value of $12.

With all the hype and anticipation, anything less than the greatest game would have been as disappointing as Dryden's play in net.

36 Baby, It's Cold Outside

Outdoor games have become all the rage in the NHL, with ice-making technology bringing hockey to the great outdoors in venues as unlikely as Dodger Stadium in Los Angeles.

But Mother Nature was all the Canadiens and the Edmonton Oilers needed to produce ice for the league's first outdoor game on November 22, 2003. When the puck was dropped at Edmonton's Commonwealth Stadium, the temperature was minus-19 Celsius (minus-2 Fahrenheit).

While subsequent games have been threatened by relatively balmy temperatures, rain, or glare from the sun, the challenge in Edmonton was shovelling out after a number of snowstorms hit the city in the days leading up to the game.

The Oilers had floated the idea of an outdoor game in the 1980s but the idea really gained momentum after Michigan and

Michigan State faced one other in an outdoor game billed as the Cold War.

The fan response to the Canadiens-Oilers game was overwhelming. After accommodating their season-ticket holders, the Oilers had 7,000 tickets for general sale and they decided to hold a lottery. More than 750,000 requests were received from around the world and 1,750 people were selected to purchase four tickets each. The attendance at the game was 57,167, an NHL record.

The regular-season contest was preceded by an alumni game which featured a collection of Hall of Famers, including the two captains, Guy Lafleur for the Canadiens and Wayne Gretzky for the Oilers.

Montreal Gazette columnist Red Fisher, who is no fan of outdoor games, noted that the old-timers got off easy because they only had to play two 15-minute periods. When asked what he remembered about the game, Fisher replied: "Cold."

Montreal goaltender José Theodore tried to compensate for the chilly weather by wearing a Canadiens toque over his goaltender's mask. The toques quickly became a fashion statement among Canadiens fans.

Montreal won the game 4–3 as Yannic Perreault and Richard Zednik each scored two goals. Most of the players said they were happy to have been part of history but also said they needed a few days to thaw out.

The Canadiens played in a second Heritage Classic in 2011 when they lost 4–0 to the Calgary Flames. That game was played at McMahon Stadium and, while there was room for only 42,022 spectators, the interest was high and the game produced record revenues for the NHL.

In 2016, the Canadiens are scheduled to become the first Canadian team to play in the Winter Classic on New Year's Day. They will face the Boston Bruins in Foxboro, Massachusetts, the home of the New England Patriots.

Montreal is also exploring the possibility of having its own outdoor game but it's going to take some imaginative thinking to make it happen.

The largest facility in the city, the Olympic Stadium, has a roof over it. McGill University's Molson Stadium is home to the Montreal Alouettes of the Canadian Football League but its capacity tops out at 25,000 and there's no room to add temporary seating.

The Canadiens are exploring the idea of building a temporary stadium, a plan that was employed several years ago to accommodate a U2 concert. One possible location is on Ile Notre Dame, a man-made island in the St. Lawrence River. The island, which was part of the Expo 67 World Fair, is home to the Montreal Grand Prix and a temporary facility would incorporate some of the permanent grandstands for the race.

37 Winning Was Everything to Blake

Hector (Toe) Blake was inducted into the Hockey Hall of Fame as a player but he is remembered today as the most successful coach in the history of the game.

Blake began his coaching career by leading the Canadiens to five consecutive Stanley Cup victories and when he retired after winning the Stanley Cup in 1968, he had won a record eight Stanley Cups in 13 seasons.

Not bad for a guy who was Frank Selke's second choice to coach the team after Dick Irvin was forced out in the wake of the Richard Riot on March 17, 1955. Irvin encouraged his players to play a physical game which sometimes strayed from the rules and

Selke felt that Irvin's attempts to fire up the Rocket led to his suspension for hitting an official.

Selke was leaning toward Billy Reay, who had retired after eight seasons with the Canadiens to be the player-coach with the Victoria Cougars in the Western Hockey League. But Ken Reardon suggested that Blake, who was coaching in the Quebec Senior League, might be a better choice. Blake had been Richard's linemate and the thinking was that he would be a calming influence on the Rocket.

Richard was generally well behaved on Blake's watch but there were times when the fiery coach could have used someone to calm him down.

"He was tough, intimidating, wise, compassionate, unforgiving, scheming, and hardworking—all of it dedicated to winning eight Stanley Cups in 13 seasons as a coach," wrote *Montreal Gazette* columnist Red Fisher. "Winning wasn't merely a worthwhile target for Blake. It was everything. It was life itself."

Fisher said Blake got the best out of the best players. The coach recognized the talent he had on his roster but also knew that even superstars had to work hard to succeed.

Stanley Cup Coaching Champions

Hector (Toe) Blake: eight (1955–56, 1956–57, 1957–58, 1958–59, 1959–60, 1964–65, 1965–66, 1967–68)
Scotty Bowman: five (1972–73, 1975–76, 1976–77, 1977–78, 1978–79)
Dick Irvin: three (1943–44, 1945–46, 1952–53)
Cecil Hart: two (1929–30, 1930–31)
Newsy Lalonde: one (1915–16)
Leo Dandurand: one (1923–24)
Al MacNeil: one (1970–71)
Claude Ruel: one (1968–69)
Jean Perron: one (1985–86)
Jacques Demers: one (1992–93)

"He would tell us, 'I can't coach you guys, you're too good,'" recalled Dickie Moore, one of the 15 Hall of Famers who would play for Blake.

"Toe Blake hated to lose so much that he made us the same way," said defenceman J.C. Tremblay.

Henri Richard, who broke into the NHL as a 19-year-old in Blake's first season as a coach, described the coach's complex personality.

"He was like a dad to me. A very severe dad, but a dad," said Richard.

When goaltender Gump Worsley was asked what made Blake special as a coach, he replied: "There are 20 guys in that dressing room and it's seldom you find even two of them alike. Toe knew each individual—the ones who worked from the needles, the ones who needed another approach. Between periods, he never blasted an individual. He'd say some guys aren't pulling their weight. The guys who weren't knew who he was talking about and you'd see the heads drop. But he'd never embarrass anyone in front of everyone."

Fisher said Blake had a sense of loyalty to his players, even those he didn't like.

Goaltender Jacques Plante fell into that category. Blake wasn't happy when Plante started wearing a mask and there were nights when Plante would balk at playing because his asthma was bothering him. But when Fisher asked Blake to name the best goaltender he had seen, his choice was Plante.

Blake went out on top with a record of 500 wins, 255 losses, and 159 ties in the regular season and an 82–37 record in playoffs.

"I had to quit," Blake said in an interview for Bill Libby's book, *The Coaches*. "Every game, every season is a new challenge. But I'd been meeting these challenges as coach of the Canadiens for 13 years. The pressure was getting to be unbearable. On the day of the game, I was getting to be unbearable. I was no good to anyone, not even my family."

Blake was diagnosed with Alzheimer's disease in 1989 and spent the last six years of his life in a nursing home, unable to recognize his family and friends. He died in 1995 but his spirit lives on. His struggle with Alzheimer's raised awareness of the disease and the Toe Blake Golf Tournament is one of several fund-raising efforts which bear his name.

38 Jack of All Trades

Jack Laviolette took on a lot of responsibility when he was asked to create the Montreal Canadiens but he didn't think that he would finish the team's inaugural game as a goaltender.

When Ambrose O'Brien decided that the newly created National Hockey Association needed a team stocked with French Canadian players, he turned to Jean-Baptiste (Jack) Laviolette to assemble the team.

Laviolette, who was a standout defenceman with the Montreal Shamrocks when O'Brien came calling, became the Canadiens' first player, first coach, first captain, and first general manager. The team he would assemble included future Hall of Famers Newsy Laonde and Didier Pitre but it would be another year before Laviolette would plug a hole between the pipes with the addition of Georges Vézina.

The goaltender for the Canadiens' first game was Pat Larochelle but he was ejected for arguing about a goal. This was in an era when there were no backup goaltenders and Laviolette replaced Larochelle, finishing on the short end of a 9–4 count against the Renfrew Creamery Kings.

The Canadiens' media guide indicates that was Laviolette's lone appearance in goal, although there are some reports that he played up to three other games and lost them all.

Laviolette, who was born in Belleville, Ontario, but raised in Valleyfield, Quebec, had far more success as a defenceman and as the architect of what would become the most storied franchise in NHL history. He scored 48 goals in 155 games with the Canadiens and was a member of the 1916 team which won the Canadiens' first Stanley Cup.

Laviolette was 39 years old when he lost his right foot in an automobile accident in 1918.

He was elected to Canada's Sports Hall of Fame as a lacrosse player a few months after his death in 1960 at the age of 80. Two years later he was inducted into the Hockey Hall of Fame.

39 Lemaire Was a Two-Way Guy

Mention Jacques Lemaire and the word *defence* immediately comes to mind.

Defence was the cornerstone of Lemaire's game as a player and later as a coach but he was also part of the most dynamic line in Canadiens history.

Lemaire was the workhorse and the defensive conscience on the line which featured fellow Hall of Famers Steve Shutt and Guy Lafleur on his wings. He would win the draws, win the battles along the boards, and use his skills as a natural playmaker to set up his linemates.

When you're between the only Montreal players to reach the 60-goal plateau, it's easy for people to forget that you could put the puck in the net as well. He scored 22 goals as a rookie in the 1967–68 season and added 13 points in 13 playoff games in what would be the last of eight Stanley Cups for Toe Blake as a coach and the first of eight Stanley Cups for Lemaire as a player.

He was a 20-goal scorer in each of his 12 seasons in Montreal. His weapon of choice was a slapshot that was both hard and on target. He developed it as a youngster by shooting with a heavy steel puck and it was said that only Bobby Hull could match the shot for speed and accuracy.

Lemaire developed a reputation for being a money player, someone who produced his best hockey in the playoffs. He scored the Stanley Cup–winning goals in 1977 and 1979. The only other players to score two Cup-winning goals were Mike Bossy, Bobby Orr, Henri Richard, Jean Béliveau, and Toe Blake.

One of those Cup winners came at 4:32 of overtime to give the Canadiens a sweep of the Boston Bruins in 1977. Lemaire had three game-winning goals in the 1977 playoffs.

Lemaire racked up 139 playoff points to stand No. 2 on the Canadiens' all-time list behind Béliveau, who had 176. He's likely to maintain that position for a while because no current player has more than 50 playoff points.

Lemaire went out on a high note, scoring the Cup-winning goal against the Rangers in 1979. He moved to Switzerland, where he served as a player-coach with Sierre. It provided him with the basis for his coaching career in the NHL, although he found the attitude a bit different from North America.

"Most guys I coached had other jobs," he said. "They would work eight to 10 hours and then come to practice. Sometimes they didn't show. I didn't know what to expect from them."

But Lemaire had another shock when he returned to Canada and eventually replaced Bob Berry behind the Canadiens bench late in the 1983–84 season. He guided the Canadiens to the Adams

Division title the following season but quit after one full season because he couldn't deal with the pressure which came with the job.

Lemaire moved into the Canadiens front office but returned to coaching with the New Jersey Devils in 1993. He won the Jack Adams Award as coach of the year in his first season with the Devils and led them to the Stanley Cup in the lockout-abbreviated 1995 season. Two of the veteran players on that team, Claude Lemieux and Stéphane Richer, played their first NHL games in Montreal when Lemaire was the coach.

He became the first head coach of the expansion Minnesota Wild and finished up his coaching career back in New Jersey from 2009 to 2011.

Lemaire was regarded as an innovator but not always in a positive light. He was the master of a defensive style employing the neutral-zone trap. Critics complained that Lemaire was bringing down the entertainment level in the NHL but his teams were often among the highest scoring in the NHL.

40 The Too Many Men on the Ice Game

The Forum Ghosts have been credited with helping the Canadiens forge miraculous results on the ice, but these ethereal spirits had to work overtime on May 10, 1979.

The Canadiens and the Boston Bruins were meeting in the seventh and deciding game of the Stanley Cup semifinals and the Bruins under coach Don Cherry felt their time was at hand.

The Canadiens had swept the Bruins in the 1977 Stanley Cup final and the teams went six games a year later, with Montreal again coming out on top. The Canadiens, who were looking for their fourth consecutive Cup, won the first two games of the semifinal series in 1979, outscoring Boston 9–4. The Bruins responded with two wins at the Boston Garden and the teams traded home wins to leave the series deadlocked at three games apiece.

The Bruins got off to a good start and took a 3–1 lead after two periods as the line of Wayne Cashman, Rick Middleton, and Jean Ratelle combined for eight points.

Doug Risebrough told the *Montreal Gazette*'s Red Fisher that the mood in the dressing room was bleak but team captain Yvan Cournoyer started talking, encouraging his teammates. Others joined in.

"Words mean a lot but if they aren't carried onto the ice, they don't mean a thing," said Risebrough. "We knew if we could get one goal, we could get another. We were unhappy but at least we were getting the shots. What a job that (Boston goaltender Gilles) Gilbert did. But we had that feeling, it we could get one...."

The Canadiens did get one from Mark Napier and then Guy Lapointe tied the game. But things looked dismal when Middleton scored at 16:01 to put the Bruins ahead 4–3. It was Middleton's second goal of the game and he had assists on the other two Boston goals.

That's when the Ghosts took over.

Or maybe it was just a brain-dead move by Bruins coach Don Cherry.

With 2:34 remaining in the third period, the Bruins were called for having too many men on the ice. They quickly learned that you can't open the door for the Canadiens because Guy Lafleur barged in and ripped a one-timer past Bruins goaltender Gilles Gilbert to tie the game.

"That was my fault," Cherry said of the penalty. "(The players) must have heard me say something. I had to grab two other guys or we would have had eight out there."

The confusion stemmed from Cherry's use of Don Marcotte as a shadow for Lafleur. When the Canadiens double-shifted Lafleur, Marcotte stayed on the ice while a new line jumped on.

There were more words from Cournoyer before the overtime. He reminded his teammates that, while they may be tired, the Bruins were tired as well.

But neither team looked weary in the overtime as they traded chances. Marcotte and Peter McNab tested Ken Dryden. Yvan Lambert and Guy Lafleur had chances, and Steve Shutt's slapshot was Montreal's 50th shot on Gilbert.

Middleton was stopped as he tried to slip past Serge Savard and the Canadiens counter-attacked, Savard to Réjean Houle to Mario Trembly to Lambert, who cemented his place in Canadiens history when he scored the winning goal at 9:33 of the overtime period.

"The first time I went in to score, I went in too deep and the puck got mixed up in my skates," Lambert explained. "This time, when I saw Mario with the puck, I put my head down and said 'I don't care, I'm getting there.' The pass was a perfect one. The goalie had no chance. It was over."

Gilbert, who stopped 47 shots, was devastated, saying, "I've lost before but this is the toughest ever."

The Canadiens would go on to beat the New York Rangers in a five-game final to give Montreal four consecutive Cup wins and their 22nd overall.

But there would be a changing of the guard at the end of the season. Future Hall of Famers Cournoyer, Dryden, and Jacques Lemaire retired. And Bowman, who had guided the team to five Stanley Cup wins in eight seasons, decided to move on. He was disappointed when he wasn't offered the general manager's job in Montreal after Sam Pollock retired in 1978 and he left to become the coach and general manager of the Buffalo Sabres.

41 The Farmer

Frank Selke was a gentleman farmer who raised prize-winning chickens but he was best known in Montreal for another type of farming. He set the stage for three decades of Canadiens success by convincing the team's owner, Senator Donat Raymond, to invest in developing young talent.

Selke had seen the value of a strong farm system firsthand when he worked for the Toronto Maple Leafs, who were poised to win the Stanley Cup four times in a five-season span from 1947 to 1951. When he joined the Canadiens as general manager in 1946, the team had won two Stanley Cups in the previous three seasons but Selke wasn't impressed with the team's talent:

"I told Senator Raymond that no other team could match his top six players—Bill Durnan in goal, Ken Reardon and Butch Bouchard on defence, and the Punch Line of Blake, Richard, and Elmer Lach. But there were no reserves, no farm system."

Selke pointed out that many of the team's players were coming to the end of their careers. The team was also losing money but Senator Raymond listened to the small, trim man and gave him a free hand—and an initial investment of $300,000—to sign young players and develop a farm system across the country. He bought the entire Quebec Senior Hockey League in 1953 to secure the services of Jean Béliveau.

"I purposely operated the farm club like a farmer," Selke said. "I always liked to spot good potential players, like plants coming up, and helped them develop and ripen until they were good enough to come up.

"We were the first to do it. We helped teams everywhere. In Winnipeg, we had 10 teams, in Regina we financed the whole amateur system, and in Edmonton we spent up to $300,000 a year in amateur development. And we were able to do it because we sold $200,000 worth of good players out of it every season."

He used Maurice Richard as the model for the type of player he wanted to develop. While Richard had a fiery temper, Selke admired him for his commitment to his family. Selke believed in character and that has remained a cornerstone of the Canadiens' ethos. Over the years, numerous players have been sent packing because of their off-ice conduct.

The Canadiens made the Stanley Cup final in Selke's first season as general manager but missed the playoffs the following season, and rebuilding the franchise took time. He didn't win his first Stanley Cup until 1953. The Canadiens lost to the Detroit Red Wings in a pair of seven-game finals in 1954 and 1955 but then set a record with five consecutive Stanley Cups.

Selke began his training as a hockey executive at the tender age of 14 in his hometown of Berlin, Ontario, which changed its name to Kitchener riding a wave of anti-German sentiment during World War I. He was too small to play but became the manager of the Iroquois Bantams. At the age of 19, he was coaching the Berlin Union Jacks and guided the team to the Ontario Hockey Association final in 1915.

Young Selke was trained as an electrician but he was making a name for himself in the world of hockey. Future Toronto Maple Leafs star Joe Primeau was the standout when Selke coached the St. Mary's juniors to an OHA title in 1925, and Selke won another OHA title with the Toronto Marlboros in 1927. Future Hall of Famer Red Horner was the star of that team.

Selke and Primeau were reunited in the 1927–28 season when he coached the Toronto Ravinas in the Canadian Professional Hockey League. The Maple Leafs bought the team in midseason and that was the start of what would turn out to be a productive but sometimes thorny relationship between Selke and Maple Leafs managing director Conn Smythe. After returning to the Marlies and leading them to the Memorial Cup in 1929, Selke became Smythe's top assistant.

Selke was involved in the development of the Maple Leafs' farm system and he used his connections in the building trades to facilitate the construction of Maple Leaf Gardens in 1931. Selke was able to convince workers to accept stock in the hockey team and the new arena as payment for their work.

He and Smythe had a good working relationship until the outbreak of World War II. Smythe, who had been a decorated hero and prisoner of war in World War I, formed an artillery brigade and served in France, where he was wounded in the leg. Selke, who was regarded as too old and too frail to serve, ran the Maple Leafs in Smythe's absence.

In 1943, Selke traded Frank Eddolls to the Canadiens for the rights to prospect Ted (Teeder) Kennedy and Smythe was angry because he wasn't consulted before the deal. Kennedy would go on to a Hall of Fame career and would become a Smythe favourite, but the man who was nicknamed the Little Dictator felt his authority had been usurped.

The reality was that Selke was doing a good job in Toronto and some of the Maple Leafs directors were in favour of giving him Smythe's job on a permanent basis. When Smythe returned from the war, he was involved in a power play to become president of Maple Leaf Gardens Ltd. and he was upset when Selke failed to support his bid.

Selke resigned in May 1946 and he joined the Canadiens two months later. He reluctantly retired in 1964, turning the reins over to his assistant, Sam Pollock, who created his own legacy in the front office.

42 Go on a Road Trip

Attendance at Florida Panthers games dropped so low in the 2014–15 season that management decided to shrink the BB&T Center by closing the upper deck, effectively reducing the capacity by about 3,000 seats.

But those seats are back in use for a few select games, including the two annual visits from the Montreal Canadiens. The Canadiens can be counted on to produce a sellout crowd made up of snowbirds who spend most of the winter in south Florida and visitors who plan their vacations to coincide with a Canadiens game.

Savvy fans who find it difficult to obtain tickets for games at the Bell Centre have discovered that it can be fun—and relatively inexpensive—to follow the team on the road.

Here are the top road-warrior destinations:

1. **Fort Lauderdale:** The Florida Panthers play 20 miles to the west in Sunrise, Florida, but no visit to the area is complete without a trip to the white-sand beaches that are rated as some of the finest in the world. While it's best to plan ahead, tickets are plentiful and accommodations are reasonable if you don't mind a short drive to the beach. There are restaurants which cater to every taste and budget. The Quarterdeck—with branches on the beach and near the arena—offers pub fare, regional specialties, large slabs of prime rib, and a happy hour that never seems to end. Coconuts on the Intercoastal has fresh seafood, half-price appetizers during happy hour, and a variety of oysters. If you're into burgers, it's worth a drive south to Hollywood to sample the 13-ounce offering at Le Tub. *GQ* magazine and Oprah Winfrey have both described it as the best

burger in America. The quintessential beach bar offers a view of boats cruising by on the Intercoastal Waterway and the only caveat is that you may have to wait for your order because grill space is limited and beauties that big take time to cook.

2. **Tampa:** The other team in Florida is located on the Gulf Coast and tickets are a little more difficult to obtain because the Lightning has done a better job of marketing a team that has had some success on the ice. There are several first-class hotels—including the Marriott Waterside and the Embassy Suites—within walking distance of the Amalie Arena. Champions bar in the Marriott is busy before and after games, while Hattrick's is a sports bar that caters to hockey fans. For a special meal, head to Bern's Steakhouse, where you're likely to see a few visiting hockey players the night before a game. Prime steaks and seafood are featured along with a wine list which runs hundreds of pages. Ask for the kitchen and wine cellar tour and leave room for dessert, which is served upstairs in the Harry Waugh Dessert Room.

3. **New York:** Tickets to Rangers games are hard to find and expensive but the Islanders and the Devils offer opportunities to follow the Canadiens and take a bite out of the Big Apple. Long Island has been a popular destination for Montreal fans because reasonably priced tickets have been readily available. The dynamics may change in 2015 when the Islanders move from the Nassau Coliseum to the Barclays Center in Brooklyn. If ticket costs and availability become a problem, there's always the option of a Devils game at the Prudential Center in Newark. New Jersey's largest city had a reputation as a high-crime area but the streets around the arena have undergone a transformation to a safe, vibrant area with two major hotels and numerous restaurants and bars. If you have a hankering for Southern cooking, you can't beat the Dinosaur Bar-B-Q, a brand already well known to AHL fans in Rochester and

Few experiences can rival invading another team's arena to cheer on the Canadiens.

Syracuse. The nearby Penn Station Newark features regular train service for the 25-minute ride to Penn Station New York.

4. **Nashville:** Here's hockey with a little Hee-Haw thrown in. The Bridgestone Arena is in the centre of the action in Music City. Wander across the street and you'll find a string of honky-tonks and barbecue joints. The most famous is Tootsie's Orchid Lounge, but Legends, the Stage on Broadway, Robert's Western World, and Rippy's are among the joints which offer nonstop music along Lower Broadway. For first-time visitors, it should be noted that most places don't have a cover charge but they pass a bucket around after each set, so you should tuck away some

bills to show your appreciation. The bands work in four-hour shifts and the general rule is the later the show, the better the musicians. The Grand Ole Opry is a short drive out of town and offers regular concerts as well as a theme park. The Country Music Hall of Fame is a three-minute walk from the arena. If you're in the mood for some culture, head out to the city's West End and check out the full-size replica of the Parthenon, which houses a collection of 19th and 20th century American art.

5. **Chicago:** A visit to the United Center should be on every hockey fan's bucket list. The United Center doesn't have as many seats as the Bell Centre but the crowds are larger because standing room is a Chicago tradition. The official capacity at the old Chicago Stadium was 16,666 but the crowds regularly topped 19,000. The Chicago fans are at least as noisy as those in Montreal and one of the highlights of any game is the stirring renditions of the national anthems by Jim Cornelison, a classically trained tenor. Before the game, drop in to the Billy Goat Tavern, a Chicago institution which was the inspiration for the "Cheeseburger, cheeseburger" routine on *Saturday Night Live*. After the game, head down to Rush Street, where the bar action continues until the wee hours of the morning.

43 Pollock Stayed One Step Ahead

Sam Pollock once said that there was no secret to building a winning team. The key, said Pollock, way staying on top:

"People have asked me many times how someone goes about building the kind of tradition that the Canadiens have. It is really quite simple. You build a top-notch organization manned by the best people at all levels. You get each man doing his job on the ice and off the ice and all of a sudden you're a winner. Believe it or not, that's the easy part. Where most sports organizations go wrong is in letting up once they reached, or are near, the top of their sport. Once you're a winner, you keep improving on perfection. You keep making trades and changes that will strengthen your team even if they aren't popular at the time. You go about your business. That is where we might have been different from other franchises. Once we started winning, we worked even harder to continue winning. Too many organizations relax at this point."

No general manager in the history of the game has come close to matching Pollock's record for success. He won nine Stanley Cups during his 14-year tenure as GM.

Pollock had a lifelong interest in sports but he had limited athletic skills and poured his energy into coaching and managing teams. He caught the eye of Canadiens GM Frank Selke, who took Pollock under his wing. Pollock coached the Junior Canadiens and later oversaw the prospects in the farm system Selke had developed.

J.C. Tremblay, Jacques Lapèrriere, Ralph Backstrom, Gilles Tremblay, and coach Scotty Bowman were in the group which became known as Sam's Boys, and they played pivotal roles as the Canadiens went through a transition after Pollock replaced Selke in 1964.

Pollock's strength was his ability to adapt to the changing face of the game. In the 1960s, he rebuilt the team with the assets from the farm system he and Selke created.

When expansion arrived in 1967, the Canadiens had the most to lose in the expansion draft because they had the deepest talent pool. Each team was allowed to protect 11 skaters and one goal-tender but Pollock pushed through a rule which exempted recently signed junior-age players and another which stipulated that first-year pros couldn't be drafted in the first 10 rounds. The first rule protected Jacques Lemaire while the second allowed the Canadiens to keep Serge Savard and Rogie Vachon because the team had lost the maximum 20 players in the first 10 rounds.

Pollock used the Canadiens' depth to ensure success through the 1970s. He would package older or less-talented players and send them to expansion markets in exchange for draft picks. From 1969 to 1974, the Canadiens had 17 first-round selections.

"People build teams in certain ways," said Pollock. "I've always traded for futures—not pasts."

Perhaps his masterstroke was engineering the acquisition of Guy Lafleur.

Pollock wasn't sure which player he wanted in the 1971 draft but he knew that he wanted the No. 1 overall pick.

The two prizes in the draft were Lafleur, who had been on everyone's radar since he dominated at the Quebec Peewee Tournament, and Marcel Dionne, a native of Quebec, who was a two-time Ontario Hockey Association scoring champion with the St. Catharines Black Hawks.

Pollock put himself in a position to get the No. 1 pick when he sent prospect Ernie Hicke and the Canadiens' first-round pick in 1970 to the California Golden Seals for François Lacombe, cash, and the Golden Seals' first-round pick in 1971.

Hicke became a useful player for two seasons in California and went on to play 520 NHL games. Lacombe never played for the Canadiens and spent most of his career with the Quebec Nordiques in the WHA. But they were pawns in this game; the key was the first-round draft choice in 1971 and it took another trade to secure that.

As Pollock expected, the Golden Seals weren't good. But there was another team that threatened to be even worse.

At the midway point in the 1970–71 season, the Los Angeles Kings had dropped below California and Pollock saw the No. 1 pick slipping away. Pollock decided to give the Kings a boost by sending Ralph Backstrom to L.A. for Gord Labossiere and Ray Fortin, two players who would never dress for the Canadiens.

The 33-year-old Backstrom had been a part of six Stanley Cup teams and had scored 20 or more goals on five occasions for Montreal. But he was unhappy with a diminished role and he requested a trade after the 1969–70 season, When Pollock refused his request, Backstrom talked about retiring. He relented after a brief holdout but he found himself spending a lot of time as a healthy scratch. He had one goal and four assists in 16 games when Pollock traded him on January 26, 1971.

The trade had the desired effect. Backstrom scored 14 goals and 13 assists in 33 games and the Kings climbed all the way to fifth place in the Western Conference.

By the time the draft rolled around, Pollock had settled on Lafleur, who helped forge the Canadiens dynasty which won five Stanley Cups in the 1970s.

Pollock weathered a challenge from the WHA in the 1970s. J.C. Tremblay, Marc Tardif, and Réjean Houle defected to the new league, although Houle would return three years later.

"The Nordiques offered me more money but it was also a chance to play more because I was behind Yvan Cournoyer and Guy Lafleur in Montreal," recalled Houle. "But my heart was always with the Canadiens and I thank Sam for bringing me back."

Pollock's continual drive to get better created some anxiety in the dressing room but Steve Shutt said it also provided some motivation.

Said Shutt: "Our joke was 'How do you spell relief? A-I-R C-A-N-A-D-A. Over and out.' It wasn't hard to stay motivated with Sam running the show, emotion or no emotion. "

"I once saw Sam on a TV show saying that running a hockey team was like running a chicken farm," said Dickie Moore. "He said it was all business, no emotion. I just think a lot of this was a front put on by a very astute man who saw the necessity of keeping his distance."

Pollock left the Canadiens in 1978 when Peter and Edgar Bronfman sold the team back to the Molson family and he moved to Toronto where he put his business acumen to good use in a number of companies controlled by the Bronfman family. He returned to his first love, baseball, when he served as chairman and chief executive officer of the Toronto Blue Jays from 1995 to 2000.

He was elected to the Hockey Hall of Fame in 1978.

 # The Quiet Leader

Don't ask Andrei Markov about his personal life. It's personal.

In fact, Andrei Markov doesn't like any questions, personal or otherwise. He simply wants to play hockey, and he has been doing that very well for 14 NHL seasons, all of them in Montreal.

For most of that time, Markov has been the Canadiens' No. 1 defenceman. P.K. Subban may get the headlines—and the richest contract in the team's history—but night after night, Markov is the man.

Early in his career, Markov ducked interviews because he couldn't—or wouldn't—speak English. Since mastering the language, he has set strict guidelines on the topics to be discussed during his rare interactions with the media.

He will talk about the team but not about individual teammates or opponents. His ban on personal topics extends even to innocuous queries about his favourite restaurants or the weather.

Markov opened up a bit in 2015 when he was the Canadiens' nominee for the Masterton Trophy, which rewards perseverance and dedication to the game. Markov demonstrated both qualities by returning to a high level after suffering two injuries which threatened his career.

Markov played only 65 games in three seasons from 2009–10 to 2011–12 as he dealt with a variety of leg and knee injuries. His misfortune began on the opening night of the 2009–10 season when he collided with Montreal goaltender Carey Price, whose skate sliced the tendons in Markov's leg. The original prognosis was that he would miss four months, but he was back in the lineup in half that time.

A hit from Pittsburgh's Matt Cooke knocked him out of the 2010 playoffs, and he suffered his most serious injury when his knee was torn up on November 13, 2010. He underwent the first of three knee surgeries on December 8 of that year.

"Sometimes, I remember the past, when I had those issues," Markov said. "That was tough for me. Right now, I feel great and try to enjoy every night because you never know what's going to happen. I'm happy to stay healthy."

When asked whether he ever thought his career might be over, Markov said he was determined to remain positive.

"I knew I could come back, but I didn't know how good I could be," Markov said. "Lots of people helped me and I thank them for that."

Markov returned for 13 games in the 2011–12 season and said a stint in the KHL during the 2012–13 lockout was key to his comeback.

A Man of Many Talents

The Salle Jacques Beauchamp, which provides pregame meals and between-period hot dogs for the media, was named to honour a former hockey writer and sports editor for the *Journal de Montreal*. But Beauchamp was also a goaltender and he regularly filled in at practice when one of the Canadiens' regular goaltenders needed a day off.

"During the lockout, I went to Russia and I started feeling comfortable," Markov said. "Those games over there helped me to come back. After the lockout, I came back and I wasn't scared about getting injured. I put all that behind me."

Markov missed only two games between 2012 and 2015, and he did so reluctantly after coach Michel Therrien insisted that he take time off. He turned 36 midway through the 2014–15 season but says he's not thinking about retirement after signing a three-year contract in the off-season.

"I know I'm getting older, but physically and mentally I feel good," Markov said. "I don't want to think I have two more years on my contract and it's going to be done. As long as I enjoy playing hockey, I want to play."

When asked if he made any concessions to age, the hardworking Markov smiled and said: "I started practicing harder, working harder. Every year, guys are bigger, stronger, and faster, and you have to try to keep up and that's what I do."

If Markov is dedicated to hockey, he's also dedicated to Montreal. He was drafted by the Canadiens in the sixth round in 1998 and made his NHL debut two years later. He has played his entire NHL career with the Canadiens and his salary cap hit of $5.75 million has been the same since 2007.

"It's the best place to play hockey," Markov said. "The passion of the fans and the organization—I never thought about leaving. It's going to be special for the rest of my life."

Markov became a Canadian citizen in 2010 but has retained his Russian citizenship and represents his native land at the Olympics and other international competitions.

Markov said he recently shared that special feeling with his 13-year-old son.

"My son came to visit me and I brought him to the practice and he sees it all and it's special for him," he said. "He plays in Russia and, hopefully, he can be a good player in the future."

45 The Mighty Atom

Aurèle Joliat didn't receive a warm reception when he arrived in Montreal at the start of the 1922–23 NHL season. The Ottawa native came from the Saskatoon Crescents of the Western Canada Hockey League in what amounted to a trade for Newsy Lalonde, who was the most popular player on the Montreal roster.

The fans didn't care that Lalonde's skills had deteriorated and that he continually fought with the club management. He was the star and was being replaced by an unknown who turned to hockey after breaking his leg while playing football.

It didn't take long for Joliat to win over the Montreal crowd. Playing left wing on a line with Billy Boucher and Howie Morenz, Joliat dazzled fans with his stickhandling and scoring ability.

He helped the Canadiens win the Stanley Cup in 1924 and had a breakthrough the following season when he led the team with 30 goals, two more than Morenz. He was part of two more Stanley Cup wins in 1930 and 1931.

But Canadiens fans had reason to be wary of the deal that brought Joliat to Montreal. Joliat had never played at the professional level and didn't play at all during the 1921–22 season because he had been suspended for a year. The reasons for that suspension have been lost to history but there are two versions of the story.

In interviews after his playing career ended, Joliat insisted that he was blackballed because he turned down a lowball offer from Tommy Gorman to play for the Ottawa Senators. Joliat, who had been playing in a senior league in Ottawa, said he was offered $250 for the season.

But there's a far more intriguing tale which involves a plot by gamblers to fix a game in the Northern Ontario Hockey Association final. After dominating the senior league in Ottawa, Joliat joined the Iroquois Falls team as a ringer for the NOHA finals. When it became obvious that Joliat was the star of the team, he was approached by some local mobsters who offered him several hundred dollars to throw the game. Joliat, who had never seen that much money, snatched it from the gambler's hand and the fix was in.

There was only one problem—Joliat didn't fulfill his part of the bargain. He scored six goals to lead Iroquois Falls to victory. The way he told the story, he eluded the angry gamblers by going out the back door of the arena and hopping on a train wearing his hockey gear.

Part of Joliat's appeal was his size. He had to stand on his toes to reach his listed height of 5-foot-6 and he never weighed more than 140 pounds. But opponents who tried to intimidate him discovered that Joliat didn't back down and wasn't shy about using his stick to settle disputes. He separated his shoulder six times and suffered five broken noses and several broken ribs, but rarely missed a game in his 16 NHL seasons.

Joliat would score 270 goals for the Canadiens, matching Morenz's career total, and he still ranks ninth on the team's all-time goal-scoring list despite the fact he played all of his career when the seasons were never longer than 48 games. He held the team record for most goals by a left winger until it was broken by Steve Shutt, who scored 408 of his 424 goals with the Canadiens.

Joliat was a crowd-pleasing showman who was instantly recognizable because he played with a peaked cap which was custom made by a Montreal hatmaker. He was an integral part of a team that became known as the Flying Frenchmen, although he was actually descended from Swiss Protestants who immigrated to Canada in the early 19th century.

Joliat won the Hart Trophy as the NHL's most valuable player in 1934 and retired after the 1937–38 season. He had a career-low six goals that season and said he lost some of his desire after his good friend Morenz died the previous year.

Joliat continued to skate on Ottawa's Rideau Canal into his eighties and an 83-year-old Joliat made a final appearance on the Forum ice when the team celebrated its 75th anniversary in 1984.

Joliat, the oldest living Canadien at the time, hit the ice running but fell after a few strides. He got up, picked up a loose puck, and was headed toward the net when he hit the red carpet and took a second fall. Again, he got to his feet and skated in on goal, where he put a shot past Jacques Plante.

As the crowd roared its approval, he doffed his hat and threw his arms into the air.

The Scoring Machine

Maurice Richard may have made history when he became the first player to score 50 goals in 50 games but nobody in the history of the National Hockey League was as prolific a scorer as Joe Malone.

Malone played most of his career for the Quebec Bulldogs in his hometown of Quebec City. He was a dominant player in the National Hockey Association but when the Bulldogs didn't make the move to the National Hockey League when it was formed in 1918, he played for the Canadiens and set the record for the highest goals-per-game average in league history with 44 goals in 20 games, an average of 2.2 goals per game.

It should be noted that Malone played in a different era. Teams carried nine or 10 players and substitutions were rare.

In an interview with *The Hockey News* a year before his death in 1969, Malone said: "Maybe I should have scored more goals, the amount of time I spent on the ice that year. In those days, the regulars played perhaps 50 minutes a game."

But Malone was quick to point out that the game was played at a slower pace.

"We didn't go up and down the ice like they do now," said Malone. "Today's game is much faster. We'd hustle when opportunities presented themselves but the rest of the time, we'd loaf—at least I did. It was the only way you could go the entire 60 minutes."

Malone had a 14-game scoring streak and he might have scored more if he hadn't missed two games in that 1917–18 season.

"I missed one game because the arena of the Montreal Wanderers burned down," he explained. "I missed another for reasons I never could remember, either I was hurt or drunk. I can't remember which."

Malone, who was a toolmaker by trade, had matinee-idol looks. In his book, *Behind the Cheering*, former Canadiens general manager Frank Selke described Malone as "handsome, good-looking, polished. Joe could make some of Hollywood's glamour boys look undistinguished by comparison."

The Bulldogs would join the NHL in 1919 and Malone was returned to his previous team. On January 31, 1920, Malone scored seven goals as Quebec defeated Toronto St. Pat's 10–6. That performance set the NHL record for the most goals in a single game.

But it wasn't Malone's best night.

"I got nine goals in a Stanley Cup game, in 1913 it was," said Malone.

Quebec won the National Hockey Association in 1912–13 with Malone scoring 43 goals in 20 games. The Sydney Millionaires issued a challenge for the Stanley Cup and Malone scored nine goals in the first of two games.

Malone won four scoring titles in seven seasons in the NHA and NHL and finished his career back in Montreal in 1923–24.

"I took a look at a kid in our training camp in Grimsby. Ontario, I knew right then that I was headed to the easy chair," recalled Malone. "He was Howie Morenz and in practice he moved past me so fast, I thought I was standing still."

47 Giving Back

Thousands of youngsters in Quebec can look forward to playing hockey and skating outdoors without worrying about global warming.

That's because the Montreal Canadiens Children's Foundation has established a program to build refrigerated rinks in underserved communities. The Bleu-Blanc-Rouge program has a goal of building one rink each year; there are currently six in operation. A study commissioned by Quebec En Forme in 2012 reported that an overwhelming number of residents felt better about their neighbourhoods after the rinks opened. The group, which promotes fitness in Quebec, said the rinks had reached 100,000 users.

The most recent rink, which opened in the South Shore community of Longueuil in 2015, is also the first built in cooperation with the Canadian Tire Jumpstart program, which is dedicated to providing sports opportunities to youngsters whose parents can't afford equipment or registration fees.

While the Canadiens have a tradition of community involvement, team president Pierre Boivin created the Children's Foundation in 2000 to give a formal structure to the club's many activities. By 2014, the foundation had distributed more than $16 million to 500 different youth groups.

"We concentrate on programs that promote active living, education, and nutrition," said Geneviève Paquette, the foundation's executive director.

In addition to the rinks, the foundation maintains a box at the Bell Centre which provides an opportunity for youngsters who would not otherwise be able see a game. It also supports programs which provide breakfast to underprivileged youngsters. Its activities during the NHL's annual Hockey Fights Cancer campaign include inviting young cancer patients to see a game and meet the players.

The foundation is funded through a variety of activities ranging from the Canadiens' annual golf tournament down to grassroots projects organized by school and community groups.

The golf tournament is the biggie, producing up to $500,000 annually. Companies and individuals pay for the privilege of playing on a world-class golf course with a Canadiens player, coach, or legend as part of their foursome. The day's activities culminate in a gourmet dinner and a live auction.

Items up for bid might include a dinner in the Canadiens dressing room with some players, a luxury box for the year's hottest concert, a trip to a road game in Ottawa on a helicopter piloted by Hall of Famer Guy Lafleur, or a chance to be part of the official team picture.

The brokers at Desjardins Securities, one of the team's major sponsors, donate their commissions for one day each year.

Rio Tinto Alcan sponsors a fund-raising event each year to benefit the foundation, while Ford sponsors an annual celebrity hockey game at the Bell Centre.

Other fund-raising efforts include a lottery and a silent auction of hockey memorabilia at each home game.

The team's involvement in the community isn't restricted to the foundation.

The Canadiens and Evenko, the entertainment arm of the Bell Centre operation, join forces each year for a blood donor clinic.

The Canadiens' wives and girlfriends are involved in a project to buy and wrap toys during the holiday season. The toys are distributed to underprivileged youngsters through several organizations.

Each year, the Canadiens players visit the city's two children's hospitals—the Montreal Children's Hospital and Hopital Ste. Justine—to visit with the youngsters and distribute gifts.

Big Jean's 500th

On the afternoon of February 11, 1971, broadcasters Dick Irvin Jr. and Ron Reusch sat in the newsroom at CFCF-TV and went over the plans for the night's newscast.

The Canadiens were playing the Minnesota North Stars that night and they were trying to decide whether to send a cameraman to shoot highlights of the game.

"It wasn't a given in those days," said Reusch. "You were dealing with film and you had to allow time for processing and editing. And Minnesota wasn't a very good team. The one thing we kicked around was that Jean Béliveau had 497 (career) goals but at that point, he had only 15 or 16 for the season.

"We talked it over it for about an hour and finally, Dick said, 'Let's do it. It's Jean Béliveau and he's likely to get a hat-trick.'"

That's exactly what happened and Reusch points out that the station wound up with the only visual evidence of the historic night.

Béliveau was 39 years old, but there were no signs that his skills had deteriorated as he victimized Gilles Gilbert, the rookie goaltender for the North Stars. Each of the goals was a classic worthy of a man who carried himself with class and dignity on and off the ice.

Béliveau's night started when he jumped on the ice on a delayed penalty. As he crossed the blue line, Béliveau unleashed a slapshot. Gilbert got a piece of the puck with his left hand but couldn't hold on.

No. 499 and No. 500 were examples of Béliveau's stickhandling ability. On both goals, he bore down on Gilbert, waited until the goaltender made his move, and then scored on a backhander. He tucked No. 500 inside the far post on the tail end of what Frank Mahovlich described as one of the nicest three-way passing plays you'll ever see. Mahovlich was stationed at the far side of the crease in case the shot needed some help, but he made no move to deflect the puck and it hit the inside of the far post and went in.

The game was delayed for several minutes as the Forum crowd threw hats on the ice and gave Béliveau a standing ovation. The game didn't attract the media horde that follows the team today, but Béliveau was kept busy after the game as he patiently granted interviews and posed for pictures, including one with a fedora perched on his head and a puck in his mouth.

Béliveau demonstrated his class later that evening when he tracked down Gilbert in the garage area at the Forum.

As Gilbert explained in a documentary commemorating the 40th anniversary of the goal, Béliveau wasn't there to apologize but he told the goaltender not to be discouraged and predicted Gilbert would go on to have a great career. Gilbert would play 416 NHL games and would figure in another memorable night at the Forum which didn't end well for the goaltender.

Gilbert was between the pipes for the Boston Bruins on May 10, 1979, the night Don Cherry forgot how to count. The Bruins were leading 4–3 late in Game 7 of their Stanley Cup semifinal when they were penalized for having too many men on the ice. Guy

Lafleur beat Gilbert to tie the game and Yvon Lambert scored the overtime winner.

The Canadiens wanted to present Béliveau with a car to commemorate his 500th goal, but instead he worked with the team to establish the Jean Béliveau Foundation to help underprivileged children. The club and other friends of Béliveau jump-started the

Jean Béliveau spent nearly his entire life as a member of the Canadiens organization. He won 10 Stanley Cups as a player and was part of seven more as an executive, the most championships by a single person in NHL history.

foundation with a check for $155,855, which was presented to him on Jean Béliveau Night, March 24, 1971. The foundation distributed more than $1.5 million to children's charities before it was turned over to the Quebec Society for Crippled Children.

On March 29, 2007, Béliveau was honoured at a $1,000-a-plate dinner at the Bell Centre that raised $1 million for children's charities.

49 The Goal-Scorer

By his own admission, Steve Shutt was never a candidate for the Ice Capades but he did know how to put the puck in the net.

"I was never a really good skater," Shutt said in a 2004 interview with Kevin Shea of the Hockey Hall of Fame. "As a kid, I tried to run on the ice but once I got near the net, I could always score."

Shutt's goal-scoring was an integral part of the Canadiens' success in the late 1970s, when the team won four consecutive Stanley Cups. He set the team record for most goals in a season with 60 in 1976–77 and linemate Guy Lafleur matched it a year later. During the Canadiens' run, Shutt scored 191 goals and added 28 in the playoffs. The only teammate to surpass him was Lafleur with 224 regular-season goals and 36 playoff goals. When asked about his role with the team, he described himself as a "specialist."

Shutt grew up as a Maple Leafs fan in Toronto and played in the Marlboros organization from peewee up to Junior A. He made the jump from midget to Junior A in one season. The Marlies wanted him to stay in his age group and play midget but he threatened to move to Montreal if he couldn't play Junior B for North York. The Marlies called him up for the playoffs.

He spent the next three seasons with a team that may have been the best junior team that never won the Memorial Cup. In 1972, four Marlies were among the first 11 players selected in the NHL draft. Billy Harris went No. 1 overall to the Islanders while Montreal selected Shutt at No. 4 and Dave Gardner at No. 8 and the Maple Leafs drafted George Ferguson at No 11. Arguably no player in that draft had as good a career as Shutt.

If Shutt was anxious to move up in the minor ranks, he learned patience in Montreal, where the roster was loaded with future Hall of Famers. He played only 50 games as a rookie, often sharing space in the press box with Lafleur. He got his name on the Stanley Cup as a rookie but said he didn't feel part of the win because he dressed for one playoff game and played only one shift.

"Being drafted by the Canadiens, I didn't know if I was going to play in the NHL," Shutt recalled. "They had a stacked team and it was extremely different for a rookie to break in there. For the first two years, I didn't really play that much but it was a real learning curve."

Shutt said the transition from junior star to NHL bench-warmer was difficult but he noted that once he became a regular, he appreciated the hard work and was determined to keep his job.

His career took off in his third season when he was placed on a line with Lafleur snd Peter Mahovlich, who was an established star. Shutt said Mahovlich "took us under his wing and gave us the confidence to play up to our capabilities."

Shutt finished his career with one season in Los Angeles and returned to the Canadiens as an assistant coach under Jacques Demers and Mario Tremblay. One of the highlights of practice in those days was when Shutt would be the best man on the ice when he joined the players for shooting drills.

"I can still shoot but the wheels are long gone," said Shutt.

He played 12-plus seasons with the Canadiens, is No. 5 on the team's all-time goal-scoring list with 408, and was part of five Stanley Cup teams. He was elected to the Hockey Hall of Fame in 1993.

50 Early Days

People talk about the Original Six—the six National Hockey League teams that were operating in the years leading up to expansion in 1967—but the Canadiens can lay claim to being the Original One.

The Canadiens predate the establishment of the NHL in 1917. They were founded in 1909 and began play in the National Hockey Association on January 5, 1910.

The team that became known as the Flying Frenchmen was the brainchild of James Strachan, who was of Scottish descent. He was the manager of the Montreal Wanderers of the Eastern League but he saw the potential for a team that would appeal to the predominantly French-speaking population of Montreal.

He brought his idea to Ambrose O'Brien, who owned the Renfrew Millionaires. O'Brien was attempting to get his team an entry into the Eastern League and, when he was turned down, he decided to start his own league, the National Hockey Association.

O'Brien took Strachan's advice and bankrolled the Canadiens as well as teams in Cobalt and Haileybury, two towns in northern Ontario which were riding a nickel-mining boom. He convinced Strachan to move the Wanderers to the new league and the Eastern League collapsed when two other teams, the Montreal Shamrocks and the Ottawa Senators, jumped to the NHA.

The Canadiens played in the Jubilee Arena and were a success at the box office, although their on-ice performance left something to be desired.

That first game, which featured seven-man teams and two 30-minute periods, drew an overflow crowd of 3,000 but the Canadiens lost 8–4 to Ottawa. When the team was formed, the *Montreal Gazette* dismissed the idea by saying there weren't enough quality French Canadian players for a competitive team and the results seemed to bear that out. The Canadiens finished last in the NHL standings with a 2–10 record.

But O'Brien made a 50 percent profit on his investment before selling the team to George Kennedy, a professional wrestler who had changed his name from Kendall because his father was ashamed to have a wrestler in the family.

Kennedy proved to be a popular owner and Newsy Lalonde, one of the team's stars, recalled years later that Kennedy led the Canadiens to their first Stanley Cup in 1916 "without once raising his voice or swearing."

Under Kennedy, the team would make one more appearance in the Stanley Cup final. After the Canadiens became one of the charter members of the new National Hockey League in 1917—they are the only one of the four teams from the 1917–18 season to play continuously to the present day—they reached the 1919 Cup final. In those days, the NHL champion played a challenge series against the Western champion, the Seattle Metropolitans.

The series was being played on the West Coast when the area was caught in the worldwide influenza epidemic that followed World War I. Several of the Canadiens became ill, including Bad Joe Hall, a veteran whose nickname reflected his physical play.

Lalonde, who was rooming with Hall, urged him to stay in bed but Hall refused and he was wearing his Canadiens sweater when he died of pneumonia on April 5, 1919. His death prompted officials to cancel the remainder of the series, which was deadlocked after five games with each team having two wins and a fifth game ending in a tie.

Lalonde had a reputation for being the meanest player in hockey but insisted that nobody was meaner than Hall.

Hall was an exception on a team largely composed of French Canadian players in its early days. There was one hybrid star in Joe Malone, who joined the Canadiens for their first season in the NHL. Malone was from Quebec City and had French-Irish ancestry. He was a star for the Quebec Bulldogs in the NHA and led them to a Stanley Cup in 1917.

When the Bulldogs didn't make an immediate transition to the NHL, Malone's rights were acquired by the Canadiens. In the 1917–18 season, he led the new league with 44 goals in the 20-game season, an average of 2.2 goals a game. He set the NHL single-game record with seven goals. To put his achievements in perspective, Wayne Gretzky holds the NHL record for most goals in a season with 92. If Malone had maintained his scoring over an 82-game schedule, he would have scored 178 goals.

Malone was injured for most of the following season and he returned to Quebec when the Bulldogs franchise was revived in 1919.

The Kennedy era ended in 1921 when he died from the lingering effects of the flu. The team was sold for $11,000 to Leo Dandurand, Louis Letourneau, and Joe Cattarinich, who had abandoned his career as a goaltender 11 years earlier to make room for a youngster named Georges Vézina.

51 Who's Next in the Rafters?

Who's next?

That's the question that was asked after the Canadiens retired Guy Lapointe's No. 5 on November 8, 2014.

Lapointe became the 18th player to have his name and number raised to the rafters, and most fans thought that it was an overdue honour for a man who was known not only as a superb defenceman but also as the ultimate prankster.

He was part of the Canadiens' Big Three on defence along with Serge Savard and Larry Robinson. Both players had their numbers retired and there seemed to an empty spot in the rafters until Lapointe's banner took its place between those commemorating his teammates.

The Canadiens have more retired numbers than any other team in the NHL, a reflection of the team's success over its long history. The decision to retire a number—the honour was first accorded to Howie Morenz in 1937—is not taken lightly. Robinson and Lapointe had to wait and so did goaltender Patrick Roy, whose selection was controversial because many fans felt he walked out on the team in 1995.

There are no hard-and-fast criteria for retiring a player's number. There are more than two dozen former Canadiens players who are in the Hockey Hall of Fame who have not been honoured with a spot in the rafters.

Goaltender Georges Vézina may have a trophy named after him but his No. 1 was retired to honour Jacques Plante and not Vézina or George Hainsworth, who set an NHL single-season record with 22 shutouts.

Frank Mahovlich's No. 27 is an honoured number in Toronto but he didn't have enough history in Montreal, even though he scored his 500th goal in a Canadiens uniform and was part of two Stanley Cup–winning teams.

Claude Provost played on seven Stanley Cup champions and won the Masterton Trophy for perseverance but he isn't even in the Hall of Fame.

Neither is J.C. Tremblay, who played on five Stanley Cup winners. He was among the top 50 NHL players in career assists when he jumped to the WHA's Quebec Nordiques.

Jacques Laperriere is in the Hall of Fame and he won a Norris Trophy as the NHL's top defenceman as well as six Stanley Cups but there has been no call for his number to be retired.

When Saku Koivu announced his retirement from the Anaheim Ducks, there was some sentiment for retiring his number. He was a popular captain when he was with the Canadiens, and he won the hearts of fans when he successfully battled cancer and later established a foundation to provide the Montreal General Hospital with diagnostic equipment to assist with the treatment of cancer and trauma victims. But there are holes in Koivu's résumé and he won no Stanley Cups in Montreal.

Canadiens Retired Numbers

1	Jacques Plante	12	Dickie Moore
2	Doug Harvey	12	Yvan Cournoyer
3	Emile Bouchard	16	Henri Richard
4	Jean Béliveau	16	Elmer Lach
5	Bernard Geoffrion	18	Serge Savard
5	Guy Lapointe	19	Larry Robinson
7	Howie Morenz	23	Bob Gainey
9	Maurice Richard	29	Ken Dryden
10	Guy Lafleur	33	Patrick Roy

But there is one glaring absentee from the rafters.

Hector (Toe) Blake is best remembered as a coach who won eight Stanley Cups in 13 years. That was a record until Scotty Bowman won a total of nine in Montreal, Pittsburgh, and Detroit.

What most people don't remember is that Blake was an outstanding player who was elected to the Hockey Hall of Fame as a player in 1966.

The Northern Ontario native made his debut with the Montreal Maroons in 1934–35. A year later, he moved to the Canadiens and became part of the Punch Line with Elmer Lach at centre and Maurice (Rocket) Richard at right wing. Lach and Richard have both had their numbers retired.

Though Blake played in an era when the seasons consisted of only 50 games, he ranks among the top 20 on the Canadiens' career list of goals (235) and points (527). He was the Canadiens captain for eight years.

Blake also has the trophies to complement his bid. He won the Art Ross Trophy as leading scorer and the Hart Trophy as the NHL's most valuable player in 1939. He scored the winning goal in overtime in Game 4 as the Canadiens swept Detroit in the 1944 Stanley Cup final and he helped the Canadiens win again in 1946.

52 The Ones Who Got Away

Every team has stories about top players who slipped away and the Canadiens are no exception.

In some cases, the team misjudged the player's talent. In other cases, the player just didn't fit in the system, or perhaps there were some disciplinary issues which dictated a change of scenery.

One deal which helped shape the good fortunes of both the Canadiens and the Toronto Maple Leafs was a trade which sent the rights to Ted (Teeder) Kennedy to Toronto for defenceman Frank Eddolls in 1943. Kennedy would play on five Stanley Cup teams in Toronto and earn a spot in the Hockey Hall of Fame.

Eddolls played parts of three seasons with Montreal but the key to this deal was that it was put together by Frank Selke, who was running the Leafs while Conn Smythe was overseas during World War II. While Selke landed a superstar, Smythe was upset because he wasn't consulted. Two years later, an unhappy Selke left Toronto and began his own Hall of Fame career as general manager of the Canadiens.

Defenceman Rod Langway had four good seasons with the Canadiens before he was traded to Washington in a blockbuster 1982 deal which saved the Capitals franchise. Langway, Doug Jarvis, Brian Engblom, and Craig Laughlin went to Washington for Rick Green and Ryan Walter.

General manager Irving Grundman made the deal because Langway was unhappy with high taxes and because his family wanted to live in the United States. He became known in Washington as the Secretary of Defence and was elected to the Hockey Hall of Fame after leading the team to 11 consecutive playoff appearances.

The Canadiens have always been protective of their image and that was a factor in the 1990 trade which sent Chris Chelios to Chicago for Denis Savard. Both players ended up in the Hockey Hall of Fame but Chelios was just coming into his prime while Savard's best years were behind him. The deal came two days after Chelios was in an altercation with two policemen in Madison, Wisconsin, where he had played college hockey.

Chelios shared the Montreal captaincy with Guy Carbonneau, who had some problems of his own. His days were numbered when he landed on the front page of a Montreal newspaper directing an obscene gesture toward a photographer who interrupted his golf game. Carbonneau was traded to St. Louis for Jim Montgomery, who played five games for Montreal before he was placed on waivers and claimed by Philadelphia.

Remember Frank Eddolls? In 1947, Selke traded Eddolls and Buddy O'Connor to the Rangers for Hal Laycoe, Joe Bell, and George Robertson. He figured that the 31-year-old O'Connor was nearing the end of his career; instead, O'Connor had a career season on Broadway with 24 goals and 60 points. He won the Hart Trophy as the most valuable player as well as the Lady Byng for the most gentlemanly player. O'Connor was posthumously inducted into the Hockey Hall of Fame in 1988.

More recently, the Canadiens found themselves on the wrong end of a deal in 2009. Canadiens GM Bob Gainey wanted to send a message by acquiring Scott Gomez and he was anxious to dump Chris Higgins, a former first-round draft pick who didn't embrace the Canadiens' ethos. There were also a few spare parts in the deal and Gainey threw in the rights to University of Wisconsin defence-man Ryan McDonagh.

The Canadiens selected McDonagh 12th overall in 2007, the same year they selected Max Pacioretty at No. 22 and P.K. Subban at No. 43. Gainey reportedly soured on McDonagh after watching him play one game in college and traded him over the objections of chief scout Trevor Timmins. Leaving Wisconsin after his junior year, McDonagh joined the Rangers in 2010–11 after half a season in the AHL. In 2014, he became the youngest captain in Rangers history.

53 A Good Bad Man

Joe Hall and Newsy Lalonde were still working on their newfound friendship when Hall died of influenza contracted during the 1919 Stanley Cup final in Seattle.

Lalonde and Hall, whose on-ice behaviour earned him the nickname Bad Joe Hall, had been bitter rivals for most of their careers.

They both had reputations for playing on the edge and there was a lively debate over which player was dirtier, although Lalonde always insisted that Hall was the meanest player in the game.

Hall's rivalry with Lalonde was forged when Hall joined the Quebec Bulldogs of the National Hockey Association and helped them win two Stanley Cups in 1912 and 1913. They became teammates when the National Hockey League was formed in 1917 and Quebec wasn't in a position to join the new league. That allowed Hall to join the Canadiens as one of the few English-speaking players in the team's early history. There was concern that Hall and Lalonde's past history would be a problem but they became close friends. They roomed together on the road and Lalonde was at Hall's bedside when he died on April 5, 1919.

The Stanley Cup final between the Canadiens and the Seattle Metropolitans was played despite the fact that the West Coast was caught up in the global Spanish flu epidemic. The problems which led to the series being abandoned resulted from a misunderstanding of the nature of the disease. The players thought they were safe because they were young and healthy. But the N1H1 strain targeted healthy young people by co-opting their immune systems. Athletes proved to be the most vulnerable to the disease.

In the best-of-five final series, Montreal and Seattle were deadlocked with two wins each and a draw, and the rules of the day most likely hastened the spread of the disease. Seattle played in the Pacific Coast Hockey Association, which had been playing for several years with the forward pass, a tactic which was banned in the East until the 1918–19 season. The speedy pace of the Metropolitans wore down the Canadiens, particularly when two of the four games went into overtime.

A few hours before the deciding game on April 1, officials announced that the game had been postponed indefinitely. Two days later, a telegram reportedly sent to the Montreal media by team manager George Kennedy reported the team was doing well, with a few members under the weather. In fact, six players and Kennedy were in the hospital and Hall died after developing pneumonia. Kennedy never fully recovered and died two years later at the age of 39.

Hall, who was born in England, grew up in Brandon and was a promising cyclist before he turned his attention to hockey. He quickly developed a reputation as a talented player whose roughhouse tactics resulted in numerous suspensions.

On December 14, 1905, he was ejected for a vicious slash while playing for the Brandon Hockey Club. When the same teams met a couple of games later, he unleashed a profanity-laced tirade on the referee and he was again ejected. When he continued yelling off the ice, the opposing team forfeited the game and said Hall would be barred from entering the arena.

A 1907 editorial in the *Winnipeg Tribune* said: "Hall's one drawback as a hockey player is his temper, which, on the ice, he appears unable to control. Joe possesses the qualities of a great hockey player and if he could only dampen this feature, his worth would be doubled."

He was in his element in 1906 when he joined Portage Lake in the International Hockey League, which was known for its rough play. Hall led the league with 98 penalty minutes but he also was an All-Star who scored 33 goals.

One of the ironies surrounding Hall is that, by all accounts, he was a gentleman off the ice. He had a reputation for being a good-natured family man.

In his book *Hockey Hall of Fame Legends*, Michael McKinley recounts that Hall deeply regretted his outbursts while playing for the Quebec Bulldogs and lamented that he was "giving a dog a bad name."

McKinley said Hall laid a beating on Lalonde one night and was embarrassed to learn that Lalonde's wife had given birth to a daughter earlier that day.

"A contrite Bad Joe showed up in the Canadiens dressing room after the game and begged Lalonde to let him go along to the hospital," wrote McKinley. "Lalonde consented, Hall went, and there he apologized to Madame Lalonde for cutting up the father of her daughter."

Hall joined Lalonde in the Hockey Hall of Fame in 1961.

54 Pursuing Howie Morenz

When Howie Morenz became the subject of trade rumors in 1934, he told a reporter that "when I can't play for (the Canadiens), I'll never put on a skate again."

Morenz didn't always feel that way. When Leo Dandurand stepped out of his comfort zone to pursue an English-speaking player from Ontario, he had to resort to some hard bargaining to get Morenz into a Canadiens uniform.

Morenz was a scoring prodigy in Stratford, Ontario, where he led the junior and senior teams in scoring in the 1922 playoffs. The following season, he led the Stratford Indians in regular-season assists and playoff goals, points, and penalty minutes.

In the age before television, the Internet, and Central Scouting, Morenz didn't appear on Dandurand's radar until December 1922 when he played in a Canadian National Railways tournament in Montreal. A friend told Dandurand about Morenz and the Canadiens owner went to Stratford in January to check him out.

Dandurand was interested but Morenz's father, William, wanted his son to finish his apprenticeship at the CNR factory in Stratford.

Dandurand reluctantly agreed to wait two years but he became worried when he heard that Morenz and his father were talking to Toronto St. Patricks. Dandurand sent Cecil Hart to Stratford with a simple message—sign Morenz at any price.

On July 7, Morenz signed a three-year deal for $3,500 a season and a $1,000 signing bonus.

It didn't take long for Morenz to second-guess his decision. He was a huge crowd favourite in Stratford and there was pressure for him to stay at home. In August, he wrote Dandurand and said he wanted to stay in Stratford. The letter included the check the Canadiens had given him as a signing bonus.

Dandurand invited Morenz to Montreal to discuss the situation. When Morenz broke down and cried, saying he wanted to stay in Stratford, Dandurand decided to play hardball. He told Morenz that if he didn't honour his contract, he could never play professional hockey. This wasn't true, but Morenz didn't know that and he agreed to report to the Canadiens' training camp.

Morenz was an immediate hit in Montreal. He had 13 goals and three assists in 24 games and helped the Canadiens finish first in the NHL. They would go on to win the Stanley Cup in 1924 by sweeping best-of-three series against the Vancouver Maroons of the Pacific Coast Hockey League and the Calgary Tigers of the Western Canada Hockey League. In the final against Calgary, Morenz had a hat-trick in a 6–1 win in Game 1 and added a goal in the second game, which the Canadiens won 3–0.

Morenz became the first NHL player to score 50 points in a season when he had 33 goals and a record-tying 18 assists in the 1927–28 season. This was in an era when there was only one assist permitted on a goal and they were awarded sparingly.

The NHL changed its rules for the 1929–30 season to permit forward passes in the offensive zone. This increased scoring chances and Morenz had a career-high 40 goals. He won the scoring title the following season and won the Hart Trophy as the league MVP in 1931 and 1932.

Morenz was booed during the 1933–34 season when he was hampered by injuries and, despite his claim that he wouldn't play for another team, he accepted a move to Chicago. But his career came full circle two years later when Cecil Hart, the man who signed him to his first contract, agreed to coach the team on the condition that Morenz would be brought back.

55 The Intimidator

By the time Sprague Cleghorn joined the Canadiens in 1921, he had won two Stanley Cups with the Ottawa Senators and had earned a reputation for being one of the fiercest—and dirtiest—players in the game.

His brother, Odie, who was his teammate with the Montreal Wanderers and later with the Canadiens, said, "He was my brother and I don't like to boast but I never saw a tougher or better defence-man than Sprague."

Odie had good reason to appreciate his brother's toughness because Sprague was quick to retaliate if he thought opponents were taking liberties with his brother.

While playing for the Wanderers in 1912, he took exception when Newsy Lalonde, who was no shrinking violet, crosschecked Odie. Sprague responded by hitting Lalonde on the back of his head with his stick. He was fined and suspended by the NHA and was also charged with aggravated assault and fined $50.

When he was with the Canadiens, he was paired with Billy Coutu and they were considered the toughest defence duo in the league.

While he won the Stanley Cup with the Senators in 1920 and again in 1921, there was no love lost for his former teammates after he joined the Canadiens. In a 1922 game, he initiated a fight in which three Ottawa players—Eddie Gerard, Frank Nighbor, and Cy Denneny—were injured. The Ottawa management unsuccessfully tried to have him banned from the game.

In the 1923 playoffs, Cleghorn struck Ottawa defenceman Lionel Hitchman in the head with his stick. He was again charged with aggravated assault and fined $50 but he also drew the ire of Canadiens owner Leo Dandurand, who suspended him for the remainder of the playoffs.

Cleghorn once boasted that he was involved in 50 incidents in which players had to be taken off the ice on a stretcher. One hockey fan who was not amused by Cleghorn's antics was Evelyn Byng, who was the wife of the Governor-General of Canada. She donated the Lady Byng Trophy to the NHL in 1925 to promote sportsmanlike play.

Clehgorn's outbursts weren't reserved for the ice. In a January 1917 game against the Toronto Blueshirts, he collided with Toronto's Ken Randall and broke his ankle when he slammed into the boards. While he was recovering, he slipped on an icy sidewalk and broke his other ankle. He was still laid up early in 1918 when he was arrested for hitting his wife with a crutch. His wife apparently forgave him for that incident but she filed for divorce in 1921 after she filed a missing-persons report and then found Sprague with another woman.

While Cleghorn was feared by opponents, he was valued by his teammates because he was a talented player who was likely to lead his team in both goals and penalty minutes. Cleghorn started his career as a forward. He once scored five goals in an NHA game in 1913 and, a year later, he had a career-high 21 goals in 19 games. He retired in 1928 after scoring 169 career goals. At the time, Harry Cameron was the only defenceman to score more goals.

When his playing days were over, he followed his brother Odie's lead and went into coaching. He coached a variety of teams and guided the Montreal Maroons to the playoffs in 1931–32, losing to the eventual champion Toronto Maple Leafs in the semifinals.

Odie revolutionized the game in the 1925–26 season when he was the player-coach with the Pittsburgh Pirates of the NHL. He introduced the concept of set lines which rotated on a regular basis. Previously, skaters stayed on the ice until they became tired.

Odie also showed his versatility by playing in goal. There were no backup goaltenders in those days and when Roy Worters was injured in the pregame warm-up, Odie donned his pads and led the Pirates to a 3–2 over the Canadiens.

Sprague Cleghorn was hit by a car in Montreal on June 27, 1956, and suffered head injuries and a fractured cervical vertebra. He was taken to St. Luc Hospital and the injuries proved to be fatal on July 12.

Two days later, Odie died from heart failure in his sleep. He was found by his sister, six hours before his brother's funeral.

56 A Tale of Two Gallys

There was a lot of confusion in the Canadiens dressing room during the training camp leading up to the start of the lockout-shortened 2012–13 season.

Namely, because there were two rookies who answered to the nickname Gally.

Brendan (Gally) Gallagher solved the dilemma by invoking seniority.

"I'm older and I've had the name longer," said Gallagher, who went on to explain that Alex (Gally) Galchenyuk would henceforth be known as Chucky.

The youngsters, who are close friends on and off the ice, are an integral part of general manager Marc Bergevin's efforts to rebuild the Canadiens and are also a testament to Trevor Timmins' acumen as a scout.

It didn't take a lot of hockey knowledge to know that Galchenyuk possessed extraordinary skills, but his stock went down after he suffered a serious knee injury during a preseason game with the Sarnia Sting in 2011. Despite the injury, Timmins felt that Galchenyuk was the No. 1 player in the draft and, three years into his career, Galchenyuk has proved him right. Timmins was impressed with Galchenyuk's work ethic and his determination to return to the ice. Galchenyuk was back for the final two games of the regular season and then scored two goals and added two assists in six playoff games.

Most of the attention was on Galchenyuk's teammate Nail Yakupov, who was selected first overall by Edmonton in 2012. The Canadiens had the No. 3 pick and Timmins held his breath until Columbus picked defenceman Ryan Murray at No. 2.

From South America to the Canadiens

The Canadiens' roster has included players from all parts of the globe, but the player with the most unusual birthplace was Rick Chartraw. He was born in Caracas, Venezuela, where his father was working as an engineer. His family moved to Pennsylvania when he was three years old. Chartraw won four Stanley Cups with the Canadiens from 1976 to 1979 and added a fifth with Edmonton in 1984.

After he was drafted, Galchenyuk said his goal was to make an immediate jump to the NHL but that seemed unlikely because of the injury and the Canadiens' history of bringing young players along slowly.

But the lockout proved to be a blessing for Galchenyuk. He answered any questions about his health when he returned to Sarnia and collected 61 points in 33 games. He was a natural center who took delight in setting up teammates but circumstances forced coach Jacques Beaulieu to use him at left wing. Martin Lapointe, the Canadiens' director of player development, urged him to shoot more and he scored 27 goals. His play earned him an invitation to the Canadiens training camp and he became the first 18-year-old to play for the Canadiens since Petr Svoboda in 1984.

Galchenyuk, who was born in Milwaukee while his Belarusian father was playing in the International Hockey League, lived in the United States, Russia, and Italy as a youngster but identifies himself as an American. His dream was to play in the NHL and his family moved from Russia to Chicago when he was 16 so that he would eligible for the Ontario Hockey League draft.

Gallagher represented more of a long shot for the Canadiens. He scored 41 goals for the Vancouver Giants in his draft year of 2010 but his size represented a concern for NHL teams. His listed height of 5-foot-8 appears to be a slight exaggeration.

But Timmins was impressed with Gallagher's tenacity and his hard work. His father, Ian, is the strength-and-conditioning coach for the Giants, and Brendan has benefitted from his father's expertise.

By the time Gallagher finished his four-year career in Vancouver, he had put together three 40-goal seasons and was the franchise's all-time leading scorer.

He impressed the Canadiens during their 2011 camp. He played with a variety of linemates and it seemed that no matter who he played with, he made them look better. Coach Jacques Martin kept putting him in the lineup until he finally had a bad game. He was sent back to junior hockey but there was no doubt that he had a future in the NHL.

Most players of Gallagher's size rely on speed and skill to create chances but Gallagher scores most of his goals by playing in the dirty areas. He led the NHL in goaltender interference penalties in 2014.

"He's frustrating to play against because guys knock him down and he bounces back up with a big smile on his face," noted teammate Dale Weise.

"Why shouldn't I be smiling? I'm playing in the NHL and I'm having fun out there," said Gallagher.

57 Little George's Remarkable Season

Georges Vézina was a tough act to follow, but the first winner of the trophy which bears Vézina's name was up to the task.

The Canadiens were in need of a goaltender after Vézina collapsed in the opening game of the 1925–26 season and died of tuberculosis four months later. Herb Rhéaume carried most of the load after Vézina was forced to retire but he had a dismal 10–20–1 record and the Canadiens finished last in the seven-team NHL.

Canadiens owner Leo Dandurand had noticed George Hainsworth in the early 1920s and felt he had talent. He couldn't use the youngster in Montreal because he already had Vézina but, at the same time, he didn't want Hainsworth playing elsewhere in the NHL. He convinced Newsy Lalonde to sign Hainsworth to a contract with the Saskatoon franchise in the Western Canada Hockey League.

Hainsworth, who was nicknamed Little George because he was only 5-foot-6, established himself in Saskatoon while playing against future Hall of Famers like Frank Boucher, Eddie Shore, and Frank Frederickson, and the timing proved perfect for Hainsworth to move back east.

The Western Canada league was in the process of folding and the top players were moving to the NHL. Toronto expressed interest in obtaining Hainsworth but Dandurand made a bold move when he paid Saskatoon $5,000 for Hainsworth's rights and then signed the goaltender for $6,500, which was a top salary in that era.

Canadien Vézina Trophy Winners

(For lowest goals-against average until 1982–83 onward, when it was decided by a vote of NHL general managers)

George Hainsworth	1927, 1928, 1929
Bill Durnan	1944. 1945, 1946, 1947, 1949, 1950
Jacques Plante	1956, 1957, 1958, 1959, 1960, 1962
Charlie Hodge	1964
Gump Worsley, Charlie Hodge	1966
Gump Worsley, Rogatien Vachon	1968
Ken Dryden	1973, 1976
Ken Dryden, Michel Larocque	1978, 1979
Michel Larocque, Denis Herron, Richard Sévigny	1981
Patrick Roy	1989, 1990, 1992
José Theodore	2002
Carey Price	2015

In those days, the Vézina Trophy went to the goaltender with the best goals-against average. Hainsworth was the inaugural winner in 1927 and repeated in 1928 and 1929.

In the 1928–29 season, Hainsworth produced the best regular season ever for an NHL goaltender, although it should be noted that the rules were a bit different and they gave netminders an edge. Forward passes were banned in the offensive zone and scoring chances were limited. But no other goaltender of that era came close to matching Hainsworth's numbers.

When he shut out Chicago 5–0 on December 18, 1928, he set an NHL record with his fifth consecutive shutout on the road. He finished the season with 22 shutouts in 44 games. That's an NHL record, and so is his 0.92 goals-against average. From February 26 to March 7, he reeled off four consecutive shutouts and went 343 minutes without allowing a goal. It's the second-longest shutout run in NHL history.

The rules changed for the 1929–30 season and, while the number of shutouts went down and his goals-against average went up, Hainsworth continued to be a dominant goaltender. He led the Canadiens to the Stanley Cup in 1930 and again in 1931. In the 1930 playoffs, he put together a shutout streak of 270 minutes and eight seconds for another record, one which stands today.

Dandurand traded Hainsworth to Toronto in 1933 in return for Lorne Chabot because Dandurand thought Chabot, a French Canadian, would help boost attendance for a team which was losing money. Hainsworth took the Maple Leafs to the Cup final in 1935 but was replaced two years later by Turk Broda, while Chabot played one season with the Canadiens before he was traded to make room for Wilf Cude, who had been born in Wales.

Hainsworth retired after being released by Toronto but he made one last stop in Montreal, playing four games while Cude was injured in 1936.

Montreal Herald sportswriter Elmer Ferguson described Hainsworth as "almost mechanical in his perfection" and Hainsworth was apologetic when he was interviewed after a shutout in 1931.

"I'm sorry I can't put on a show like some of the other goaltenders," Hainsworth said. "I can't look excited because I'm not. I can't shout at other players because it's not my style. I can't dive on easy shots and make them look hard. I guess all I can do is stop pucks."

Hainsworth didn't live to see his induction into the Hockey Hall of Fame in 1961. He died in a car accident in Gravenhurst, Ontario, in 1950.

58 The Semi-Conscious Goal

Concussions are a major topic of conversation in today's game. With the threat of lawsuits and a concern over permanent brain damage, the National Hockey League and its players take head injuries seriously. There is a league protocol to follow after a player has taken a hit to the head and the player isn't allowed back on the ice until he has been cleared by a doctor.

This was not the case in 1952 when Maurice (Rocket) Richard scored one of the most dramatic goals in franchise history after being knocked out in the second period.

The 1951–52 season was not a particularly memorable one for Richard. He was bothered by a knee injury which forced him to miss 20 games. He missed another two games in February when coach Dick Irvin Sr. took him out of the lineup and sent him to Florida for rest and recuperation. He still finished the season with 27 goals, which was the fourth-best total in the league.

The Canadiens finished second in the regular season and were matched against the Boston Bruins in the best-of-seven semifinal. The Bruins took a 3–2 lead in the series as the teams headed back to the Boston Garden. Montreal staved off elimination when it defeated the Bruins on an overtime goal by Paul Masnick, a 20-year-old who had played only 15 games than season.

On April 8, 1952, the series returned to the Forum where a standing-room-only crowd greeted the Canadiens for the seventh and deciding game in the series. But the festive atmosphere in the building turned somber early in the second period when Richard was injured.

The Rocket employed his trademark button-hook move to go around Bruins defenceman Hal Laycoe. Boston forward Leo Labine read the play and he slipped behind Laycoe and hit an unsuspecting Richard low, sending him head-first into the boards. The Forum went silent as Richard lay unconscious on the ice. After he was revived, he needed help to leave the ice and blood flowed from a cut over his eye.

Richard spent most of the game in a dazed state in the Forum clinic. Gordon Young, the team doctor, suggested that Richard take a ride to the hospital for X-rays but Richard refused.

Richard returned to the bench late in the third period. There was blood on his face and a towel around his neck. The game was tied 1–1 and there were five minutes remaining, although Richard did not know that because he was unable to focus on the scoreboard. He had to ask linemate Elmer Lach for the score and the time remaining.

Irvin looked at his star as he took a seat on the bench. He had been around long enough to suspect that Richard was concussed but he asked: "Can you go?"

Richard nodded and said: "Sure."

"Okay, get out there," replied Irvin.

Frank Orr and Chrys Goyens describe the action in their book, *Maurice Richard: Reluctant Hero*:

"Four minutes remained in regulation time when Richard took the puck from Butch Bouchard deep in his zone and evaded Fleming Mackell at the blueline. He eluded Woody Dumart and another Bruins forward in the neutral zone, and broke into the Boston end. He tried to angle big defenceman Bill Quackenbush into the middle, driving him into his partner, Bob Armstrong, but Quackenbush was stronger and forced the Rocket wide and into the corner.

"Suddenly, the Rocket leaned into the defender, pushing him off with his arm and cutting to the Boston goal. Armstrong cut over and Richard button-hooked him and moved in on Sugar Jim Henry, who as Andy O'Brien recollected 'was squinting through a mess of a face that had suffered a broken nose and two black eyes earlier in the series.'

"Richard faked Henry to the ice and put the puck in the net with what some observers called the 'Goal of the Century.'"

"That beautiful bastard scored semi-conscious," observed *Montreal Herald* columnist Elmer Ferguson.

The game produced one of the memorable pictures in the game's history. Roger St-Jean of *La Presse* caught Henry and Richard at game's end and Henry, with his black eyes, appears to be bowing as he shakes hands with the bloodied Richard.

On his return to the dressing room, Richard went into convulsions and had to be sedated. It was several hours before he was able to go home.

59 The Defenceman's Defenceman

Tom Johnson had no illusions about his role on one of the greatest hockey teams ever assembled.

"I was classified as a defensive defenceman; I stayed back and minded the store," said Johnson, who played alongside Doug Harvey on the Canadiens team that won a record five consecutive Stanley Cups from 1956 through 1960. "With the high-powered scoring teams I was with, I just had to get them the puck and let them do the rest."

In an interview for Dick Irvin Jr.'s oral history of the team, *The Habs*, Johnson, who wore No. 10 before Guy Lafleur made it famous, said he accepted his anonymity early in his career.

"When I first came up, we would play a lot of exhibition games all around Quebec, even during the season," said Johnson. "They would introduce the players in the order of their numbers, and of course Rocket (Richard) was No. 9. The cheer he got would last a long time. I always say I used to skate out at the end of the Rocket's cheer. They could never hear my name so not too many people in those towns ever found out who I was."

Johnson was a junior star in his native Manitoba and Frank Selke signed him as a free agent in 1947. His transition to the NHL was a difficult one because it soon became apparent that Johnson's skating wasn't up to NHL standards, particularly on a Canadiens squad that played an uptempo game. But Johnson worked hard through two seasons in the minors and, after he joined the Canadiens on a full-time basis in 1950, coach Dick Irvin described him as "the steadiest defenceman in the league."

Johnson was never mistaken for a great skater but he made up for his lack of speed with his stickhandling and passing as well as his physical play. He was a proficient penalty-killer and he was a tough opponent who wasn't above using his stick to settle grudges on the ice. He was an integral, although often overlooked part of the Canadiens' offensive success because his teammates could press the attack and take chances knowing that Johnson had their backs.

He stepped out from under the shadow of his defence partner Doug Harvey in the 1958–59 season when Harvey was hampered by injuries. While Harvey missed only nine games, his production suffered when he did play and Johnson picked up the slack. He had his best offensive season with 10 goals and 29 assists and won the Norris Trophy as the league's top defenceman.

Johnson dealt with some injuries of his own and legendary sportswriter Red Fisher noted: "Of all the great players I covered in Montreal in the 1950s, I don't think there was anyone who played with more pain when he had to. He'd take shots in his knees. They were ripped up and he'd come out and play. Injuries didn't matter to this guy. He'd never make any kind of big deal about it. The guy came out and played like no other player did. I admired him a great deal for it."

It was an injury which ended Johnson's stay in Montreal after 13 seasons. He collided with rookie Bobby Rousseau during a practice in March 1963. He suffered a fractured cheekbone and an eye injury and his season was over.

The Canadiens thought his career was over and left him unprotected in the waiver draft. The injury didn't concern Bruins general manager Lynn Patrick, who had recovered from a similar injury. He paid $20,000 to claim Johnson and it would be the start of a 30-year association with the Bruins as player, coach, and executive.

His playing career would end on February 28, 1965, when Chico Maki severed the nerves in Johnson's leg, leaving him with a permanent limp. He coached the Bruins to a Stanley Cup in 1972 and later served in a number of capacities in the Bruins front office.

He was elected to the Hockey Hall of Fame in 1970 in what was seen as a controversial selection. Eddie Shore, who was no shrinking violet, opposed the selection because of Johnson's reputation as a dirty player.

60 O Capitaine, Mon Capitaine, Bon Voyage

Freezing temperatures and blowing snow greeted mourners as they gathered at Mary, Queen of the World Cathedral for Jean Béliveau's funeral on December 10, 2014.

As one commentator noted: "It's a hockey day."

It was a day when the world said its last good-bye to Béliveau, who passed away on December 1 after a lengthy illness. The church was overflowing with former teammates and rivals, members of the current team, politicians and celebrities, and some of the ordinary people who remembered Béliveau as the most beloved Canadien. Millions more watched it on national television in Canada.

Béliveau had asked for a simple funeral but it was difficult to follow his wishes. The province of Quebec accorded him the honour of a state funeral and the family allowed his fans a chance to offer their condolences. Béliveau's body lay in state for two days at the Bell Centre and thousands of fans, many of whom were too young to have seen him play, filed past his casket.

People were also encouraged to post their memories of Béliveau on the team's website.

His wife, Elise, his daughter, Hélène, and his granddaughters, Magalie and Mylene, kept the vigil at the Bell Centre for hours on end. When an onlooker expressed his amazement at the long hours the family members spent talking to strangers, one of his granddaughters noted that her grandfather had done it for 60 years and they were only being asked to do it for two days.

Four of his former teammates delivered eulogies.

Dickie Moore talked about being lucky to have played with Béliveau during the glory years of the 1950s, lucky to have him as a friend.

"What would you rather be, good or lucky?" asked Moore. "I was lucky, he was good. I'll miss you, Jean. The man I always looked up to. I'm only 5-foot-10."

Yvan Cournoyer, who is only 5-foot-7, also talked about the height disparity between himself and the 6-foot-3 Béliveau:

"The first time I sat next to Jean, we had our shin pads on the floor while we were getting ready and I realized pretty fast that his were a bit longer than mine. I understand why once he stood up next to me."

Serge Savard talked about listening to the radio as a six-year-old the night Béliveau was called up from the Quebec Aces and scored three goals against the New York Rangers. Savard said that was the night Béliveau became his idol alongside Rocket Richard and Doug Harvey.

Savard would grow up to be Béliveau's teammate for three Stanley Cups and later worked beside him in the Canadiens front office. He praised Béliveau's humility; leadership; and devotion to the team, his family, and the foundation he established to help crippled children,

Noted Savard: "When a journalist asked him how he wanted to be remembered, his first response was, 'I want to be remembered as a team player.'"

Ken Dryden recalled rooming with Béliveau in the latter stages of the 1971 season and into the playoffs. Dryden was a rookie while Béliveau was playing his final season and Dryden said he learned by watching the captain. He noted that the Canadiens were not legendary when Béliveau joined the team. They had won the Stanley

Perhaps the most beloved Canadien of all time, Jean Béliveau passed away in 2014. His body lay in state at the Bell Centre for two days, where thousands of fans paid their respects.

Cup only seven times. By the time Béliveau retired, the Canadiens had won 17 Cups.

Dryden also touched on Béliveau's second career with the Canadiens as an executive and ambassador:

"No place was too small or too remote because no fan—no person—was too unimportant. He was the great Jean Béliveau, tall, handsome, and graceful and gracious with the warm dignity and friendly smile, yet there he was. He treated everyone with such respect. He said the right thing in the right way, in French and in English, because that's what he believed and that's the way he was."

The most emotional words were delivered by Cournoyer, who recalled a conversation with Béliveau early in his career:

"When I started with Jean, I was 20 years old and he told me all the time: 'Your time moves very quickly. Time moves very quickly.' Jean, for 51 years you've been my friend, my captain, an idol for an entire people. Jean, there's a hole in our hearts today. I'll never forget the memories we made together. The rose I'm wearing today, Jean, I'll keep it with me the rest of my life in your memory.

"O capitaine, mon capitaine, bon voyage."

61 The Rocket Has Left the Building

Sports Illustrated's Michael Farber is fond of saying that nobody in Western civilization understands ceremony better than the House of Windsor and the Canadiens.

The team has demonstrated this understanding of ceremony on numerous occasions as it retires numbers or honours fallen heroes but the night which best supports Farber's thesis was March 11, 1996, the night they closed the Forum.

The Canadiens opened the building on November 29, 1924, with a 7–1 win over Toronto and they closed it by beating the Dallas Stars 4–1.

The game was merely a prelude to an emotional closing ceremony that was highlighted by the introduction of the Canadiens players who had been inducted into the Hockey Hall of Fame. After honouring three builders—coach Scotty Bowman, general manger Sam Pollock, and owner Hartland Molson—the players were introduced, starting with Guy Lapointe and continuing through to Maurice Richard, whose appearance unleashed an ovation which became the subject of a debate.

In *Rocket Richard: Reluctant Hero*, authors Chrys Goyens and Frank Orr had this description of the event: "When Maurice Richard brandished the torch, the building erupted in an ovation that had veteran observers shaking their heads and the Rocket in tears. On and on it went, four minutes, six minutes, eight minutes, an incredible wall of sound that cascaded down to ice level for 10 minutes until Maurice could pass the torch to another great, Jean Béliveau. On another evening, Béliveau's accolade would rival the Rocket's, but this crowd was emotionally spent."

The ovation was the main topic of conversation and its length grew faster than Pinocchio's nose. It was 10 minutes in one news report, 12 in another. A guy who was there said he timed it and it clocked in at a shade over 15 minutes.

To many in the arena, it seemed like the ovation was endless, but a video of the event posted on YouTube puts the event in perspective. From start to finish, the ovation lasts a few seconds over seven minutes. The Rocket appears touched by the outpouring of love and at the same a bit embarrassed. When he motions to the crowd to end the ovation, the cheers get louder. There are chants of "Mau-rice, Mau-rice" and "Go Habs Go." His glaring eyes are softened and he appears close to tears but he holds them back.

For the record, there was no torch being passed—that part of the ceremony involving former captains came earlier in the evening—and Béliveau had been introduced 10 minutes before the Rocket.

When the 45-minute ceremony ended, reporters sought out Richard for his thoughts about the ovation but he had quietly left the building.

Richard did have some comments a few days later: "I appreciated the applause—who wouldn't?—but sometimes I wonder what they were applauding. I've been retired for 36 years now; it wasn't even their fathers who saw me play but their grandfathers! I think the fans that night were applauding the building and the Stanley Cup banners and I appreciate that because to me, winning was everything and we won much more than the others."

And if Richard didn't shed any tears on closing night, he didn't express any regrets over the decision to move to a new building.

"(The Forum) was the right building for our time and now the Molson Centre will be the building for today," said Richard.

But the man of the people did have one reservation:

"The only thing that bothers me is that the public will end up paying too much to go to hockey games from now on."

62 The Cannonball

Didier Pitre was an original member of the Canadiens but he nearly missed the team's inaugural game in the National Hockey Association because he signed a contract with the wrong team.

When Jack Laviolette was asked to put together a team of French Canadian players for the newly created NHA, he immediately thought about Pitre, who was his boyhood friend from Valleyfield, Quebec.

Pitre made a name for himself playing for the Michigan Soo Indians in the rough-and-tumble International Hockey League. While he was known as a gentlemanly player, he packed a solid 190 pounds on his 5-foot-11 frame. He was able to handle himself against physical opponents although he most often used his speed and skating ability to avoid trouble. In two seasons in Michigan, he won a scoring title and earned All-Star honours, as well as the nickname Cannonball.

He later played for the Montreal Shamrocks and the Renfrew Creamery Kings. In the summer of 1909, he was back in Sault Ste. Marie working during the off-season when he received a telegram from Laviolette, which read: "New League formed. New Canadien team formed. Big money available. Come to Montreal."

What Laviolette and Pitre didn't know was that the Nationals, a team in the rival Canadian Hockey League, also had their eye on Pitre. A Nationals representative met up with Pitre on the train ride from the Soo to Ottawa. Pitre thought he was dealing with someone from the new team Laviolette was pitching and he signed a contract.

Upon his arrival in Montreal, Pitre learned that he had made a mistake and he signed a second contract with the Canadiens. The dispute wound up in court and wasn't resolved until a judge ruled in favor of the Canadiens on January 5, 1910, saying that, under Quebec law, no man should be forced to do anything against his will. The ruling came mere hours before the team played its first game.

Pitre was an instant success. He played on a line with Laviolette and Newsy Lalonde and they were the original Flying Frenchmen. He scored 11 goals in 13 games in the inaugural NHA season and, over the next three seasons, he scored 70 goals in 51 games.

Pitre moved to the Vancouver Millionaires for the 1913–14 season but returned to the Canadiens the following season and would remain with the team until his retirement in 1923.

He led the Canadiens to their first Stanley Cup in 1916, leading the team in scoring during both the regular season and the playoffs. During the NHA era from 1909 until the creation of the National Hockey League in 1917, Pitre was the team's leading scorer with 156 goals and 25 assists in 128 games.

Pitre and the Canadiens made another Stanley Cup run in 1919. They won the NHL title but the final against the Seattle Metropolitans of the Pacific Coast Hockey League was abandoned after the Canadiens were caught up in the worldwide Spanish flu epidemic which would claim the life of Montreal forward Joe Hall.

On January 16, 1919, Pitre and Jack Darragh of the Ottawa Senators made history when they each had a natural hat-trick—three consecutive goals—in a game which Montreal won 10–6.

It was reported that Pitre could skate as fast backward as he could forward and he was put to the test in his final two seasons with the Canadiens. At age 38, he was moved to defence. It was a seamless transition for Pitre, who had played rover in the era when the game was played with seven-man lineups. The Canadiens lost to Ottawa in a two-game, total-goals series for the NHL title in 1923 but Pitre, the last of the original Canadiens, was praised for his solid defensive play.

An account in *La Presse* read: "One expected him to be exhausted after a few minutes but he was like a wall against the Ottawa attack."

When he retired after the series, he had scored 220 goals and added 58 assists in 255 games with the Canadiens.

He also left behind a reputation as one of the game's most likeable players.

"Many played brutally but Pitre was not one of them," legendary sportswriter Elmer Ferguson wrote in the *Montreal Herald*. "It is doubtful if the big, good-natured Frenchman ever did a mean or unsportsmanlike thing in his whole career."

He was popular with the fans and he would often appear between periods to toast the crowd with a glass of champagne.

Pitre died following a heart attack in 1934 and was elected into the Hockey Hall of Fame in 1962.

63 Trader Sam

Sam Pollock earned the nickname Trader Sam by engineering a series of trades which sent excess players from the talent-rich Canadiens organization to expansion teams in return for their draft picks.

This practice, which laid the groundwork for the team which would win four consecutive Stanley Cups from 1976 to 1979, wouldn't have been possible if the teams had listened to Pollock.

When NHL president Clarence Campbell asked for Pollock's help in formulating the rules for expansion and the universal entry draft, the Canadiens general manager proposed a moratorium on the trading of draft picks by the new teams. Pollock, who was a great believer in thinking ahead, felt that the best way for expansion teams to be competitive was to develop a nucleus of young players.

The other teams in the league shot the idea down. They would regret not listening to Pollock.

During the 10-year period from 1969 to 1978, the Canadiens amassed 26 first-round picks. In 1972, they held four of the first 14 picks and they did even better two years later when they had five picks among the first 15.

It would be unreasonable to expect all of the draft picks to be winners but they did yield some key players, including three members of the Hockey Hall of Fame.

The most celebrated deal led to the acquisition of Guy Lafleur with the No. 1 overall pick in 1971. The Canadiens swapped first-round picks with the California Golden Seals and also gave up rookie Ernie Hicke in return for Francois Lacombe. And Pollock ensured that the Golden Seals would finish last when he sent Ralph Backstrom west to shore up the Los Angeles Kings.

But there were four other deals that stand out in that era.

In 1968, Pollock sent minor-league goaltender Gerry Desjardins to Los Angeles for the Kings' first-round picks in 1969 and 1972. Desjardins had moved on to Chicago by the time the Canadiens used the 1972 pick to select future Hall of Famer Steve Shutt with the fourth overall pick.

On January 20, 1970, the Canadiens traded Dick Duff to Los Angeles for Dennis Hextall and the Kings' second-round pick in 1971. Duff was on his way to the Hall of Fame after winning two Stanley Cups in Toronto and four more in Montreal but he was coming up on his 34th birthday and there wasn't much left in the tank. Hextall never played for the Canadiens but Pollock used that second-round pick to draft future Hall of Famer Larry Robinson.

The Kings finally found a deal that paid off for them on May 29, 1973, when they sent cash and a 1974 first-round pick to Montreal for defenceman Bob Murdoch and forward Randy Rota. Murdoch had six productive seasons with the Kings. As for the Canadiens, they used that pick to select Mario Tremblay.

On March 9, 1974, the Canadiens traded Dave Gardner to St. Louis for the Blues' first-round pick in 1974. Gardner, who had been drafted eighth overall in 1972, played 350 NHL games but only 36 of them for Montreal and 23 for the Blues. The Canadiens used the pick to select Doug Risebrough seventh overall.

64. Play a Game at the Bell Centre

Have you ever dreamed of streaking down the Bell Centre ice with the roar of the crowd ringing in your ears?

The Canadiens can make your dreams come true—for a price.

While the Bell Centre is one of the busiest arenas in North America, there is ice available for hockey games, ringuette, or skating parties. Corporate groups, recreational leagues, and hockey players looking for that once-in-a-lifetime experience have displayed their skills on the Bell Centre ice.

Before we go any further, we should mention that the experience isn't cheap. A basic two-hour rental for a game costs $8,000 and when you add in the tax, it comes to a shade under $9,200. That covers the use of the ice, the services of a public address announcer, a recorded national anthem before the game, and a dressing room.

If you want to play in the afternoon on a game day, the price goes up to $8,500. There's a 20 percent discount if you want to play after attending a Canadiens game (game tickets are, of course, extra).

That's not the end of the extras.

If you want to look the part, you can rent regulation Canadiens jerseys. That will set you back $760 for up to 32 players. Each additional jersey costs $25.

You have to give the jerseys back but if you want a keepsake to take home you can order dressing room name plates for the gang. That will set you back $340.

If you want your company logo or other message flashing on the electronic power ring, that's a $680 option.

The Canadiens will be happy to provide a former player to sign autographs for $1,500. For another $1,000, the alumni player will lace them up and play in the game.

A referee will cost $125 and if you forgot to bring a puck, the Bell Centre will provide a genuine NHL puck for $5.

Some players may want a DVD of the game to prove they made it to the big time and those are available for $20, with the price dropping to $15.50 if you order 10 or more.

Finally, you can have the services of your own team photographer for $750.

The Canadiens have also joined the ranks of teams offering an annual fantasy camp experience. The first camp was held in January 2015 and featured a range of activities on and off the ice with a price tag of $3,900. There were three on-ice sessions, including a full game at the Bell Centre in the afternoon prior to the game between the Canadiens and the New York Islanders which the fantasy campers watched from a luxury suite.

The package also included a road trip to watch the Canadiens play in Ottawa, three nights at a luxury hotel in downtown Montreal, a Canadiens jersey, and CCM hockey equipment worth $1,800, plus a chance to meet and share the ice with former players like Guy Lafleur, Réjean Houle, Patrice Brisebois, Murray Wilson, Mathieu Dandenault, Yvon Lambert, and Chris (Knuckles) Nilan.

65 Saving His Best for Last

Boston Bruins general manager Art Ross made a severe error in judgment when he traded Albert (Babe) Siebert to the Canadiens in 1936.

Siebert was a first-team All-Star in 1935–36 but Ross felt that the 32-year-old had lost a step or two, which was why he moved Siebert to defence. Ross was also concerned that there was obvious friction between Siebert and his defence partner, Eddie Shore, who was also a first-team All-Star.

The two had fought earlier in their careers when Siebert was with the Montreal Maroons. Siebert, who was known as one of the fiercest battlers in the NHL, administered a beating to Shore, who later claimed that he was unable to fight back because he was being held down by another Maroons player. He and Siebert never talked although they did form a strong, physical tandem.

Canadiens coach Cecil Hart welcomed Siebert and named him the captain of the team. In his three seasons with the Canadiens, he was named to the All-Star team twice and he won the Hart Trophy as the most valuable player in the 1936–37 season.

Before Ross moved him to defence, Siebert was the 1920s' equivalent of a power forward. After playing junior and senior hockey in Kitchener, he signed with the Maroons in 1925. He scored 16 goals in his first season and helped his team win the Stanley Cup.

When Hooley Smith arrived in Montreal in 1926, he joined Siebert and Nels Stewart in what became known as the S Line. The three players complemented each other: Stewart was a pure goal scorer, Smith was a playmaker, and Siebert used his speed and his strength to break out of the defensive zone and create space for his linemates.

His physical play occasionally landed him in trouble. In December 1927, he was suspended after he sent Billy Boucher of the New York Americans to the hospital following a brawl which began when Siebert elbowed Boucher. The New York player then hit Siebert over the head with his stick and Siebert responded with a flurry of wild swings.

Siebert had 39 points for his best offensive season in 1931–32 but the financially strapped Maroons sold him to the New York Rangers. He would win his second Stanley Cup in 1933 but his production was down and he was traded to Boston early the next season.

Ross moved him to defence after Shore was suspended for an assault which ended Ace Bailey's career, and an Associated Press poll named him comeback player of the year. Siebert insisted that he had never been away and he said his production went down in New York because coach Lester Patrick didn't use him properly.

While Siebert would rack up close to 1,000 penalty minutes in his career, he had a soft side which endeared him to the fans in Montreal. His wife, Bernice, was a paraplegic as the result of complications during the birth of the couple's second daughter. He would do most of the housework and would bring his wife to each home game, carrying her to a seat at the Forum before heading to the dressing room.

Here's how legendary sportswriter Elmer Ferguson described Siebert:

"The Babe would become embroiled in fistic battles. Perhaps he would suffer penalties, earn the disfavor of the crowd by his bruising style of play. Perhaps the game would make him seem like a crude and uncouth person, rough and brutal. From the dressing room, the Babe would stride along the promenade until he reached the chair where his fragile bit of an invalid wife sat. Bending down, he would kiss her, then he would gather her up in his muscular arms, stride out of the rink, and deposit her in a waiting car that would take her home to the kiddies that he adored so much."

Hart would retire after the 1938–39 season and Siebert was named to replace him but the Babe never coached a game. On August 25, 1939, he and his family traveled to his cottage on the shore of Lake Huron to celebrate his father's 80th birthday. He was a strong swimmer but he apparently suffered a cramp when he went into the lake to retrieve an inflatable tire and he drowned.

On October 29, 1939, the Canadiens played an NHL All-Star team in a benefit to assist Siebert's family and raised $15,000, the equivalent of $300,000 today.

Siebert was inducted into the Hockey Hall of Fame in 1964.

The First Star

Edouard (Newsy) Lalonde came by his nickname honestly. He was a reporter and a printer in his hometown of Cornwall, Ontario, before he accepted a $35-a-week deal to play for Sault Ste. Marie of the International Hockey League.

Lalonde's pro debut was both unexpected and eventful. As Michael McKinley relates in *Hockey Hall of Fame Legends*, Lalonde arrived in the Soo after a long train ride and expected to be a spectator for his first game. When Soo star Marty Walsh was injured 20 minutes into the game, Lalonde was pressed into service wearing a borrowed pair of skates.

At one point, Lalonde was shaken up by a hard check but there were no other substitutes and he had to gut it out. Jack Hammond, a local boxer, tried to help Lalonde by giving him a swig of whisky.

"It burned my mouth, and my gums and my throat. I thought I was a goner," said Lalonde.

It seems that Hammond had two bottles and Lalonde took a swig from a bottle of ammonia used to revive boxers when they were knocked out. He survived the experience and scored two goals, which prompted the Soo's American opponents to offer him $50 a week. The Soo team matched that offer and Lalonde began a 30-year odyssey.

When the National Hockey Association was formed in 1909, Lalonde joined the Canadiens and he scored the franchise's first goal. Midway through his first season, he was traded to the Renfrew Creamery Kings, where he won the league scoring title playing alongside Frank Patrick and Cyclone Taylor.

Lalonde returned to the Canadiens in 1911 and then jumped to the Vancouver Millionaires of the newly formed Pacific Coast Hockey Association, where he won another league scoring title in 1912. Vancouver would trade him back to the Canadiens the following season and he would remain in Montreal for 10 seasons.

He won the scoring championship seven times in four different leagues and he guided the Canadiens to their first Stanley Cup in 1916.

Lalonde also scored in the first-ever National Hockey League game on December 19, 1917, when the Canadiens posted a 7–4 victory over the Ottawa Senators.

He might have won another Stanley Cup in 1919 when the Canadiens won the NHL title behind Lalonde's league-leading 32 points in 17 games. He added 17 goals in 10 playoff games and the Canadiens were within a victory of winning the Cup in the challenge series against the Seattle Metropolitans when the global flu epidemic caught up to the team.

Lalonde, Joe Hall, Billy Coutu, Jack McDonald, Louis Berlinguette, and owner George Kennedy were all hospitalized with the flu. Kennedy offered to forfeit the series but the Metropolitans declined and no champion was declared that season.

Lalonde was immensely popular with fans but less so with opponents, team management, and even some of his teammates.

He held out in a contract dispute in 1915 and played only six games that season. Despite the holdout, he was named player-coach.

After Kennedy died and the team was sold to Leo Dandurand, Lalonde battled with management and left the team for four games in the 1921–22 season.

The Canadiens sold him to Saskatoon in 1922 and, when it was pointed out that the sale contravened the waiver rules, Montreal accepted prospect Aurèle Joliat in a trade. Joliat quickly replaced Lalonde as a fan favourite in Montreal and when the Canadiens and Saskatoon met in a game later that season, Lalonde greeted Joliat with a crosscheck to the face.

He had a reputation for being one of the meanest players in the game. When he was a coach, he once punched one of his players who talked back to him. After his playing days ended, he coached the New York Americans, the Ottawa Senators, and the Canadiens. Montreal fired him 16 games into the 1934–35 season.

Lalonde was also one of Canada's leading lacrosse players and was honoured as the top player for the first half of the 20th century. He has been elected to the Canada Sports Hall of Fame, the Lacrosse Hall of Fame, and the Hockey Hall of Fame.

67 Too Much, Too Soon

When José Theodore arrived at the Canadiens' charity golf tournament in 2003, he had some explaining to do. It had nothing to do with his lackluster performance the previous season.

There was a feeding frenzy because the media was told that this was the one and only time Theodore would talk about the summer in which he was linked to a notorious biker gang while his father, a brother, three half brothers, and an uncle were arrested and charged with offences ranging from loan-sharking and racketeering to weapons possession and issuing death threats.

After Theodore failed to replicate his heroics of the 2001–02 season—when he won the Vézina Trophy as the NHL's top goaltender as well as the Hart Trophy, which goes to the player most valuable to his team—his personal life began to unravel.

Allo Quebec, a weekly tabloid dedicated to crime news, published pictures of Theodore partying with the Hells Angels following a 1998 golf tournament sponsored by a strip club. A second photograph published by the daily *Le Journal de Montreal* showed Theodore in 2000 with members of the gang at one of their clubhouses outside the city. In July, there was a further revelation that his father, Ted Theodore, had opened a joint bank account with José's name attached. Police determined that José had no knowledge and that his father used his name because he didn't think there would be any questions about large deposits into an account of an athlete with a seven-figure income.

As Theodore stood on the grass outside the Elm Ridge Country Club clubhouse, he said, "When you're young, you don't have the same judgment as today. These photos were taken five or six years ago. I learn from experience. But I'm not perfect. These are the things that come with my fame."

The source of Theodore's fame was that brilliant 2001–02 season. Taking over from an injured Jeff Hackett early in the season, Theodore played a career-high 67 games and saved more shots than any goalie in the league. He posted a 2.11 goals-against average and a .931 save percentage. The photogenic 25-year-old was at the top of the world.

But the success went to Theodore's head. During the off-season, he was everywhere except in the gym and on the ice. He played a lot of golf, made public appearances, filmed commercials, and enjoyed Montreal's nightlife. After making $1.65 million, he was looking for a raise but general manager André Savard was cautious. It didn't matter because owner George Gillett was in love with Theodore and, as the Canadiens gathered for their 2002 golf tournament, the team announced that Theodore had become the highest-paid player in team history with a three-year deal worth $15 million.

Rollie Melanson, the Canadiens goaltending coach, didn't have to search for an explanation when Theodore's performance tailed off.

"When you're No. 1 in the world, the only place you can go is down," said Melanson. "What we didn't anticipate was him coming into camp not in the condition he should have been in."

Theodore bounced back in the 2003–04 season when he won a career-high 33 games, but there were more distractions.

He was back on the front pages of the tabloids after he was photographed cavorting with Paris Hilton at a 2006 music awards show in Toronto. And he was handed a two-year ban by the International Ice Hockey Federation after he tested positive for finasteride, a masking agent for steroids. The drug was contained in Propecia, a prescription hair-loss treatment. The NHL had granted him a medical exemption to use the drug but it was banned by international governing bodies.

Another dip in his performance and the emergence of Cristobal Huet led to his being traded to Colorado in 2006. The trade served as a wake-up call for Theodore. He played seven more seasons and was the No. 1 goalie in Colorado, Washington, Minnesota, and Florida before an injury ended his career in the 2012–13 season.

He experienced a tragedy in the summer of 2009 when his son Chace died two months after he was born prematurely.

Theodore founded Saves for Kids, a charity to benefit the neo-natal intensive care unit at the Children's National Medical Centre in Washington. He won the 2010 Bill Masterton Memorial Trophy for perseverance and dedication to the game.

In 2014, he returned to Montreal as an analyst for the French-language telecast of Canadiens games on TVA Sports.

68 Hard Work Paid Off for Reardon

When Ken Reardon was growing up in Winnipeg, he played hockey in the shadow of his older brother, Terry.

Terry Reardon was a high-scoring forward who was the leading goal-scorer in the Manitoba Junior Hockey League for two seasons. He was still junior age when he made his NHL debut with the Boston Bruins.

His kid brother took a bit longer to develop but would go on to have a longer and more successful career.

Ken saw limited ice time as a midget and juvenile and dressed for only 19 regular-season games over two seasons with the Edmonton Athletic Club Roamers junior team.

But Reardon emerged as an overnight sensation in the Memorial Cup playdowns in 1940. The Roamers didn't match their 1939 march to the final but the seldom-used Reardon scored 18 goals and added 13 assists.

The following season he was playing for the Canadiens, where he established a reputation for hard work and even harder checks.

Reardon once summed up his career by saying: "I couldn't skate, I couldn't shoot, and I wasn't very intelligent. But I was spectacular."

Reardon's Hall of Fame career was short. He played only seven seasons and retired in 1950, nearly a year short of his 30th birthday. He lost three seasons while serving overseas with the Canadian Army during World War II and his rugged style of play led to numerous injuries which hastened his retirement.

When he returned from the war, Reardon settled in alongside Emile (Butch) Bouchard and became a perennial All-Star. In five seasons, he was named to the first team twice and the second team three times. He was a major part of the Canadiens' Stanley Cup victory in 1946.

Reardon also developed a reputation for being one of the toughest players in the NHL. He was involved in a long-running feud with Cal Gardner, which began when Gardner crosschecked Reardon in the face during a 1947 game at Madison Square Garden.

That ignited a bench-clearing brawl which eventually involved a number of fans. One fan took a swipe at the bloodied Reardon and police were hard-pressed to keep the Canadiens from attacking the crowd.

The feud was still simmering prior to the 1949–50 season when Reardon said: "I'm going to make sure that Gardner gets 14 stitches in his mouth. I may have to wait a long time, but I'll get even."

In November 1949, Reardon and teammate Leo Gravelle spent a few hours in a Chicago jail cell after they were accused of attacking fans with their sticks. The charges were dismissed but NHL president Clarence Campbell came down hard on Reardon later that month when he made good on his threat against Gardner. He delivered a devastating shoulder check to Gardner, who was playing with the Toronto Maple Leafs. Reardon broke Gardner's jaw and Campbell ordered Reardon to post a $1,000 good behaviour bond.

New York Rangers defenceman Gus Kyle may have ended Reardon's career when he hit him during the 1950 playoffs. Longtime broadcaster Dick Irvin Jr. said that was one score

Reardon wasn't able to settle. According to Irvin, Reardon used to say: "I just want to play one more game…one more game against Kyle."

When he retired from playing, Reardon turned his effort to developing the Canadiens' farm system. General manager Frank Selke sent Reardon back to his roots in Western Canada and he managed the Regina Pats. Under his leadership, the Pats reached the Memorial Cup final four times in the 1950s. The Pats lost in the 1958 final to the Ottawa-Hull Junior Canadiens, who were managed by Sam Pollock.

Red Berenson, Terry Harper, Dave Balon, and Bill Hicke were among the Pats who graduated to the Canadiens in that era.

Reardon also convinced Selke that Toe Blake would be the best man to coach the Canadiens, when Selke was leaning toward Billy Reay.

When Selke reluctantly retired as general manager in 1964, the Molson family chose Pollock over Reardon as Selke's successor but there were no hard feelings on Reardon's part.

"Sam Pollock is the smartest man I know, in hockey and in life," said Reardon, who remained in the Canadiens organization as a vice-president.

He was inducted into the Hockey Hall of Fame in 1966.

69 Born to Be a Canadien

P.K. Subban was born to be a Canadien.

Subban's father, Karl, was 11 when his family moved from Jamaica to Sudbury, a mining town in Northern Ontario. French Canadians made up a significant portion of the population and they cheered for the Canadiens. When young Karl became a hockey fan, he adopted the local favourites as his team.

Karl Subban played basketball at Lakehead University in Thunder Bay, earned a degree in education, and moved to Toronto where he taught and eventually became a respected middle-school principal in one of the city's toughest neighbourhoods.

P.K. Subban has become a stalwart defenceman for the Canadiens since joining them in 2010. He won the Norris Trophy as the NHL's top defenceman in 2013.

He and his wife, Maria, also raised a family. First there were two daughters, who followed their father into education. And then there were the boys, P.K. (his full name is Pernell Karl), Malcolm, and Jordan. All three would become hockey players. Malcolm is a goaltender in the Boston Bruins organization while defenceman Jordan has been drafted by the Vancouver Canucks.

P.K. was the oldest and he became indoctrinated into rooting for the Canadiens, a heresy in a city that worships the Toronto Maple Leafs.

The term "hockey parents" has a negative connotation and Maria Subban said she and her husband tried to keep their support in perspective.

"Karl was a principal and he had to be reserved but I cheered a lot, not just for our kids but for all the kids," said Maria. "We tried to get to as many games as possible but it was hard sometimes with three boys at different ages."

Karl Subban used to get up at 5:00 AM and drive a teenaged P.K. an hour to Guelph, where he would work with a private trainer before school. There would be late-night outdoor skating sessions at a public rink in the shadow of Toronto's City Hall.

P.K. was big for his age and dominated minor hockey but, by the time he was ready for junior, most of his peers had caught up. He was still available to the Belleville Bulls in the sixth round of the Ontario Hockey League draft because there was a feeling he was too small.

By the time Subban was ready for the NHL draft in 2007, his size—he's a shade under his listed height of 6 feet—wasn't as big a factor as his playing style. Scouts admired his skating skills and his booming shot but had questions about his defence.

High risk, high reward, said most of the reports.

Trevor Timmins, the Canadiens director of amateur scouting, focused on the high reward. Where some scouts saw cockiness, Timmins saw confidence.

"I visited the family and saw the character, the work ethic he grew up with," said Timmins.

The Canadiens had two first-round picks that year and went with defenceman Ryan McDonagh at No. 12 and forward Max Pacioretty at No. 22. They selected Subban in the second round at No. 43.

It was difficult to tell who was happier that day—P.K. or his father. While Karl Subban talked about his longtime love for the Canadiens, P.K. addressed the Montreal media for the first time and said: "I'm going to make Mr. Gainey happy he drafted me."

Bob Gainey had stepped down as general manager by the time Subban made his first splash in the NHL but he was happy to see Subban's development. After spending most of the 2009–10 season in the minors, P.K. was called up when Andrei Markov injured his knee in the playoffs. Subban played 14 games as the Canadiens went to the Eastern Conference final. The plan was to ease him into the lineup, but one night in Pittsburgh he was on the ice for almost 30 minutes. He had arrived in the NHL.

Over the past few years, Subban has become one of the most recognizable players in the NHL, a black superstar in a sport whose personnel and fan base are predominantly white. Like most minority players in the NHL, he has been subjected to racist taunts but he has managed to dismiss them, drawing on lessons learned from his father.

"You're always going to have ignorant people who say and do ignorant things," said Karl Subban. "I learned a long time ago and I've told my kids that if you waste time and energy on these people, it distracts you from what you're trying to accomplish."

Subban was pulled into a controversy during the 2014 playoff series against the rival Boston Bruins. He scored two goals, including the overtime winner in Game 1, and that prompted a handful of Boston fans to post racist taunts on social media. Subban took the high road, saying that he was concentrating on the next game and that he didn't feel the comments reflected the majority of the Boston fan base.

That doesn't mean Subban was universally loved in Beantown. In a feature later that year, *Sports Illustrated* described Subban as the "most hated" player in the NHL, and before Game 7 of the Boston series, Subban told NBC's Pierre McGuire that he was looking forward to a nasty game and that the Canadiens wanted to take all the excitement away from the Boston crowd.

They did exactly that with a 3–1 win.

Maria Subban said one of the things that upsets rival players is that P.K. is always smiling and that it's difficult to get under his skin.

But Subban does get under the skin of rivals—and, on occasion, coaches and teammates. Subban and his defence partner, the ultra serious Andrei Markov, have reached a respectful détente, while coach Michel Therrien is less likely to bench Subban when he gets burned on a goal.

That's because the high-risk, high-reward scale has swung decidedly to the reward side. Subban has won a Norris Trophy and he entered the 2014–15 season with a new eight-year, $72-million contract. It's the longest and richest in team history.

70 Toe Loses It

When Dick Irvin left the Canadiens to coach the Chicago Blackhawks in 1955, general manager Frank Selke had the ideal candidate to replace him.

Toe Blake had experience as a player and as a minor-league coach but the most important factor in the decision was Blake's relationship with the fiery Maurice (Rocket) Richard. They played together on the Punch Line with Elmer Lach and, in the aftermath of what became known as the Richard Riot, Selke thought Blake would be able to control Richard's temper.

What Selke didn't count on was Blake's temper, which got him into trouble on several occasions. The man who won the Lady Byng Trophy in 1946 as the league's most gentlemanly player morphed into the coach who engaged in verbal—and the occasional physical—battles with players, sportswriters, on-ice officials, and fans.

One of his most infamous transgressions occurred on March 26, 1961, in a playoff game between the Canadiens and the Chicago Blackhawks. Referee Dalton McArthur called a penalty on Dickie Moore in the third overtime and Murray Balfour scored the winning goal to end a contest that veteran sportswriter Red Fisher described as the greatest game he ever saw.

Blake, who was also upset that McArthur had disallowed a goal in the second overtime because Doug Harvey's stick was too high, walked across the Chicago Stadium ice, threw a punch at McArthur, and continued to the visitors' dressing room.

In his postgame comments, Blake admitted that he threw a punch but insisted that he missed his target. The problem was that NHL president Clarence Campbell was sitting in the stands and saw the punch land—as well as the bright red welt on the side of McArthur's face.

The following day Campbell announced that Blake was being fined $2,000. At that time, it was the largest fine in league history; Blake noted: "There goes my new car for next year." (There was also a suggestion that Blake's wife was upset because it cost her a new washing machine.)

Campbell defended McArthur's officiating performance but the referee felt that the incident led to a premature end to his career. In a television interview with sportswriter Scott Young—younger readers should know he's Neil Young's dad—McArthur said that was his last playoff game. He found his schedule cut back the following season and was told his services were no longer required after he worked only five games in the 1962–63 season.

Eddie Powers, who was the standby official that night in Chicago, ran into problems of his own when he tangled with Blake.

After the Toronto Maple Leafs defeated the Canadiens 6–3 on January 31, 1963, Blake questioned Powers' integrity and suggested that he refereed as if he had a bet on the game. The quote appeared the following day in the French-language newspaper *Montreal-Matin* and was disseminated across Canada.

Campbell fined Blake $200, the standard fine for criticizing an official, but Powers wasn't satisfied. He resigned and blasted Campbell for not backing up his officials. He then filed a slander suit against Blake in the Ontario Supreme Court. The suit was eventually settled for an undisclosed amount of cash along with apologies from Blake, the Canadiens, the reporter, and the newspaper.

In the Eyes of the Law

Julian Porter is regarded as one of the leading litigators in Canada and he credits Eddie Powers' lawsuit against Toe Blake for sparking his interest in libel and slander law.

He was an articling student with a prominent Toronto firm when Jean Béliveau, Kenny Reardon, Frank Selke, and Blake arrived in the office to meet with senior partner Walter Williston to discuss Blake's defence.

"I was a hockey nut," he recalled in a 1999 profile in *The Lawyers Weekly*. "I didn't know libel from my left foot but I walked in with the crowd. I knew hockey."

Williston assigned him to research the law on libel and he spent three weeks in the library.

"In three weeks you can learn an awful lot of law. It gave me a foothold," he said.

Porter's research told him that Powers had a strong case and Blake agreed to settle before the case reached the courtroom.

Blake did find himself before a judge when two fans in Los Angeles accused him and Claude Provost of hitting them with hockey sticks during a game at the Los Angeles Sports Arena on November 19, 1967. The two were arraigned in March but were acquitted of malicious assault in July.

The incident also produced two civil suits which went nowhere. Bernard Weisman sought $405,000 in damages, claiming that he needed 23 stitches to close a wound. He testified that he was booing Blake and found himself with a gash in the head after he moved closer to the Montreal bench. A second plaintiff, a woman, claimed that she suffered a concussion when she was struck by a stick in the same incident.

71 The Torch

The Canadiens dressing room provides a vivid reminder of the team's history.

There are plaques containing the rosters of each team dating back to the inaugural 1909–10 season. Above the stalls where the players stow their equipment, there are the faces of the 45 Canadiens who have been inducted into the Hockey Hall of Fame and the words To YOU FROM FAILING HANDS WE THROW THE TORCH; BE YOURS TO HOLD IT HIGH.

The words are taken from the poem "In Flanders Field." It was written on the battlefield in 1915 by John McCrae, a Canadian military surgeon, after he presided over the funerals of soldiers killed during World War I.

Canadiens general manager Frank Selke enjoyed reading poetry and he was moved by McCrae's words. In 1952, he lifted two lines from McCrae's work, hoping that they would inspire his players.

The torch has gone from being a metaphor to a tangible symbol of the team's past and its ties to the future. The torch has been a staple of special events, first at the Forum and now at the Bell Centre.

One of the most memorable nights in the team's history was the closing of the Forum on March 11, 1996. The evening opened with the team's former captains passing the torch from one to another until it reached the hands of the current captain, Pierre Turgeon.

Today, the Canadiens begin each season with the passing of the torch from a veteran—the late Jean Béliveau and Guy Lafleur have handled the chore in recent years—to members of the current team.

"I grew up in Connecticut and I didn't know much about the history of the team but I got butterflies the first time I carried the torch," said Max Pacioretty.

P.A. Parenteau, who grew up in Longueuil on Montreal's South Shore, had a similar reaction after he joined the Canadiens prior to the 2014–15 season.

"As a Quebecois, I grew up watching the Canadiens and it was one of the proudest moments of my career when I stepped on the ice with the torch in my hand," said Parenteau.

The Canadiens are also aware of the origins of McCrae's poem and the torch. The poem inspired the team's coaching staff and other members of the organization to wear poppies in their lapels in the weeks leading up to November 11, the anniversary of the armistice which ended World War I. The commemoration is known as Remembrance Day in Canada and Veterans Day in the United States and celebrates those who served in the armed forces.

72 The Price Is Right

If there is a 25th Stanley Cup in the Canadiens' near future, you can bet that goaltender Carey Price will play a major role.

Under the guidance of goaltending coach Stéphane Waite, Price has become one of the most consistent goaltenders in the NHL, but his critics won't be happy until he hoists the Cup.

An ongoing complaint from fans is "He's never won the big game," an opinion that fails to recognize that Price's résumé is littered with big-game performances, starting with the world junior championships in 2007.

Canada defeated Russia 4–2 in the final but Price sewed up the tournament MVP honours with his play in the semifinals. Canada defeated the United States 2–1 in a shootout. The Americans had a 4-on-3 power play in the 10-minute overtime and outshot Canada 12–2 in the extra period but Price was a rock.

He led Team Canada to a third consecutive gold medal, going 6–0 with two shutouts, a 1.14 GAA, and a .961 save percentage.

Later that year, Price was called up to the Hamilton Bulldogs and led them to their only American Hockey League title. He started every game and became the first teenage goaltender to win the Jack Butterfield Trophy as the playoff MVP.

Need more evidence of Price's ability to play on the big stage?

In 2014, he backstopped Canada to the gold medal at the 2014 Winter Olympics in Sochi, Russia. His critics have dismissed that performance, saying that anyone could have won behind a lineup stacked with many of the world's top players.

Canadiens coach Michel Therrien disagrees.

"Team Canada played a very disciplined system and they didn't score a lot of goals," said Therrien "That puts more pressure on the goaltender because he can't afford to make a mistake."

And Price didn't make many. He allowed only three goals in five games and went undefeated with a 0.59 goals-against average and a .971 save percentage. He was nearly flawless in the knockout phase of the event. In the quarterfinals, the Canadians survived a scare to beat Latvia 2–1. Canada defeated the United States 1–0 in the semifinals as Price made 31 saves. He posted another shutout in the final as Canada defeated Sweden 3–0. Price needed to be stingy because Canada scored only 11 goals in those games, an average of 2.2 goals a game. He was selected as the outstanding goaltender in the tournament.

Price has yet to duplicate those results in the NHL playoffs, but general manager Marc Bergevin believes in building a team from the goal out and said Price is an excellent start. In the 2014 playoffs, Price continued his Olympic success as he led the Canadiens to a sweep of Tampa Bay and then showed his ability to win the big game in a seven-game upset of the Boston Bruins.

The Canadiens trailed the best-of-seven series 3–2 but Price shut out the Bruins 4–0 at the Bell Centre and then made 29 saves as Montreal clinched the series with a 3–1 win in Boston.

Price's playoff run ended in the first game of the conference final against the Rangers. He was injured when New York's Chris Kreider crashed into him. Without Price, the Canadiens lost in six games but his performance gave Montreal fans hope that their first Stanley Cup win since 1993 was within reach.

In 2014–15, Price would post a season for the ages: he led the NHL in goals-against average (1.96), save percentage (.933), and wins (44), all career highs, as the Canadiens won the Atlantic Division. After the season, he was awarded the Hart Trophy as the league's most valuable player, the Vézina Trophy as best goaltender, the Ted Lindsay Award as most valuable player as voted by the

NHLPA, and the Jennings Trophy for fewest goals allowed (shared with Chicago's Corey Crawford).

73 Wickenheiser and Savard

Contrary to popular belief, Doug Wickenheiser wasn't the worst player ever drafted by the Canadiens.

It just seemed that way back in 1980.

The Hockey News rated Wickenheiser as the top prospect in the draft that year and he was named the Canadian Hockey League Player of the Year after scoring 89 goals for the Regina Pats. The Canadiens had the No. 1 pick that year and Irving Grundman, who became the general manager after a successful career as the owner of a string of bowling alleys, didn't hesitate to draft the rangy center.

The reaction from Montreal fans was immediately negative. The fans, particularly the French Canadians, wanted Grundman to select Denis Savard, who was the star player for the Montreal Juniors.

Savard wasn't as big as Wickenheiser and he didn't score as many goals, but he was a flashy playmaker. He teamed with Denis Cyr and Denis Tremblay to form a high-scoring line known as Les Trois Denis. It didn't matter to the fans that the Winnipeg Jets also passed on Savard and selected Dave Babych with the No. 2 pick (Chicago grabbed Savard at No. 3).

Through no fault of his own, Wickenheiser was regarded as a bad guy and fans piled on Grundman when Savard quickly became a star and a popular figure in Chicago while Wickenheiser became the No. 1 draft pick nobody wanted.

Wickenheiser quickly learned that the Canadiens' philosophy was to bring young players along slowly. He made the NHL roster as a rookie but played only 41 games, scoring seven goals and dishing out eight assists.

Savard? He had 28 goals and 75 points as a rookie.

Wickenheiser played in 56 games in his second year and had 12 goals and 23 assists but Savard left him far behind as he scored 32 goals and added 89 assists for a 119-point season.

Wickenheiser's best NHL season was in 1982–83 when he scored 25 goals and added 30 assists. But the pressure weighed heavily on him and when he started the next season with five goals and five assists in 27 games, the Canadiens traded him to St. Louis.

Savard would return to Montreal in 1990 as part of what would be regarded as one of the worst deals engineered by general manager Serge Savard. Denis Savard's Hall of Fame career was on the wane. He was still a good player but not a great one and the Canadiens sent a great player to Chicago in the person of defenceman Chris Chelios.

A Chicago-area native, Chelios had helped the Canadiens win their 23rd Stanley Cup in 1986 and won the Norris Trophy as the NHL's top defenceman in 1989. But he ran into some problems a year later when he was arrested in Madison, Wisconsin. Two police officers accused him of trying to fight with them after he was spotted urinating in an alley next to a bar. The image-conscious Canadiens took a dim view of the incident and traded him the following day.

When Savard reported to the Canadiens' training camp in 1990, Wickenheiser was in Asiago, Italy. His NHL career was over and he finished with 556 games played, 111 goals, and 165 assists. He would play two seasons in Europe and two more in the minor leagues.

Savard played three seasons in Montreal and was part of the Canadiens' last Stanley Cup win in 1993. If you look at the picture of the Canadiens' on-ice celebration after beating the Los Angeles Kings, Savard stands out because he is not in uniform. He is in a suit as he sits on the ice next to the Cup. He appeared in 14 of Montreal's 20 playoff games but he was a healthy scratch down the stretch. Coach Jacques Demers decided that Savard had lost a step and he wanted to go with a quicker lineup. But Demers had so much respect for Savard that he deputized him to serve as an assistant coach and he was behind the bench for the final game.

Savard moved to Tampa Bay the following season and finished his career back in Chicago. He retired with 473 goals and 865 assists for a total of 1,338 points. He was elected to the Hockey Hall of Fame in 2000.

Wickenheiser's career ended in 1994 when a cancerous sarcoma was removed from his wrist. The cancer returned in 1997 and, by the time doctors diagnosed the disease, it had spread to his lungs and he was told it was inoperable. He died on January 12, 1999, at the age of 37.

74 Picking the Wrong Guy

Expansion brought a major change to the way hockey teams were put together. In the days of the Original Six, each team had an extensive farm system which included junior teams. NHL teams signed promising players to C cards when they were 13 and the team would control the players' development through junior and into the professional ranks.

The system changed with expansion and amateur players were available to any team through an annual entry draft.

While not every first-round player is a guaranteed superstar, the majority of them have decent careers. But here are 10 first-rounders who didn't pan out for the Canadiens:

The strangest case may have been that of **Robin Sadler**, a defenceman who was drafted ninth overall in 1975. He reported to the Canadiens training camp in September but left after a week because he couldn't handle the stress. He had signed a three-year contract with a hefty signing bonus but returned the money. He went home to North Vancouver, where he worked for a delivery service for $250 a week. The following season he went to Austria, and in 1977, he signed a contract with Edmonton of the WHA but again left camp without playing a game. He rejoined the Canadiens organization in February 1978 and played nine games with the Nova Scotia Voyageurs before heading back to Europe, where he enjoyed several seasons of stress-free hockey, winning two championships in the low-key Dutch league.

The Canadiens looked to the Western Hockey League for a big winger and found 6-foot-3 **Lindsay Vallis** with the 13th pick in 1989. His only NHL appearance in a 13-year pro career was in a game for the Canadiens in the 1993–94 season.

Defenceman **Brent Bilodeau** was drafted 17th overall from the Seattle Thunderbirds in 1991. He played with nine different teams over a 12-year minor-league career.

Terry Ryan was a bruising left winger with the Tri-City Americans when he was selected eighth overall in 1995. He played eight games over three seasons with the Canadiens but concussions and an ankle injury ended his NHL dreams. He played his last professional game in 2003 and he continues to play senior hockey in his native Newfoundland. He chronicled his career in a memoir titled *Tales of a First-Round Nobody: My Life as an NHL Footnote.*

David Fischer was named Mr. Hockey as the outstanding high school hockey player in Minnesota a few months before the Canadiens selected him 20th overall out of Apple Valley High School in 2008. He was headed to the University of Minnesota, where the Canadiens expected him to put some meat on his 6-foot-3, 190-pound frame. But Fischer never filled out and his progress was slowed by a virus, injuries, and a death in his family. When he graduated from Minnesota, the Canadiens elected not to offer him a contract. He played two seasons in the ECHL with a brief two-game stint with Houston of AHL before heading to Germany.

Goaltender **Ray Martyniuk** was the fifth overall choice in 1970 after playing for the Flin Flon Bombers. He played nine seasons in the minors, most of them as a backup. The high point in his career was in 1974–75, when he posted a 31–15–6 record with the Salt Lake Golden Eagles of the Central Hockey League.

Gord McTavish was the last of five first-round picks for the Canadiens in 1974, going 15th overall. Over six pro seasons, he played one game for the St. Louis Blues and 10 for the Winnipeg Jets.

Bruce Baker was the last of three first-rounders in 1976. The Ottawa 67's winger played five seasons with Nova Scotia before retiring.

Left winger **Jan Ingman** was selected 19th overall in 1981 but never left his native Sweden. He helped Farjestads win three Swedish League titles.

Alain Heroux was drafted 19th overall out of Chicoutimi in 1982. He retired and returned to school after one season with the Sherbrooke Canadiens.

75. A Rivalry Like No Other

As the Canadiens prepared to meet the Boston Bruins in Game 7 of their Eastern Conference semifinal in 2014, defenceman P.K. Subban was asked about playing in Boston's TD Garden.

"It's going to be great," he replied. "I can't wait for the crowd, the noise, the energy in the building. I can't wait to take that all away from them."

Subban and the Canadiens did just that, beating the Bruins 3–1 to win a series which reflected hockey's oldest and most bitter rivalry.

The series began with the Canadiens winning Game 1 on a Subban goal in double overtime and ended with Boston's Milan Lucic threatening Canadiens Dale Weise and Alexei Emelin during the traditional handshake at the end of the series.

In between, there was a lot of great hockey punctuated by online racial taunts directed at Subban, charges of diving, and a fine when Shaun Thornton squirted a water bottle at Subban.

"There's a real rivalry here," said Montreal coach Michel Therrien. "Rivalries are created in the playoffs and over the years these teams have had some great series."

The Canadiens and the Bruins have faced off in the postseason a record 34 times, dating back to 1929 when the Bruins defeated the Canadiens 3–0 in a best-of-five semifinal series. The Canadiens have enjoyed the upper hand for most of the rivalry; they have won 25 of the 34 meetings and are a perfect 7–0 when the teams have met in the Stanley Cup final.

The rivalry has produced some of the most famous moments in NHL playoff history.

On April 8, 1952, a bloodied Maurice (Rocket) Richard emerged from the clinic at the Montreal Forum and scored on Sugar Jim Henry for the series-clinching goal in the semifinals.

The Canadiens won 18 consecutive playoff series from 1946 to 1987 and posted a few upsets in that string.

The Bruins, led by Phil Esposito and Bobby Orr, were a worthy contender in 1969 but the Canadiens beat them in six games in the second round of the playoffs. Jean Béliveau notched the series winner in the second overtime in Game 6.

Esposito and Orr shattered scoring records in the 1970–71 season but an untested goaltender named Ken Dryden started the Canadiens' run to the Stanley Cup by eliminating Boston in seven games. Dryden would beat the Bruins again in the 1977 and 1978 Cup finals and the 1979 semifinal, which ended with a 5–4 Canadiens win in overtime. There's more than a trace of irony in Dryden's success against the Bruins, since the team drafted him in 1964 but traded him to the Canadiens a few hours later.

The Bruins had that final game in the bag before they were called for having too many men on the ice with less than three minutes left in regulation. Guy Lafleur tied the game on the ensuing power play and Yvan Lambert delivered the winner in overtime.

The Bruins were favoured again in 2002 and 2004 but were upset on both occasions. In 2002, the Canadiens won their first playoff series since 1998, and in 2004, they made history by coming back from a 3–1 deficit.

76 Béliveau Passes the Torch to Dryden

The 1971 Stanley Cup playoffs had a little bit of everything—an unknown goaltender who morphed into a most valuable player, a feud between the winning coach and a star player, a rookie shutting down one of the most feared goal-scorers in the NHL, and a 10th Stanley Cup to mark Jean Béliveau's final season.

The Canadiens weren't expected to contend for the Cup after finishing third in their division in the regular season. That put them up against the defending champion Boston Bruins in the opening round of the playoffs.

There were raised eyebrows when coach Al MacNeil announced that Ken Dryden would start in goal in place of Rogie Vachon. Dryden, who was a law student at McGill University, had spent most of the season playing for the Montreal Voyageurs of the American Hockey League. He was called up to the Canadiens late in the season and played only six NHL games. But MacNeil liked what he saw—Dryden went undefeated in those games with a 1.65 goals-against average and a .957 save percentage. Dryden played every game in the playoffs and won the Conn Smythe Trophy as the most valuable player in the playoffs, a year before he won the Calder Trophy as the NHL's top rookie.

The Canadiens upset the Bruins in seven games and then eliminated the Minnesota North Stars in six games. That set up an Original Six final between the Canadiens and the Chicago Blackhawks.

Controversy erupted when MacNeil benched future Hall of Famer Henri Richard in Game 5 of the series. After Chicago won 2–0 to take a 3–2 lead in the series, Richard told reporters that MacNeil was incompetent and "the worst coach I ever played for." MacNeil, who spoke only English, was perceived as anti-French, and after he received death threats, a police guard stood beside him behind the bench as the Canadiens posted a 4–3 win in Game 6 at the Forum.

Richard apologized for his remarks and general manager Sam Pollock attempted to calm the waters when he said: "If I know Richard as well as I think I do, I bet you he'll score a big goal for us."

Pollock would have won that bet because Richard scored the tying goal and then added the winner as the Canadiens won 3–2. It was only the second time in NHL history that a road team had won Game 7 in a Cup final.

MacNeil and Richard hugged at the end of the series but the win wasn't enough to save MacNeil's job. Scotty Bowman took over as head coach while MacNeil returned to coaching the Voyageurs, who moved to his native Nova Scotia.

Chicago coach Billy Reay also had problems in the Cup final. He was criticized for limiting Bobby Hull's playing time but Hull was being brought to a standstill by Canadiens rookie Réjean Houle.

"Hull was a strong player, not dirty, but when he was carrying the puck he was difficult to handle," recalled Houle. "I tried to make sure I stayed in front of him and I tried to keep him from getting the puck. In the final game, we were trailing 2–0 and I lost him and I thought he was going to score and it was going to be all over. But he hit the crossbar and then Jacques Lemaire scored to get us back into the game."

Béliveau, who had been persuaded by Pollock to play one more season, had six goals and 16 assists in 20 games.

Brothers Frank and Peter Mahovlich combined for nine goals in the final series. Pollock acquired Frank Mahovlich from Detroit in midseason and the Big M collected 41 points in 38 games. He was even more productive in the playoffs as he scored 14 goals and added 13 assists.

77 Age No Obstacle for Gardiner

The list of Canadiens who have won the Hart Trophy as the league's most valuable player contains many well-known names—Richard, Béliveau, Lafleur, Geoffrion.

And then there's Herb Gardiner.

Gardiner and Wayne Gretzky share the distinction of being the only players to win the Hart Trophy in their first NHL seasons, but there's an important difference between the two. Gretzky was 19 years old when he was honoured; Gardiner was 35.

Gardiner played senior hockey in Winnipeg as a 17-year-old but he was more intent on establishing his business career. He started out as a banker and then quit playing when he took a job as a surveyor for the Canadian Pacific Railway. His hiatus from hockey would last a decade. He enlisted in the Canadian Army and fought for three years in World War I before receiving a medical discharge in 1918.

He resumed playing hockey and turned professional when the Calgary Tigers joined the newly formed Western Canada Hockey League. He and Red Dutton provided the Tigers with a formidable pair on defence and he made an impression on the Canadiens in the 1924 Stanley Cup playoffs. Aurèle Joliat and Howie Morenz used their speed to wear down the Tigers but Gardiner stood out with his physical play. When the Western League folded in 1926, the Canadiens bought his contract.

At 5-foot-10 and 190 pounds, Gardiner was one of the biggest players in the NHL and one of the most physical. He teamed with fellow Hall of Famer Silvio Mantha for two seasons and won the Hart Trophy in 1927. He earned the nickname "ironman of hockey" after he reportedly played every minute of every game for two seasons.

The Canadiens loaned him to Chicago for the 1928–29 season and he served as a player-coach. He had a 5–23–4 record as a coach before finishing his final season with the Canadiens.

He had more success coaching the Philadelphia Ramblers in the American Hockey League and became a strong advocate for hockey in that city. In 1947, there was a plan to relocate the dormant Montreal Maroons franchise in Philadelphia and Gardiner was poised to be the franchise's general manager. The idea died when the proposed owners ran short of cash.

Gardiner settled in Philadelphia and lived long enough to see the Flyers be part of the first expansion. He was elected to the Hockey Hall of Fame in 1958 and died in 1972.

78 A Not-So-Good Friday

Wilf Paiement of the Quebec Nordiques and the Canadiens' Mike McPhee dropped the gloves 23 seconds into a playoff game on April 20, 1984, but that was merely a teaser for what was to come in a game which became known as the Good Friday Massacre.

The fierce rivalry between these teams boiled over at the end of the second period as they engaged in a bloody bench-clearing brawl which produced a record 252 minutes in penalties and resulted in 12 players being tossed from the game.

The Canadiens were looking to win the Adams Division final but the Nordiques had a 1–0 lead in Game 6 when Dale Hunter knocked Guy Carbonneau to the ice in front of the Quebec net.

Chris (Knuckles) Nilan came to Carbonneau's defence and the brawl was on. Both benches emptied and the result was a 40-man riot.

Mario Tremblay of the Canadiens broke Peter Stastny's nose. Louis Sleigher of the Nordiques sucker-punched Jean Hamel and knocked him out. Hamel also suffered a broken nose, as well as an eye injury which hastened his retirement from hockey.

Backup goaltenders Steve Penney and Clint Malarchuk traded punches and were both ejected.

It took a while for referee Bruce Hood to sort out the penalties and the delay led to two critical mistakes. He handed out a number of game misconduct penalties at the end of the second period but he didn't notify the teams. As a result, players who had been tossed from the game returned to the ice for the third period and another brawl broke out. The players were able to resume swinging unimpeded because Hood and his linesmen were tardy returning to the ice.

Sleigher was among the players ejected from the game but when the Canadiens saw him back on the ice, several players went after him. Mark Hunter of the Canadiens swung his stick at Sleigher and found himself being challenged by his brother Dale.

There was almost an hour delay between the end of the second period and resumption of play in the third.

"For me, it was one of the most embarrassing games," said Michel Goulet, who polished his Hall of Fame credentials in 11 seasons with the Nordiques. "I thought it was totally stupid, totally out of control. You look at it and say, 'Wow, it's just amazing that we end up everybody's punching everybody.'"

Goulet said the heated rivalry contributed to the mayhem but he pointed a finger at Hood for "letting everything go. When you know the referee is letting everything go, you go harder, you punch harder, you slash harder. That's what happened.

"It's sad because we played so many good games and that's the one they keep showing."

When play finally resumed, both benches were thin.

"You got a lot of ice time," said Goulet. "It was hard for the coach to bench you."

Goulet scored at 2:02 to put the Nordiques ahead 2–0 but Steve Shutt scored twice to tie the game and Rick Green, John Chabot, and Carbonneau added goals as the Canadiens went on to win 5–3 to complete the series upset.

By the early 1990s, much of the animosity between the teams had petered out. Chris Nilan told Michael Farber of the *Montreal Gazette* that was the result of a changing attitude among the players.

"The difference is now you don't find guys who are willing to carry the flag into battle, who are willing to get shot down so the men behind them can fire," said Nilan. "That's what Steve Shutt said after the Good Friday brawl in 1984: 'Now that the idiots are gone, we can go out and play hockey.'"

Hood retired at the end of the season but there was speculation that NHL officials encouraged him to quit.

79 The Quotable Guy Lafleur

Guy Lafleur's reputation as a straight shooter extends far beyond the ice.

Lafleur is associated with the Canadiens as a team ambassador but his role is not to be confused with that of team cheerleader. Ask Lafleur what he thinks of the team or a particular player and you will get an honest answer.

Brutally honest, in some cases.

A classic example was the night in November 2007 when the Canadiens dropped a 3–0 decision to the Buffalo Sabres and Lafleur dropped this bomb during a postgame show: "The Canadiens don't have a first line; they have four fourth lines."

In 2010, the Canadiens advanced to the Eastern Conference final but Lafleur was less than impressed when he said: "Let's just say it was better than last year."

Lafleur conceded that the Canadiens exceeded expectations by beating Washington and Pittsburgh but he had issues with their performance against Philadelphia in the conference final.

"When we went up against Philadelphia, we could see that size was an important factor on a team," said Lafleur. "Not only size, but sustained intensity. In the first two games against Philadelphia, the team didn't show up, and that's where the series played out."

Lafleur noted that centre Scott Gomez ate at his restaurant prior to the playoffs and Lafleur tried to impart some advice. He said Gomez did a good job of moving the puck into the opponent's

In 1971, Guy Lafleur was Montreal's first overall pick in the NHL draft. He won five Stanley Cups with the Canadiens and retired with 560 career goals.

zone and then froze. He urged the veteran to shoot the puck more often but that advice fell on deaf ears.

Lafleur talked about the enthusiasm of the fans during the playoffs but injected a note of reality when he said that, in his day, the fans saved that outpouring of love for the Stanley Cup parade.

Lafleur was also not impressed with the 2014 run to the conference final which ended in a six-game series loss to the New York Rangers. In an interview with the French-language daily *La Presse*, Lafleur called out Thomas Vanek and Max Pacioretty.

"You can't keep guys like Vanek and Pacioretty on the team," said Lafleur. "They should stay home if they're not willing to pay the price. Your team won't win with players like that who disappear under adversity."

Lafleur, who played in an era when Stanley Cup wins were commonplace in Montreal, said: "We can't be satisfied with a good season. You don't play hockey just to have a good season. You play to win the Stanley Cup."

But Lafleur may have been a bit too harsh with Pacioretty, who was playing in only his second playoffs. In 21 playoff games, he had 11 points for an average of 0.52 points a game. Lafleur started his career with 14 points in his first 29 playoff games, an average of 0.48 points a game. He moderated his views on Pacioretty after the forward's strong performance the following season.

Lafleur was proud of his achievements; when he had only two goals and three assists in 19 games to start the 1984–85 season, he retired for the first time, saying: "After 13 years, I couldn't accept to be No. 2."

He said he considered himself a leader even though he never wore the captain's C. "The day you hear someone call me captain will be the day I buy a boat," said Lafleur.

80 He Died of a Broken Heart

Howie Morenz was regarded as the most exciting player of his day, but his exploits on the ice have been overshadowed by his tragic death at the age of 34.

Morenz, who was a three-time winner of the Hart Trophy with the Canadiens, was traded to Chicago in 1934 because the Montreal franchise was in deep financial trouble. When Cecil Hart returned to coach the Canadiens in 1936, he insisted that he wouldn't take the job unless they brought back Morenz.

The veteran showed occasional signs of the speed which earned him the nickname The Stratford Streak and the Canadiens were enjoying a successful season when they played the Chicago Blackhawks at the Forum on January 28, 1937.

The game took a tragic turn in the first period when Morenz lost his balance while chasing a loose puck. His left skate became jammed into the boards and didn't move when Chicago defenceman Earl Seibert was unable to stop and landed with full force on Morenz. The impact snapped Morenz's left leg and there were reports that the noise could be heard throughout the Forum.

Morenz was taken to Hôpital St. Luc, where it was determined that the leg was broken in four places. Over the next month, Morenz would suffer from depression. He was concerned about the team's decline in the standings and the fear that he would never play again.

When he first entered the hospital, his room was a beehive of activity with family, friends, teammates, and players from other NHL teams. In his book *The Montreal Canadiens: 100 Years of Glory*, D'Arcy Jenish recounts that many of the players brought drinks and one player noted "the whisky was on the dresser and the beer was under the bed."

In late February, team physician Hector Forgues imposed a ban on all visitors except for family and team officials after diagnosing Morenz with a nervous breakdown.

On March 8, Morenz complained of chest pains. His wife, Mary, and Cecil Hart were called to the hospital but Morenz collapsed and died minutes before they arrived. The cause of death was a blood clot but teammate Aurèle Joliat created a popular myth when he said that Morenz died of a broken heart because he knew he would never play again.

The Canadiens and the Montreal Maroons were scheduled to play on March 9 and the Maroons offered to postpone the game. But Mary Morenz said her husband would have wanted the game to be played. Players from both teams wore black armbands and two minutes of silence were observed prior to the game.

Morenz's funeral was held at the Forum on March 11. His casket was placed at center ice and more than 50,000 people filed past it to pay their respects. The Canadiens players took turns

Canadiens Hart Trophy Winners

Herb Gardiner	1927
Howie Morenz	1928, 1931, 1932
Aurèle Joliat	1934
Albert (Babe) Siebert	1937
Hector (Toe)	Blake 1939
Elmer Lach	1945
Maurice Richard	1947
Jean Béliveau	1956, 1964
Bernard Geoffrion	1961
Jacques Plante	1962
Guy Lafleur	1977, 1978
José Theodore	2002
Carey Price	2015

forming an honour guard around the casket which was covered with flowers including a large wreath in the shape of the No. 7 from Joliat.

On November 2, 1937, Morenz became the first player in Canadiens history to have his number retired. That night, a benefit all-star game was played at the Forum to raise money for the Morenz family. A team composed of players from the Canadiens and the Maroons lost 6–5 to a team representing the other teams in the league. When the Hockey Hall of Fame was established in 1945, Morenz was among the first nine players honoured.

Morenz was the league's leading scorer in 1928 and 1931 and won the Hart Trophy as the most valuable player in 1928, 1931, and 1932.

But he was recognized as a star from the time he joined the Canadiens in 1923 and he was credited with bringing the NHL to the United States. After Charles Adams, the owner of the grocery store chain in New England, watched Morenz play in the 1924 Stanley Cup final between the Canadiens and Ottawa, he secured a franchise for Boston.

Boxing promoter Tex Rickard was similarly impressed by Morenz and agreed to install ice in Madison Square Garden and pursue an NHL franchise. Rickard insisted that his franchise play its first home game against Morenz and the Canadiens, and the New York Americans made their Madison Square Garden debut on December 15, 1925.

81 Perfect Attendance

Doug Jarvis' mother once recalled that he had nearly perfect attendance at school when he was growing up in Brantford, Ontario. Once, he insisted on going to school with a bruised leg only to discover later that the leg was broken.

Jarvis had perfect attendance during an NHL career which spanned 12 seasons with three different teams. When his run ended two games into the 1987–88 season with the Hartford Whalers, he had played 964 consecutive games beginning with his first NHL game as a Canadien on October 8, 1975.

"You could say the record snuck up on me," Jarvis said in Hartford on December 26, 1986, when he played his 915th game to pass Garry Unger as the NHL's ironman. "You'd pass some guy on the ladder and the next guy would be 200 games ahead and you'd put it out of your mind."

Jarvis' streak is even more impressive because it started when his career started. Of the 20 players who have played more than 500 consecutive games, only five had streaks start with their first game. The only player in that group with an active streak is Andrew Cogliano, who has a chance to pass Jarvis early in the 2019–20 season.

Jarvis was drafted by the Toronto Maple Leafs in the second round in 1975 after he put together a 133-point season with the Peterborough Petes. Within days of the draft, the Leafs traded him to Montreal for defenceman Greg Hubick, whose NHL career lasted 77 games.

Canadiens coach Scotty Bowman wasn't as impressed with Jarvis' dazzling numbers in junior hockey as he was with Jarvis' defensive play. Jarvis had been well schooled in that aspect of the game by Roger Nielson, and Bowman inserted him at centre on a checking line with future Hall of Famer Bob Gainey and Jimmy Roberts on his wings.

Jarvis would play seven seasons—the first 560 games of his streak—with the Canadiens, and he was part of another streak as he played on four consecutive Stanley Cup–winning teams from 1976 through 1979.

"It's incredible what he's done," said Gainey. "I played in 50 to 60 percent of the games in his streak and I know what he went through some nights."

In his book *Hockey's Greatest Moments*, Lance Hornby recounted the night the Canadiens beat up on the Colorado Rockies and Jarvis had a hat-trick.

"As we were a checking line, he was almost embarrassed," said Gainey. "But inside every defensive player, there's an offensive player waiting to get out."

Jarvis' tenure with the Canadiens ended in 1982 when he was part of a blockbuster trade with the Washington Capitals. Future Hall of Famer Rod Langway, Brian Engblom, Craig Laughlin, and Jarvis went to the Capitals for Ryan Walter and Rick Green.

Jarvis and Langway would help the Capitals become a Cup contender. In 1984, Jarvis won the Selke Trophy as the top defensive forward in the NHL while Langway won the Norris Trophy as the top defenceman in 1983 and 1984.

After he broke Unger's record, Jarvis was awarded the Bill Masterton Memorial Trophy in 1987. The award is presented annually by the Professional Hockey Writers Association to "the player who best exemplifies the qualities of perseverance, sportsmanship, and dedication to hockey."

Jarvis was a superbly conditioned athlete who credited his strong Christian beliefs for his record.

The only time the streak was in jeopardy was in Game 761. During a game in Detroit, the Red Wings' Randy Ladouceur hit

Jarvis and he suffered a concussion. With the league-mandated protocol on head injuries in effect today, Jarvis' streak would have been over. But after spending the night in a Detroit hospital for observation, Jarvis joined his teammates the following day in St. Louis.

82 The French Canadian Rule

One of the enduring myths surrounding the Canadiens' success in the 1970s was the existence of a rule which gave the Canadiens first chance to draft French players from Quebec.

The rule did exist but the impact on the Canadiens' performance was minimal.

From 1963 until 1968, there was a draft for players who had not previously signed C-cards which bound them to an NHL team. Montreal had the option of selecting two French players from Quebec before the other teams started picking but exercised this option only once.

In 1968, Montreal jumped the line to select goaltender Michel Plasse and center Roger Belisle. Plasse would play 32 games with the Canadiens as Ken Dryden's backup. Belisle's pro experience was limited to 11 games in the International Hockey League.

A universal draft was introduced in 1969 and that was the last year the Canadiens had the pick of the Quebec litter. They selected two players from the Junior Canadiens, Réjean Houle and Marc Tardif.

Houle was the No. 1 pick after winning the Ontario Hockey Association scoring title but it was Tardif who would have the better career. He was establishing himself as a fan favourite when he jumped to the Los Angeles Sharks of the World Hockey

Association. He signed a three-year deal worth $350,000, a considerable jump from the $40,000 he was making in Montreal.

The Sharks moved to Michigan and became the Stags after that season, and a few months into the 1974–75 season, Tardif was traded to the Quebec Nordiques. He won two scoring titles in Quebec and is the all-time leading scorer in the WHA. The Canadiens reclaimed his rights when the NHL and the WHA merged in 1979 but he was made available in an expansion draft and played four more seasons after being reclaimed by the Nordiques.

Houle also jumped to the WHA in 1973, signing with the Nordiques. Money was a factor in Houle's decision but he also saw an opportunity for more ice time. Houle was behind Yvan Cournoyer and Guy Lafleur on the Montreal depth chart.

The Canadiens were loaded with Hall of Fame talent and Houle was overwhelmed at times by the attention from the fans and the media. He returned to the Canadiens in 1976 in time to become part of three consecutive Stanley Cup winners. He retired after the 1982–83 season as a five-time Stanley Cup champion.

The Canadiens selected one other French Canadian star with the No. 1 overall pick—that was Guy Lafleur in 1971.

83 The Brothers Mahovlich

Frank and Peter Mahovlich were brothers but they couldn't have been more different personalities.

Frank, the elder by nine years, was thoughtful, quiet, and moody on occasions. Pete was the gregarious life of the party.

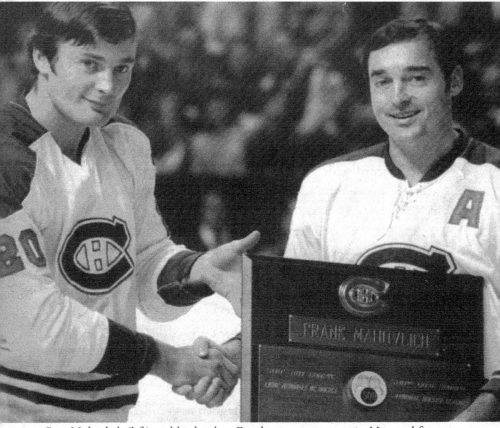

Pete Mahovlich (left) and his brother, Frank, were teammates in Montreal for parts of four seasons and won two Stanley Cups together.

They were teammates in Montreal for parts of four seasons and shared in Stanley Cup wins in 1971 and 1973.

Frank was the missing piece in the 1971 drive to the Cup. An established star, he was happy playing in Detroit after a successful but pressure-filled start to his career in Toronto. But when Ned Harkness arrived in Detroit as coach and general manager, he started making changes. On January 13, 1971, he traded Mahovlich to the Canadiens for Mickey Redmond, Guy Charron, and Bill Collins.

A few weeks later, Mahovlich was a part of history when he assisted on Jean Béliveau's 500th goal. Earlier in his career, he assisted on Gordie Howe's 700th and he reached the 500-goal plateau himself while playing with the Canadiens.

The 1971 playoffs featured an upset win over the Bruins in the first round, Béliveau's farewell, and the emergence of goaltender Ken Dryden, who won the Conn Smythe Trophy as the playoff MVP. But Frank Mahovlich also played a key role as he set a playoff record with 14 goals. Frank had won four Stanley Cups with Toronto but he said there was a different feeling when he won in Montreal.

In *The Big M: The Frank Mahovlich Story*, Ted Mahovlich quotes his father: "In Montreal, you felt like cheering, you felt like having a party—it was very enjoyable."

Peter Mahovlich, who had 10 playoff goals in 1971, didn't need a Stanley Cup to be in the mood for a party.

In his book *The Game*, Ken Dryden described Mahovlich as a "big, handsome, talented man who wouldn't play it straight—the guy who wears lampshades at parties, the perennial conventioneer in search of a good time."

That search for a good time often led to conflicts between Pete Mahovlich and coach Scotty Bowman. While Pete had his most productive seasons under Bowman's watch—he topped the 100-point mark twice—he and Bowman had an uneasy relationship.

Pete had a way of getting under Bowman's skin. When he was singled out to skate extra laps after practice, Pete would yell out: "This is fun, Scotty. Can we have some more?"

There's an often-repeated story about a road trip where Bowman announced there would be a $50 fine for anyone missing curfew. Peter Mahovlich took out a $100 bill, handed it to Bowman, and said: "This will cover tonight and tomorrow night."

It's a great story but Bowman said it never happened.

"We had to watch Pete, especially on the West Coast, but he was a very good player and had some big games for us," said Bowman. "And it was good when Frank joined us because he helped Pete."

Frank Mahovlich was nicknamed the Big M after he arrived in Toronto and Pete was dubbed the Little M although he was a good three inches taller than his brother.

While they had different personalities and there was a gap in their ages, they were close. Frank was protective of his brother, a trait that didn't always go over well with Pete. The younger Mahovlich told Ted Mahovlich about a fight he had with Buffalo's Reggie Fleming:

"Fleming had my shirt and we were struggling with each other to land a punch. Well, over my shoulder comes this fist which tagged Fleming—it was Frank. After the fight broke up, I was angry and said: 'Hey! I can take care of myself.' But he was looking out for me."

After four seasons with the Canadiens, Frank Mahovlich moved to the WHA, playing with the Toronto Toros and the Birmingham Bulls. At the end of his career, he found himself playing with Frank Beaton and Dave Hanson, who was featured as one of the Hanson brothers in the movie *Slap Shot*. According to John Brophy, Frank was asked why his production was down and he replied: "I don't know but I think I played better when I was with Howe and Delvecchio."

Peter Mahovlich turned to coaching and scouting when his playing career ended while Frank concentrated on running a successful travel agency in Toronto. He received an appointment to the Canadian Senate in 1988 and served until 2012, when he reached the mandatory retirement age of 75. Not surprisingly, Mahovlich's farewell speech was noted for its brevity.

84 Better Late Than Never

When teams strike gold in the late rounds of the draft, it raises questions about a team's scouting. Did they see something the 29 other teams missed? Did the team itself screw up by not picking the guy earlier? Was it just dumb luck that they found a potential All-Star in the seventh round?

Here are 10 players who were drafted by the Canadiens after the fifth round and went on to have productive NHL careers—although not necessarily in Montreal:

1. **Andrei Markov** was a three-year veteran of the Russian League when the Canadiens drafted him in the sixth round (162nd overall) in 1988. He was available because many teams thought that he was reluctant to leave Russia. He made the jump in 2000 and went on to become the Canadiens' most complete defenceman.

2. **Brian Savage** played parts of nine seasons with the Canadiens and reached the 20-goal plateau four times. Savage was drafted in the eighth round (171st overall) in 1991 after his first season at Miami University in Ohio. He slipped in the draft because he dropped out of junior hockey as a teenager and played for his high school in Sudbury while also competing as one of the top junior golfers in Canada. He joined the Canadiens in 1994 after helping Canada win an Olympic silver medal at Lillehammer and he was the first Montreal player to register a hat-trick at the Bell Centre on October 7, 1996. He later played with Phoenix, St. Louis, and Philadelphia.

3. **Oleg Petrov** was selected two rounds before Savage in the 1991 draft (127th overall) and a year later he became the first Russian

to play for the Canadiens. He scored 70 goals over parts of eight seasons but he achieved his greatest success playing in Switzerland and the KHL.

4. **Craig Conroy** was drafted in the sixth round (123rd overall in 1990) and played four seasons at Clarkson University before joining the Canadiens in 1994. He played only 13 games over two seasons with the Canadiens but went on to play a total of 1,009 regular-season games with Montreal, St. Louis, Los Angeles, and Calgary. On two occasions, he was among the top three candidates for the Selke Trophy as the NHL's top defensive forward.

5. **Jaroslav Halak** was selected 271st overall in the ninth and final round of the 2003 draft. Halak wrested the No. 1 job away from Carey Price in the latter stages of the 2009–10 season and led the Canadiens to the Eastern Conference final. Halak became a popular figure in Montreal but the Canadiens felt Price had a brighter future and traded Halak to St. Louis for Lars Eller.

6. **Sean Hill** was an eighth-round pick (167th overall) and joined the Canadiens after playing at the University of Wisconsin. He played 31 games as a rookie in 1992–93 and was part of the Canadiens' last Stanley Cup winner. He was claimed by Anaheim in the 1993 expansion draft. He played 876 games over 15 seasons with eight different teams.

7. **Michael Ryder** was drafted in the eighth round (216th overall) in 1998 from the Hull Olympiques and was given an opportunity to play when his junior coach Claude Julien was hired by the Canadiens. The Newfoundlander scored 25 goals in his rookie season in Montreal and followed up with back-to-back 30-goal seasons. He fell out of favour with Guy Carbonneau, who had replaced Julien, because the coach wasn't happy with Ryder's defensive play. He scored 14 goals in 70 games in 2007–08 and was often a healthy scratch as the season wore

on. During the off-season, he was reunited with Julien when he signed with the Bruins as a free agent. Ryder had another shot with the Canadiens when he was brought in at the trading deadline in 2013. He had 10 goals and 11 assists in 27 games and added a goal and an assist in five playoff games.

8. **Stéphane Robidas** was a seventh-round pick in 1995 (164th overall). The defenceman played two seasons with the Canadiens but was selected by Atlanta in the waiver draft in 2002. The Thrashers flipped him to Dallas and he became a fan favourite. He missed most of the 2013–14 season with a broken leg but made a successful comeback the following season with the Toronto Maple Leafs.

9. **Chris Nilan** was a Boston native drafted out of Northeastern University in the ninth round (231st overall) in 1978. Nilan would play for the Canadiens, the Rangers, and the Boston Bruins, and his willingness to drop his gloves earned him the nickname Knuckles. He retired as one of the most penalized players in NHL history with 3,043 penalty minutes.

10. **Keith Acton** was a prolific scorer with the Peteborough Petes but was ignored until the sixth round of the 1978 draft because he was only 5-foot-8 and 170 pounds. He played three full seasons with the Canadiens; his most productive season was 1981–82, when he had 88 points in 78 games while centering Steve Shutt and Guy Lafleur. He played 1,023 games over 15 seasons with Montreal, Minnesota, Edmonton, Philadelphia, Washington, and the Islanders.

85 Working Overtime

Hockey people will tell you that once you reach the playoffs, anything can happen. There may be no greater proof than the 1993 Canadiens and their improbable run to a 24th Stanley Cup.

The Canadiens finished third in the Adams Division and, while they had 102 points, they weren't expected to get out of the Eastern Conference. Pittsburgh had an NHL-best 119 points and was a two-time defending champion, while Boston had eliminated Montreal from the playoffs in three consecutive years.

As luck would have it, the Canadiens didn't have to face either team on their way to the Cup final against Wayne Gretzky and the Los Angeles Kings. Pittsburgh lost to the New York Islanders in the Patrick Division final while Boston lost to Buffalo in the first round.

The playoffs did not get off to a good start for the Canadiens. They were matched against their archrival, the Quebec Nordiques, and they lost the first two games in Quebec City. Patrick Roy, who was a Quebec City native, struggled and a columnist in the Quebec City newspaper *Le Soleil* suggested that the Canadiens should consider trading their star goaltender.

But the Canadiens turned things around. They won the next four games against the Nordiques, with two of the wins coming in overtime. They swept Buffalo in the division final, though three of those games were decided in overtime. In the Eastern Conference final, Montreal took a 3–0 series lead against the Islanders to tie a playoff record with 11 consecutive wins. The Islanders won Game 4 but the Canadiens closed out the series with a 3–2 win in the next game. The series produced another two overtime wins.

The Kings were as improbable a finalist as the Canadiens. They didn't have the home-ice advantage in any of their Western

Conference series but defeated Calgary and Vancouver in six games and then edged Toronto in seven.

The final series opened at the Montreal Forum and the Kings dominated the game. They won 4–1 and the lone Montreal goal was credited to Ed Ronan when Wayne Gretzky defected a pass into the Kings' net.

The series turned on Game 2. L.A. had a 2–1 lead late in the game when Montreal coach Jacques Demers called for a measurement of Marty McSorley's stick. McSorley was handed a two-minute penalty because the curve on his stick was too big. Demers pulled goaltender Patrick Roy to create a 6-on-4 advantage and Eric Desjardins scored his second goal of the game from the point to send the game into overtime. Desjardins scored the winner 51 seconds into OT to become the only defenceman to score a hat-trick in the Stanley Cup final.

The McSorley incident upset the Kings, who thought someone had sneaked into their locker room and measured their sticks. Another theory had a member of the Canadiens equipment staff spotting the illegal stick when he was helping the visitors settle in. Demers denied any skullduggery and said Canadiens captain Guy Carbonneau spotted the illegal curve.

There was more controversy as the series moved to Los Angeles for Game 3. The Kings rallied from a 3–0 deficit to tie the score and, with time running out, it appeared that Carbonneau covered the puck in the crease, which should have resulted in a penalty shot. But referee Terry Gregson ruled that the puck was shot into Carbonneau's equipment. The game went into overtime and John LeClair scored after only 34 seconds. After the series, Gregson admitted that he made a mistake on the call.

LeClair was the overtime hero again in Game 4 as he scored 14:37 into the extra period for a 3–2 victory. It was the Canadiens' 10th overtime win, a playoff record.

The Kings were a dispirited lot as the series moved back to Montreal. The Canadiens went ahead 2–1 early in the second period and won the game 4–1. There were suggestions that Gretzky was hurt and he failed to get a shot on goal. Roy, who had let in some soft goals in the first two games in Quebec, won his second Conn Smythe Trophy as the most valuable player in the playoffs.

86 What If Dryden Had Been a Bruin?

Over the course of his career, Ken Dryden enjoyed some of his most memorable moments playing against the Boston Bruins, beginning in 1971 when he led the Canadiens past the defending Stanley Cup champions in the first round of the playoffs.

He never lost to the Bruins in the playoffs, beating them again in the 1977 and 1978 finals and in the semifinals in 1979.

The irony is that, for a few hours, Dryden's NHL rights were once held by the Bruins.

From 1963 until the introduction of the first universal NHL entry draft in 1969, teams participated in the NHL amateur draft. Most of the best players signed C cards which bound them to NHL teams and the players available in the amateur draft were usually late-bloomers who had been overlooked earlier in their playing days.

In 1964, the Bruins selected Dryden with the 14th pick overall. He was playing for a Junior B team in Etobicoke and, while his older brother Dave was working his way through the minors en route to the NHL, Ken's priority was to get an education at Cornell University.

The details of what happened on the day Dryden was drafted have been lost to history but there was a suggestion that the Bruins were interested in Guy Allen, a Junior B defenceman who had been selected 12th overall by the Canadiens.

Within hours, the Canadiens and Bruins worked out the details of a trade involving the players they drafted that day. The Canadiens sent Allen and Paul Reid, a winger from the Kingston midgets who had been drafted 18th overall, to Boston for Dryden and Alex Campbell, a winger who was the second overall pick.

The draft was such a low-key event that it was years later before Dryden learned that he had been selected by the Bruins. His agent simply told him that he had been drafted by Montreal.

The 1964 draft produced a handful of NHL players including Mike Pelyk, Jim Dorey, Tim Ecclestone, and Syl Apps Jr., but Dryden turned out to be the prize.

None of the other players involved in the Dryden trade had significant pro careers.

Campbell had one outstanding season at St. Lawrence University, where his teammates included future NHL coach Mike Keenan. He played one pro season in the International Hockey League.

Allen also got as far as the IHL, while the highlight of Reid's career was part of a season as Bobby Orr's teammate with the Oshawa Generals. Reid always thought he had been drafted by the Bruins and it was 38 years later when he learned that he was selected by the Canadiens.

87 Gainey's Pain

Bob Gainey was a popular choice when he was named general manager of the Canadiens in 2003.

He had been the captain of the Canadiens for eight of his 16 NHL seasons, winning over many fans by learning to speak French because it was the right thing for a captain to do. He was a major part of the Canadiens dynasty which won four consecutive Stanley Cups from 1976 to 1979, and he won the Conn Smythe Trophy as the playoff MVP in 1979.

He had success as a coach and general manager in Minnesota and Dallas—he was the GM when the Stars won the Cup in 1999—and he was coming home to guide a franchise which had gone an unimaginable decade without winning the Cup.

By the time he walked away from the GM job during the 2009–10 season, it was clear that Gainey was no miracle worker. His teams never won more than one round in the playoffs. He fired coach Claude Julien to create an opening for Guy Carbonneau and then dumped Carbonneau for reasons which remain a mystery to this day.

Given a chance to rebuild a team that was short on size, he made a series of deals in 2009 which resulted in an even smaller lineup and, in the process, gave away franchise defenceman Ryan McDonagh.

However, the legacy of Gainey's second run in Montreal isn't marked by the team's performance but by a family tragedy.

Montreal Gazette columnist Red Fisher once wrote that nobody ever played through as much pain as Bob Gainey. But the emotional pain Gainey suffered in his personal life went deeper than what he endured as a player on the ice.

Gainey's wife, Cathy, battled brain cancer for five years before she died at the age of 39.

Her death had a traumatic effect on the couple's four children, particularly daughter Laura, who was 10 when her mother died. In her teen years, she turned to drugs and spent nine months in a rehab center.

In her midtwenties, Laura found her passion when she signed on as a trainee seaman on the Picton Castle, a tall ship which sails out of Lunenburg, Nova Scotia. She fell in love with life on the high seas and delighted in climbing the towering masts to set the sails.

But tragedy struck on December 8, 2006. Nobody is sure why Laura was on deck that night as the ship sailed through a raging storm in the Atlantic Ocean. What is clear is that she wasn't wearing a life jacket and she wasn't secured by a safety tether when what was described as a "rogue wave" swept her overboard. A three-day search-and-rescue operation failed to find a trace of her body.

Gainey visited the ship several weeks after the incident and, as he talked with crew members, his grief turned to anger as he tried to understand what happened to his daughter.

The ship was registered in the Cook Islands, whose investigation concluded that Laura was an "unlucky victim." But Gainey noted that the report was incomplete and ran contrary to an investigation conducted by Andrew Scheer, a retired U.S. Navy captain who works as a marine safety consultant.

Scheer noted that the ship's crew wasn't adequately trained in man-overboard drills, safety equipment wasn't employed, and the ship was understaffed. Scheer found that many of the crew members, including Laura, were assigned to tasks for which they weren't qualified and crew members were asked to work long hours.

Gainey believed that his daughter was exhausted and confused when she was swept overboard.

He established a family foundation to honour his wife and daughter. The foundation's website notes that Bob and Cathy shared a love and concern for children but the direction of the foundation was influenced by Laura's interests and concentrates on arts education and environmental awareness for children.

According to the foundation's mission statement, "Laura took a great deal of inspiration both from exploring her own artistic side and even more from teaching children's art classes. She found endless inspiration on her walks through the woods near our home north of Peterborough, Ontario, kayaking along the coast of British Columbia, or hiking through the jungles of Costa Rica. She believed deeply in environmental conservation, and sustainability."

88 The American

Canadiens fans emerged from their New Year's revelry on January 2, 2001, to what was perceived as bad news. Their beloved team had been sold to George Gillett Jr., an American with a shadowy past.

There were fears that Gillett, a high-flyer who once filed for bankruptcy with more than $900 million in debts, would move the team to the United States. That concern was only slightly eased by the fact that Molson Brewery would retain a 19.9 percent stake in the franchise and had the right of first refusal if Gillett decided to sell the team.

Gillett, who rebuilt his financial empire with holdings in ski resorts and meatpacking, proved to be a good steward for the storied franchise. A lifelong sports fan, Gillett had once owned the Harlem Globetrotters and a 20 percent stake in the Miami Dolphins. A year prior to buying the Canadiens, he joined with Pat Bowlen and John Elway in a failed bid to buy the Colorado Avalanche and the Denver Nuggets. His name came up in connection with other NHL teams, including the Islanders, the Florida Panthers, and the Ottawa Senators. But none of those deals was as attractive as the Canadiens.

While the Canadiens were an iconic brand, Molson Brewery was anxious to sell the team because it had decided to concentrate on its core brewing business. It put the Canadiens on the block along with two hardware chains and several chemical companies in the United States and Canada.

Molson would have preferred a Canadian buyer but there was no interest in a team that was mediocre on the ice and was having trouble filling its new arena, which was the largest in the NHL with 21,273 seats. The team was also involved in a battle with the city of Montreal over an annual $9 million property tax bill. The team thought it deserved a break because the arena was built without a penny of public money.

Gillett wasn't the only bidder but he was the only one to come up with $275 million to buy 80.1 percent of the franchise. The brewery threw in the arena to sweeten an already sweet deal.

In the eight years he owned the team, Gillett proved to be a generally competent and popular owner. His timing proved to be impeccable, as he was one of the owners who benefitted from the 2004–05 lockout. The collective bargaining agreement provided the owners with some certainty in regard to payroll and there was a new hunger for the game when play resumed in the fall of 2005. As a gesture to the fans, the team set up a lottery to distribute 500 free upper-level seats for each game but the Bell Centre would sell out every game for most of the next decade. The sellout streak ended on December 9, 2014, when the team left a seat empty to honour the late Jean Béliveau.

Gillett embraced the tradition of the team and not coincidentally found a way to cash in on the team's history. The Canadiens franchise predates the National Hockey League and it celebrated its 100th anniversary in 2009. Montreal became the center of the hockey world. It served as the host for the 2009 All-Star Game and the 2009 NHL entry draft.

The plaza on the west side of the Bell Centre was turned into an outdoor museum. There were statues of Maurice (Rocket) Richard, Jean Béliveau, Guy Lafleur, and Ken Dryden. There were plaques commemorating the team's 24 Stanley Cups and a block of marble inscribed with the names of all of the players from the first 100 years of the franchise. Fans were invited to purchase bricks inscribed with messages attesting to their love of the team.

(The contents of the plaza went into storage in 2012 when the developers who owned the land decided to build La Tour des Canadiens, a high-rise condominium. The plaza will be reconstructed on the east side of the building once construction is completed on an adjoining office tower.)

The Canadiens marketed the centennial with vintage jerseys, souvenir books, and other memorabilia.

Gillett also set up the Gillett Entertainment Group to handle the concert business at the Bell Centre and other venues throughout eastern Canada. While he was a unilingual Anglophone, he saw the potential to promote more French-speaking performers. He featured Céline Dion and worked with Cirque du Soleil to fashion arena shows.

Gillett's downfall was his ambition. In February 2008, he joined with Texas businessman Tom Hicks to buy another iconic franchise, the Liverpool Football Club, one of England's top soccer teams. A few months later, he bought a controlling interest in the Evernham Racing NASCAR team, and in 2008, he joined with Joey Saputo in a bid for an MLS franchise.

The Liverpool venture did not go well. Fans quickly became disillusioned with the new owners after they failed to deliver on the promise of a new stadium, and the team dropped in the Premier League standings. Pressed for cash to keep Liverpool afloat, Gillett sold the Canadiens for $550 million to a group headed by Geoff Molson on June 20, 2009.

By the end of 2010, Gillett was out of the sports business. The Royal Bank of Scotland, which had financed the Liverpool purchase, took control of the team and sold it to New England Sports Ventures, the group that also owns the Boston Red Sox. He also lost his stake in the NASCAR team, which had merged with Petty Enterprises and became Richard Petty Motorsports.

89 The Lost Art of Penmanship

Former Canadien Dollard St. Laurent was reminiscing after a round of golf when the discussion turned to autographs.

St. Laurent said he and Phil Goyette were playing in a charity golf tournament outside Ottawa when St. Laurent put on his fan hat and asked one of the current players for an autograph.

"He scribbled on a piece of paper, adding his number at the end," said St. Laurent. "When I looked at it, I couldn't recognize a single letter. The number was the only way you could even guess at whose signature it was. It was different in our day. You were happy that someone wanted your autograph and you took your time and made sure it was legible."

The Canadiens have had scores of legendary players and two of the best—Maurice (Rocket) Richard and Jean Béliveau—produced iconic signatures.

Shortly after he was diagnosed with abdominal cancer in 1998, Richard was the guest of honour for the launch of a new edition of *Maurice Richard: L'idole D'un Peuple* (The Idol of a People), a biography of the Rocket by Jean-Marie Pellerin. The book looked at Richard's career against the backdrop of the social, economic, and political change that became known in Quebec as the Quiet Revolution.

Pellerin portrayed Richard as an example of that change, a young man from a working-class background who became one of the greatest hockey players in the world.

Richard was undergoing chemotherapy and he appeared uncomfortable in the gathering of politicians, academics, and journalists. When the speeches ended, Pellerin said that he and Richard would be happy to autograph copies of the book.

The Rocket became more animated as he interacted with his fans. He modestly accepted their praise and then signed their books, painstakingly forming each letter. You didn't have to guess about the genesis of the signature. You could almost imagine a nun standing over his shoulder and saying: "Très bon, Maurice."

Béliveau's signature has a little more flair to it. It's a signature befitting a corporate executive, which is what Béliveau became after his playing days.

While Richard was known for his fiery demeanor, Béliveau was most often described as a gentleman. He had a successful career with Molson Brewery and the Canadiens after his playing days and he continued serving as an ambassador for the team.

When Canadiens fans booed the U.S. national anthem in 2008, the club called on Béliveau to address the crowd and urged them to treat the anthem with respect.

A Signature Moment

Jean Béliveau was honoured at a Hockey Canada Foundation gala in 2010. The following spring, insurance executive Barry Lorenzetti represented the foundation when Béliveau and his wife, Elise, presented a check to the Quebec Society for Crippled Children.

"As we arrived at Camp Papillon, there must have been about 300 people waiting," recalled Lorenzetti. "Mr. Béliveau got out of the car and immediately people surrounded him asking for his autograph. To my amazement he stood there like a rock star and signed each and every one of the sweaters or papers that were presented to him!

"As we were leaving, he said to me that he had practiced getting his signature right after a recent setback in his health. In fact, he said writing his signature and signing the number 4 next to it had caused him some embarrassment because when he was writing checks he would add the number 4 on the check."

Béliveau's penmanship was put to the test on March 29, 2007, when he was honoured at a dinner in the Bell Centre. The ice surface was transformed into a gourmet dining room and 1,000 guests paid $1,000 each to honour Béliveau and feast on a lobster martini, filet of veal, asparagus, salad with Brie cheese, and a decadent dessert described as the Chocolate Temple. The dinner raised $1 million, which was donated to six different children's charities.

There were messages of congratulations from Canadian prime minister Stephen Harper, Quebec premier Jean Charest, and Montreal mayor Gérald Tremblay. Former teammates were in attendance. Hall of Famers Eddie Giacomin, Rod Gilbert, Gerry Cheevers, Red Kelly, Johnny Bower, and Gordie Howe were among the former foes representing the NHL's Original Six teams.

The head table was littered with Quebec's business elite and international singing star Céline Dion appeared on a video feed from Las Vegas.

Each guest received a souvenir booklet chronicling the highlights of his career and a gift box which contained a puck and a stick blade commemorating the evening.

As Béliveau took a break between courses, one of the guests approached the head table. He said he was sorry to bother Béliveau but asked for an autograph.

"I already have," said a smiling Béliveau as he opened the box and pointed to the perfectly formed signature on the stick blade. He had spent two days earlier in the week to sign his autograph more than 1,000 times and each one was perfect.

90 Game Called on Account of Fire

It would be an understatement to say the Canadiens played in some rickety firetraps before they began sharing the Montreal Forum with the Montreal Maroons in 1926.

The Canadiens were forced to move out of the first two arenas they played in because the buildings burned down.

The Jubilee Arena in Montreal's east end was the Canadiens' home in the inaugural 1909–10 season in the National Hockey Association. They shared the rink with the Montreal Wanderers, who had helped establish the new league after the Wanderers were rejected for membership in the Canadian Hockey Association.

The Wanderers were blackballed because owner J.P. Doran wanted to move the team from the much larger Montreal Arena to the 3,200-seat Jubilee Arena, which he owned. Doran had the last laugh because the CHA folded eight weeks into the 1909–10 season because of poor ticket sales.

The Canadiens moved in 1911 to the Montreal Arena, which was also known as the Westmount Arena. It was built in 1898 and was one of the first arenas built specifically for hockey.

There were 4,300 seats in the building and there were large areas devoted to standing room, which brought the capacity to 10,000. There were a restaurant and smoking rooms reserved for men, and fans could rent rugs to provide some warmth and comfort while sitting on the hard benches.

The rink offered a unique design—boards in the corners were rounded, replacing the squared-off style. This allowed players to rim the puck, shooting it along the boards, behind the net, and out the other side.

The rink featured several other innovations. The height of the boards was set at four feet, a considerable increase from the one-foot boards at the Victoria Skating Rink. The rink featured natural ice when it opened but it became home to Montreal's first artificial ice-making plant in 1915.

A fire broke out in the ice-making machinery on January 2, 1918. The arena burned to the ground, leaving two teams in the infant National Hockey League—the Canadiens and the Wanderers—without a home.

The Wanderers, who had won four Stanley Cups, had lost key players Odie Cleghorn and Sprague Cleghorn and had won only once in their first four NHL games. They were looking for players when the fire left them homeless. They forfeited games to the Canadiens and Toronto before disbanding.

The Canadiens moved back into the Jubilee Arena but again found themselves homeless when that building burned down on April 23, 1919.

Construction began almost immediately on the Mount Royal Arena on the corner of Mount Royal Avenue and St. Urbain Street in the area currently known as the Plateau Mont-Royal. The arena had seating for 6,000 spectators with room for an additional 4,000 willing to stand. A week after it opened, a balcony partially collapsed before a game against Ottawa and police limited ticket sales to 6,500.

The Canadiens were unhappy with the arena because it had natural ice and the quality of the playing surface varied from game to game. The players complained about bad bounces and dangerous ruts. Owner Thomas Duggan promised on several occasions to install ice-making equipment but the Canadiens management felt he devoted most of his time to getting American teams to join the NHL.

Frustrated by the lack of progress, the Canadiens moved in 1926 to the Montreal Forum, which was built two years earlier as the home of the Montreal Maroons. The Canadiens had to break their lease to move and a court ordered them to pay Duggan $83,000 in compensation. They quickly recovered that with the additional revenue generated by playing in the Forum.

While the Forum was built for the Maroons, the Canadiens played the first hockey game there on November 29, 1924, because there was no ice available at the Mount Royal Arena. They beat Toronto St. Pats 3–0 that night. The Mount Royal Arena was converted into an auditorium after the Canadiens left and was later used as a commercial space which included a bakery and an upholstery shop. The building was destroyed by an early morning fire on February 29, 2000.

91 Dryden vs. Dryden

When Ken Dryden was growing up, he honed his skills on a small backyard rink his father, Murray, had built behind their home in the Islington neighbourhood of Toronto. He was usually the youngest kid in the game but his brother Dave, who was six years older, had a hard and fast rule: if you wanted to play on the Drydens' rink, Ken had to play.

The brothers both made their way to the NHL, although they took different routes. Dave, who played junior hockey, made his NHL debut with the New York Rangers when he was 20 years old, although it was several more years before he found regular employment in the NHL.

Ken opted for the U.S. college route, earning All-American honours at Cornell University. He joined the Canadiens organization in 1970, reporting to the Montreal Voyageurs of the American

Hockey League while studying law at McGill University. He was called up to the Canadiens late in his first pro season and found himself facing his older brother in an unscheduled showdown.

Ken's promotion sparked speculation about a Dryden-versus-Dryden matchup when the Buffalo Sabres traveled to Montreal on March 20, 1971. But Canadiens coach Al MacNeil decided not to put any undue pressure on his young goaltender and told him that Rogie Vachon would play. But after Vachon was injured, the brothers found themselves at opposite ends of the ice.

Here's how Dryden described the night in his book *The Game*:

"I didn't enjoy that game very much. I had played only two previous NHL games and seeing Dave in the other end was a distraction I didn't want or need. And while I became more comfortable as the game went on, I was surprised and disappointed that I didn't feel more.... I could sense the curious excitement of the crowd, I could feel its huge vicarious pleasure, but my own excitement was vague, it had no edge to it, as if somehow, it wasn't new, as if in fact we had done it before.

"When the game was over, proud and relieved we shook hands at center ice. A few hours later, I began to feel differently. What had surprised and disappointed me earlier, I found exciting and reassuring. It really had been no different. Those backyard games, the times we stood at opposite ends of the yard, the times we dreamed we were Sawchuk and Hall, there had been a connection, we just never knew it."

92 Nicknames

Nicknames in hockey today tend to be banal and devoid of imagination.

Carey Price becomes Pricer, Brandon Prust is Prusty, and even though he hates the name, Lars Eller is Larry to his teammates.

Brendan Gallagher and Alex Galchenyuk both arrived in Montreal with the nickname Gally. Gallagher claimed seniority and kept the name while Galchenyuk became Chucky.

In the early days of the NHL, players had more colourful monikers that reflected their origins or a particular skill. Here are some classics from the past:

Maurice Richard: The Rocket: There isn't a better term to describe his explosive play on the ice. Richard's first nickname was the Comet but teammate Ray Getliffe noted that Richard skated in on the opposing goal like a rocket and the name was picked up by reporters. Baz O'Meara of the *Montreal Star* and Dick Carroll of the *Montreal Gazette* have both been credited with popularizing the name. When Richard's younger brother, Henri, arrived on the scene, he was dubbed the Pocket Rocket.

Jean Béliveau: Le Gros Bill: Béliveau's 6-foot-3 frame was a factor in this name which was adopted by Quebec City journalist Roland Sabourin when Béliveau was playing with the Quebec Aces. The name is derived from a French Canadian folk song, "Le voilà, le Gros Bill" (Here Comes Big Bill). His grace on and off the ice also earned him the nickname Gentleman Jean.

Bernie Geoffrion: Boom Boom: *Montreal Star* sportswriter Charlie Boire gave Geoffrion this nickname when he played for the Laval National junior team. Geoffrion claimed to have invented the slapshot and the nickname celebrated his booming blasts.

Hector Blake: Toe: This one goes back to his childhood. His younger sister had trouble saying Hector and Blake became Toe. Blake was also known during his playing career as the Old Lamplighter because of his goal-scoring ability.

Howie Morenz: The Stratford Streak: He was from Mitchell, Ontario, but the speedy forward took his alliterative nickname from the neighbouring town of Stratford. He was also known as the Mitchell Meteor, the Phantom of the Ice, the Canadiens Catapult, and the Hurtling Habitant, although the Stratford Streak was the name which stuck throughout his career.

Bill Durnan: Doctor Strangeglove: The dominant goaltender of the 1940s was a natural right-hander but he trained himself to be ambidextrous. Instead of a blocker, he wore two modified gloves and would switch hands on his stick depending on the direction of the rush.

Edouard Lalonde: Newsy: One of the Canadiens' earliest stars had been a reporter and a printer with the *Cornwall Freeholder* newspaper before launching his hockey career.

Didier Pitre: Cannonball: At 5-foot-11, Pitre was one of the bigger players in his day and his nickname derived from his size, speed, and blistering shot.

Jack Laviolette: The Speed Merchant: It's a self-explanatory description for the player who was also the Canadiens' first captain and coach.

Aurèle Joliat: Mighty Atom, The Little Giant: One of the smallest players on the ice, he earned the respect by never backing down from a confrontation.

Georges Vézina: The Chicoutimi Cucumber: The man whose name is on the trophy awarded to the NHL's top goaltender was discovered when the Canadiens were barnstorming in Chicoutimi in the remote Saguenay region 130 miles from Quebec City. Frank Boucher of the New York Rangers remarked on Vézina's cool demeanor and described him as "imperturbable."

Albert Leduc: Battleship: Though he was only 5-foot-9 and 190 pounds, Leduc was known as a punishing defenceman.

Lorne Worsely: Gump: His nickname was derived from his resemblance to comic-strip character Andy Gump.

Dickie Moore: Digging Dickie: This nickname was a tribute to Moore's determination on the ice.

Larry Robinson: Big Bird: One of the Canadiens' Big Three on defence, the 6-foot-4 Robinson's lanky physique conjured up images of the *Sesame Street* character.

Serge Savard: The Senator: His political connections allowed him to obtain one of the first lottery franchises in Quebec. While he received overtures to run for public office, he concentrated on a business career. While he serving as the Canadiens general manager, he was also a partner in a real estate development firm.

Yvan Cournoyer: The Roadrunner: His speed and his ability to elude checks from larger opponents invited comparisons to the popular cartoon character. Cournoyer said the nickname first appeared in *Sports Illustrated* after he scored a couple of goals and had several breakaways in a game at Madison Square Garden.

Guy Lafleur: The Flower: It's simply the English translation of his family name.

Partrick Roy: St. Patrick: Roy's fiery temper often landed him in trouble and a feud with coach Mario Tremblay led to his departure from Montreal. But his nickname derives from his ability to perform miracles on the ice. He's generally credited with leading mediocre teams to the Canadiens' most recent Stanley Cup wins in 1986 and 1993.

Emile Bouchard: Butch: Teammate Bob Fillion gave him the name, explaining that his last name resembled the English word *butcher*.

Alex Kovalev: AK-27: The Russian sniper's nickname combined his number with a reference to the Kaleshnikov assault rifle.

93 Danny Boy

The pews at St. Ignatius Loyola Church were full on the morning of March 2, 1993, for Danny Gallivan's funeral and there wasn't a dry eye in the building as Dennis Ryan, the leader of the Canadian folk group Ryan's Fancy, sang "Danny Boy."

The congregation was composed of Hockey Hall of Famers; fellow broadcasters; politicians; and ordinary folk, fans who had listened to Gallivan describing Canadiens games for 32 seasons on *Hockey Night in Canada*.

Gallivan once taught Latin after graduating from St. Francis Xavier University in Antigonish, Nova Scotia, but his reputation as a broadcaster was built on his unique use of the English language.

He brought a new lexicon to the game. A spectacular save became "scintillating" or perhaps "larcenous." Goaltenders would kick out a shot in "rapier-like" fashion. If a puck was lost in the goaltender's equipment, it was caught in his "paraphernalia."

If a team had trouble getting shots on goal, Gallivan would say "there has not been a multitudinous amount of shots" or he would refer to a "dire dearth of chances."

When he couldn't find words to describe a play to his satisfaction, he would make up a word. He referred to hard shots as "cannonading" drives and when an English teacher wrote to say there was no such word as *cannonading*, Gallivan wrote back and said, "There is now."

Another such word was spinarama, which Gallivan used to describe the action when a player made a sudden 180-degree or 360-degree turn to elude a check. Canadiens defenceman Serge Savard had made this his trademark move and it became known as the Savardian spinarama. Spinarama was subsequently added to the Oxford Canadian Dictionary.

Montreal Gazette columnist Red Fisher shared the broadcast booth with Gallivan on occasion and offered this glimpse of the announcer at work:

"He would be there, often on his feet, gripping a microphone in his fist, his voice rising and falling with the ebb and flow of the action taking place on the ice. He was never more comfortable than when he gripped that microphone, never more sure of himself than when he was completely immersed in the game.

"Somehow, he was able to shut out everything else, and that often included instructions barked into his earphones from the television truck. The game was all that mattered, everything else had its own time, its own place."

Gallivan was uncomfortable wearing a headset and had the ability to tune out messages from the producer in the truck. On some occasions, he would simply disconnect the set, which also meant there was no sound coming through the attached microphone. On more than one occasion, viewers were mystified as they watched Gallivan conduct an interview with no sound.

Gallivan hooked up with HNIC by accident. He was working in Halifax and he travelled to Montreal in 1950 to do the play-by-play of a junior playoff game between Halifax and the Montreal Junior Canadiens. Doug Smith, who was the play-by-play announcer for the Canadiens, become ill and Gallivan was pressed into service. He had never seen an NHL game but he did a good job even though he didn't know any of the players on the ice.

When Smith decided to concentrate on broadcasting football in 1952, Gallivan replaced him in the HNIC booth and remained there until he retired in 1984.

Dick Irvin joined him in the early 1960s and they set the standard for hockey broadcasts. While they worked together well,

Gallivan had one habit which irked Irvin. Gallivan would call him Richard despite the fact that Dick was derived from Irvin's middle name, Dickinson.

94 The French Fact

When Randy Cunneyworth was appointed interim coach of the Canadiens in December 2011, he knew one thing: no matter how well the team did under his tutelage, there was no way he was going to be hired on a permanent basis.

There was an uproar in the French media and among some fans after Cunneyworth, who didn't speak French, replaced Jacques Martin. Team owner Geoff Molson made Cunneyworth's temporary status clear when he stressed that the coach of the Montreal Canadiens must be able to communicate in French.

Cunneyworth, who had an 18–23–9 record in his 50 games at the helm, was let go at the end of the season and was eventually replaced by Michel Therrien. Molson had said that Cunneyworth would return to his role as an assistant but Therrien and general manager Marc Bergevin cleaned house and Cunneyworth was out of work.

The insistence on having a French-speaking coach upsets some fans who point out that it limits the number of possible candidates for the job.

When Therrien was hired for his second go-around with the Canadiens, there were complaints that his only qualification for the job was his ability to speak French. He has his detractors even though he's the first coach to guide the team to three consecutive playoff appearances since Pat Burns made it four in a row from

1989 to 1992. Burns' mother tongue was English but he polished his French while walking the beat as a policeman in Hull, Quebec.

There are arguments for and against the French-only rule. It does limit the pool of available candidates although, strangely, even the strongest proponents of the rule have suggested that there could be an exception made for a popular former captain like Kirk Muller or a proven winner like Mike Babcock, who didn't pick up much French when he was pursuing his undergraduate degree at Montreal's McGill University.

And the Canadiens players of today are far removed from the Flying Frenchmen of the past. Montreal's cosmopolitan atmosphere is attractive to European players and the Canadiens roster is one of the most diverse in the NHL.

But these factors must be balanced against the environment in the city. Montreal's population is overwhelmingly French and the language is understood by the majority of people in the English-speaking and other ethnic communities.

There is also a need for French-speaking players. This is a problem because the percentage of francophone players in the NHL has shown a steady decline and the introduction of the entry draft means that the Canadiens no longer have their choice of the best talent in Quebec.

In the past 25 years, the Canadiens have drafted only two Quebec players in the first round. Eric Chouinard was the 16th

No Ticket Required

Toronto Maple Leafs and Canadian Olympic team coach Mike Babcock said he regularly attended games at the Forum when he was a student at McGill University. Babcock said Brian Skrudland, his teammate with the junior Saskatoon Blades, would sneak him in through the garage at the Forum and he would watch the game from the standing-room areas.

pick overall in 1998—he was selected over Simon Gagné—and he would play 13 of his 90 NHL games with Montreal.

The fans expressed their desire for a local hero when they cheered the selection of Louis Leblanc at No. 18 in the 2009 draft, which was held at the Bell Centre. He bounced back and forth between the Canadiens and Hamilton for three seasons before the Canadiens gave up on him. In 2014, he was traded to Anaheim for a fifth-round draft pick.

95 The Canadien Way

They say that imitation is the sincerest form of flattery, and many teams aspired to imitate the Canadiens' success from the 1950s to the late 1970s. Teams believed that the best way to achieve that result was to hire men who had been schooled in the Canadien way of doing things.

The list of former Canadiens who moved on to other organizations as coaches and general managers is exhaustive but here are some notables who moved on with varying degrees of success:

Scotty Bowman tops the list. He was miffed when he was passed over as general manager after Sam Pollock retired. Bowman went to Buffalo as coach and general manager. He added to the five Stanley Cups he won in Montreal by winning one in Pittsburgh and three more in Detroit. He continues to play a role as senior advisor to his son, Chicago GM Stan Bowman.

Glen Sather spent only one season as a player in Montreal but he absorbed enough from Bowman and Pollock to build a dynasty of his own in Edmonton, where he won five Stanley Cups.

The tenure of **Bob Gainey** as GM of the Canadiens wasn't very successful but he had a good run with the Minnesota North Stars/ Dallas Stars. He guided Minnesota to the Stanley Cup final in his first year as coach in 1991. After the team moved to Dallas, he was the general manager when the Stars won the Stanley Cup in 1999.

Jacques Lemaire quit as coach of the Canadiens after his first full season because he couldn't handle the pressure but he went on to coach 15 seasons in New Jersey and Minnesota, winning a Stanley Cup with the Devils in 1995.

Doug Risebrough was an assistant coach with the Calgary Flames when they beat the Canadiens in the 1989 Stanley Cup final. He later became the head coach and GM of the Flames and served as GM of the Minnesota Wild and vice-president of hockey operations for the Edmonton Oilers.

Pat Burns, Claude Julien, Michel Therrien, and **Alain Vigneault** all made their NHL head coaching debuts with the Canadiens but achieved their greatest success later in their careers. Burns was a three-time winner of the Jack Adams Award as coach of the year and won a Stanley Cup with New Jersey in 2003. Julien was fired by the Canadiens and the Devils before leading Boston to the Stanley Cup in 2011. Vigneault has guided the Vancouver Canucks and the New York Rangers to the Cup final. Therrien, who has returned to the Canadiens for a second stint as head coach, took the Pittsburgh Penguins to the Cup final in 2008.

Larry Robinson was never comfortable in a head coaching role but he was behind the bench when the Devils won the Stanley Cup in 2000. He has served as a longtime assistant with the Devils and the Los Angeles Kings.

Ron Caron was the Canadiens' head scout and assistant general manager during six Stanley Cup seasons in the 1970s. As GM of the St. Louis Blues, he assembled a winning team built around Doug Gilmour, Brett Hull, and Adam Oates.

Maurice Richard and Boom Boom Geoffrion both tried their hand at coaching with limited success. Richard coached the Quebec Nordiques in 1972 but he quit after two games because he couldn't handle the pressure. Geoffrion coached the Rangers and the Atlanta Flames but had to abandon both jobs because of health problems.

Ralph Backstrom and Red Berenson both took their talents to the U.S. college ranks. Backstrom set a Denver University record with 34 wins in 1985–86 and took his team to the Frozen Four. Berenson won the Jack Adams Award in 1981 with the St. Louis Blues but he returned to his alma mater, the University of Michigan, in 1984. He has taken the Wolverines to the Frozen Four 11 times and won two NCAA titles.

96 The Cop on the Beat

When the Canadiens' run of five Stanley Cups ended in 1960, it was obvious to the team's brain trust that the game was changing. Speed and finesse were giving way to size and strength; Chicago won the Cup in 1961 and the Toronto Maple Leafs would win back-to-back titles in 1962 and 1963.

Sam Pollock recognized the need for a player who could neutralize players like Toronto's Eddie Shack and Chicago's Reggie Fleming.

Their first attempt at filling the void was the acquisition of Lou (Leapin' Louie) Fontinato in the deal which sent Doug Harvey to the New York Rangers. Fontinato proved to be a temporary solution because late in his second season with the Canadiens, he missed a check on Vic Hatfield and crashed head-first into the boards. He suffered a neck injury which ended his career.

The injury opened the door for John Ferguson, who claimed to have invented the role of enforcer in his autobiography *Thunder and Lightning*.

"That is how the enforcer was born in the NHL," Ferguson said of his arrival in Montreal in the fall of 1963. "As Casey Stengel used to say: 'You could look it up.' It was September 1963 and the cop on the beat was John Bowie Ferguson."

Emile Francis, who had scouted Ferguson in the American Hockey League, described him as a "bad skater with no finesse but he seems to overcome this by sheer determination." Francis went on to say that he never saw Ferguson lose a fight.

Former Canadien John Ferguson, shown here plying his trade, has claimed to be the NHL's first true enforcer.

Horsing Around

John Ferguson's middle name, Bowie, was not related to Jim Bowie, the American pioneer who popularized the Bowie knife. In fact, Ferguson's parents were horse-racing enthusiasts and he was named for the Bowie Race Track in Maryland. As a youngster, he would spend time at Hastings Park in Vancouver. He handicapped standardbred races for the *Montreal Gazette* and spent his final years as the general manager of Windsor Raceway.

Toe Blake liked what he saw in training camp. He put Ferguson on a line with Jean Béliveau and Bernie (Boom Boom) Geoffrion and told him to look after his linemates.

Ferguson didn't waste any time announcing his arrival. On October 8, 1963, the Canadiens traveled to Boston and Ferguson took on Terrible Ted Green, a former Canadiens prospect who had been claimed on waivers by Boston.

"Fergie would destroy Green in record time," Geoffrion would recall in his memoir. "Bam! Bam! Bam! Three straight right crosses and the fight was over. Ted Green was dead meat and for the first time since I became a Canadien, I could say we had a full-time enforcer."

But Ferguson's teammates were aware that his skills went beyond fighting. He could change the tempo of a game with a big hit. Ferguson conceded that the fighting ended up in the headlines but he scored 145 goals in 500 games, including 29 in the 1968–69 season. He had a career-high 52 points that season and added four goals—and 80 penalty minutes—as he won his fourth Cup. He had the winning goal in the last game of the final series against St. Louis. He would retire as a player after winning a fifth Stanley Cup in 1971. He had his most productive playoffs that year with four goals and six assists.

He was known as the heavyweight champion of the NHL and there was a proposal for Ferguson to meet a real boxer, Canadian heavyweight champion George Chuvalo, in a three-round exhibition bout. The idea was quickly rejected by Canadiens general manager Sam Pollock.

Ferguson paved the way for other enforcers, tough players who could contribute in ways other than dropping their gloves. He was the inspiration for Dave (Tiger) Williams, whose 241 NHL goals were overshadowed by his NHL-record 3,966 penalty minutes. Williams recognized Ferguson's contribution by wearing Ferguson's No. 22.

Ferguson was an assistant coach with Team Canada in the 1972 Summit Series and he urged Bobby Clarke to take out Soviet star Valeri Kharlamov. Clarke obliged with a slash which broke Kharlamov's ankle. Ferguson defended the incident later, saying, "that guy is killing us."

He remained involved in hockey as coach and general manager of the New York Rangers and later as GM of the Winnipeg Jets in the WHA and from 1979 on in the NHL. He later worked in the front office with the Ottawa Senators and the San Jose Sharks. He beat prostate cancer in 2005 but the cancer returned and he died on July 14, 2007.

97 How Many Cups Have You Won?

Canadiens coach Toe Blake and legendary Montreal sportswriter Red Fisher once went eight months without speaking to each other.

Blake was upset over something Fisher had written and confronted the reporter in the Montreal Forum before a game.

"I should biff you one," Blake yelled.

Back to the Future

Toe Blake won eight Stanley Cups in 13 seasons before he retired to serve as a consultant. He coached in an era when there were no assistant coaches, no videotape, and no advanced statistics. In fact, teams weren't keeping track of such basic information as hits, blocked shots, and plus-minus figures.

Blake had one vision of the future of the game shortly after he retired and he rejected it out of hand.

Paul Arsenault, who was at the beginning of a long, successful career as a Canadian university coach, went to Oregon to pursue a master's degree and when he returned to Montreal, he met with Canadiens general manager Sam Pollock, who had shown an interest in the college game.

"What did you learn down there?" asked Pollock.

"There's a new thing called videotape," Arsenault replied. "It's like film but you can play it back right away and you can slow it down and you can see where players have made a mistake and where they've done something good and you can point it out to them."

"That's very interesting," said Pollock. "Is there anything else?"

Arsenault explained that researchers had looked into the value of stretching before and after practices. He noted that hockey teams were starting practice sessions by stretching on the ice.

Videotape and stretching are integral parts of hockey today but they seemed foreign in the late 1960s. But Pollock, who was always looking for a way to be a step ahead of the pack, was intrigued by the ideas and he suggested that Arsenault discuss them with Blake, who had assumed the role of a consultant.

Arsenault and Blake met over lunch at the Texan restaurant, a popular spot across the street from the Forum. Blake listened silently as Arsenault made his pitch. He nodded once or twice, thanked the young coach for his input, and returned to the Forum.

"What did you think of the kid's ideas?" Pollock asked.

"Not much," replied Blake. "This videotape thing? I don't have to watch television to tell me that someone screwed up. I've been around this game long enough that I can tell when a guy's screwed up, and the guy knows when he's screwed up."

Blake paused before saying, "And I don't get that stuff about exercising on the ice. What happens if a guy gets a cold from lying on the ice? And can you see me asking Béliveau to do push-ups on the ice? He seems like a nice kid but tell him to come back and see me when he's won eight Stanley Cups."

"A Toe Blake about to lose control was not a comforting sight in those days," Fisher wrote in his memoir *Hockey, Heroes and Me.* "The situation needed a strong and, I hoped, brave response."

Fisher said: "Go ahead, you son of a bitch, I can use the money."

"You're so goddamn cheap, you probably would sue," replied Blake as he stormed out of the room.

The eight-month chill between two proud, stubborn men was finally broken when Fisher's wife, Tilly, and their son, Ian, were riding in a cab that was involved in an accident. Ian was bruised and Tilly broke her shoulder.

The next day, Fisher received a phone call from Blake, who inquired about Fisher's family. The two were back on speaking terms.

While they weren't talking, there was at least one occasion when they did communicate. Fisher and Blake both lived in Montreal's West End and they would get a lift home after games from broadcaster Danny Gallivan.

After a close loss one night, Fisher addressed Gallivan: "Why don't you ask the Hall of Fame coach why he waited so long before pulling the goaltender?"

Blake didn't miss a beat as he replied: "Why don't you ask the hack writer how many Stanley Cups he's won?"

98 Saving Trent McCleary

Hockey can be a violent game but team doctors are rarely placed in a position where they deal with a life-or-death situation.

But that's the position Dr. David Mulder found himself in on January 29, 2000.

It was the Saturday of Super Bowl weekend and the stands were filled with youngsters as the Canadiens played an afternoon game at the Molson Centre. The Canadiens were deadlocked 2–2 with the Philadelphia Flyers when Trent McCleary, a 27-year-old journeyman forward, went down to block a slapshot by Flyers defenceman Chris Therien.

The shot hit McCleary in the throat and fractured his larynx. McCleary staggered to his feet and struggled toward the bench. Dr. Mulder rose from his seat in the stands directly behind the Canadiens bench and made his way to the ice as McCleary collapsed 15 feet away. He was quickly joined by his assistant, Dr. Vincent Lacroix, and by Dr. David Fleiszer, an oncologist who was a top college football player a decade earlier at McGill University.

There was a hush in the arena as the doctors attended to McCleary with a shaken Therien looking on.

"I got all of the shot," said Therien. "It's like the whole thing, the puck, everything, was in slow motion. I could hear him breathing. It sounded like something was stuck in his throat."

Mulder and Fleiszer performed an emergency tracheotomy in the ambulance on the way to Montreal General Hospital.

Mulder said McCleary nearly died on the way to the operating room. When he was asked how close McCleary was to death, Mulder replied: "It was about as close as I think you could come."

Mulder said the injury was similar to those suffered by a driver whose throat hits the steering wheel in a head-on collision.

"It's like drowning in your own blood," said Mulder.

The fractured larynx was only part of McCleary's problem. His right lung collapsed and his heart shifted to the right side of his body.

"That could be just as life-threatening as the airway," Mulder said at a news conference a few days after the incident.

It was the latest in a series of career-threatening injuries for McCleary. On Super Bowl weekend in 1995, he nearly lost an eye when he was hit by Boris Mironov's stick in an AHL game. Earlier in the 1999–2000 season, he suffered a severed tear duct when he was cut by a skate.

McCleary, who was known as one of the most vocal players in the Canadiens locker room, was unable to speak but was able to send a written message of encouragement to his teammates as they prepared to play Carolina the day after he was injured.

The message, delivered by general manager Réjean Houle, read: "Doing great everybody. Here's $500 on the board for the win. Battle hard. I'll be listening. Go Habs! Trent #6."

McCleary met the media a week after the accident and answered questions via a notepad. He underwent several other surgeries and speech rehabilitation before regaining his speech six weeks after the accident.

While there were serious doubts whether he could resume playing, the Canadiens signed him to a one-year contract worth $300,000 prior to the 2000–01 season and he reported to training camp. He played one exhibition game and found that he was gasping for breath midway through a shift. A medical examination revealed that his air passage was 15 percent narrower than before his injury and posed a serious risk to his health.

On September 20, a day he called the toughest in his career, he announced his retirement. McCleary remained with the Canadiens for several years as their Western Hockey League scout.

The incident provided Dr. Mulder with a unique experience. In their haste to get McCleary to the operating room, the operating room staff only had time to cut away his sweater and remove his shoulder pads.

Said Mulder: "I told Trent this was the first time I ever finished an operation and looked up and the patient was wearing skates."

99 The Depth Player

If you want to understand the depth of talent in the Canadiens organization in the 1960s, consider the case of Bob Berry.

Berry was one of Montreal's most versatile athletes while growing up in the suburb of Mount Royal. As a baseball catcher, he was good enough to be offered a contract by the Houston Colt .45s. The University of Kentucky wanted him to play football. But Berry's first love was hockey, and in 1963–64 the Canadiens assigned him to the Peterborough Petes, a junior team affiliate.

Berry had a good start in Peterborough with four goals and three assists in his first 11 games but he was unhappy with the way he was being used.

The Canadiens viewed Berry as an enforcer, a physical player in the style of John Ferguson, who was just beginning his NHL career. Berry saw himself as a scorer and went back home to attend Sir George Williams University, a commuter school with a high-rise campus and a hockey team with no rink. The Canadiens placed Berry on their suspended-player list.

The Georgians became a Canadian college powerhouse with Berry in the lineup but he had few options when he graduated in 1967. He joined the Canadian national team in Winnipeg with an eye on playing in the 1968 Olympic Games. But this was the era of strict amateurism and Berry was ruled ineligible because he had played semipro football for the Quebec Rifles.

Expansion in the NHL offered new opportunities but Berry's rights were controlled by the Canadiens. He made his peace with the team and was assigned to the AHL. The Canadiens were stacked at left wing with Marc Tardif, Dick Duff, and Ferguson, and he only played two games with the Canadiens before he was sold to the Los Angeles Kings in 1970.

The 27-year-old Berry was an immediate hit with the Kings and collected 63 points as a rookie, nine fewer than Calder Trophy winner Gilbert Perreault. That was a team record for a rookie until Luc Robitallle arrived in 1986. Robitaille also would erase Berry's team record of 159 goals for a left winger. His willingness to go to the net in search of rebounds earned Berry the nickname Crease.

In seven seasons with the Kings, Berry had 159 goals and 191 assists for 350 points.

Berry turned to coaching when his playing career ended. He started with Springfield in the AHL and replaced Ron Stewart behind the Kings bench in 1978. After three seasons in L.A., he resigned and replaced Claude Ruel in Montreal in 1981. He guided the Canadiens to a first-place finish but lost to the Quebec Nordiques in the first round of the playoffs. He had a second-place finish in 1982–83 but the Canadiens couldn't get past Buffalo in the playoffs. After a 28–30–5 start in his third season, he was replaced by Jacques Lemaire.

Berry, who later coached the Pittsburgh Penguins and St. Louis Blues, has a place in Canadiens history as the last non-interim coach who wasn't fluently bilingual.

100 Wait 'Til Next Year?

The Canadiens' Stanley Cup drought extended to 22 years with a second-round loss to the Tampa Bay Lightning in the 2015 play-offs, but general manager Marc Bergevin, who is not one to raise expectations, saw reasons to be optimistic as the season came to an end.

His post mortem on the 2014–15 season focused on the positives.

The Canadiens won the Atlantic Division and finished with the second-best overall record in the National Hockey League.

Carey Price established himself as the No. 1 goaltender in the NHL, leading the league in wins, goals-against average, and save percentage. He shared the Jennings Trophy with Chicago's Corey Crawford for fewest goals allowed, and took home both the Vézina and Hart trophies.

P.K. Subban continued his development. Armed with a team-record eight-year, $72 million contract, the 26-year-old Subban was a finalist for the Norris Trophy for the second time in his career.

Bergevin acknowledged that the Canadiens wanted to score more goals, but he and coach Michel Therrien share the belief that there's something beautiful about a 1–0 game—as long as they're on the winning end.

When asked if he had thought about trading for a big center, Bergevin replied: "There aren't any out there. I made a trade last night on my Xbox, but when I called the other general manager this morning, he hung up on me."

Bergevin said the team will continue to rely on the draft and its developmental system to beef up the offence, and there are two prospects who could be in a position to help in a year or two.

Nikita Scherbak is coming off a strong year with the Everett Silvertips in the Western Hockey League. He was a first-round pick in 2014 and could fill the continuing need for right wingers.

But the player who has made the most progress may be Michael McCarron, a first-rounder in 2013. He was drafted as a right winger but was moved to center after he was traded from the London Knights to the Oshawa Generals, and he helped lead the Generals to the Memorial Cup.

McCarron is 6-foot-6 and weighs 225 pounds, 15 fewer pounds than when he was drafted. He shed the excess weight so that he would be quicker on his skates but remains a physical force on the ice.

Bergevin disappointed the many fans who have been waiting to see Alex Galchenyuk playing center on a full-time basis in 2014–15. Bergevin suggested Galchenyuk may never play in the middle. One reason is that Galchenyuk has enjoyed some success at left wing, but the major concern is that the youngster hasn't been able to handle the defensive responsibilities that go with playing center.

Bergevin also disappointed fans who were hoping there might be some money in the cookie jar to entice a free-agent forward. Bergevin got a head start on the free-agent market by signing defenceman Jeff Petry to a six-year, $33 million contract. Petry signed nearly a month before he was in a position to test the market as an unrestricted free agent.

The Canadiens acquired Petry from the Edmonton Oilers at the trading deadline in March, and the expectation was he was just a rental. But Petry said he and his wife were impressed with Montreal and the Canadiens organization and wanted to stay. The Canadiens were equally impressed with how quickly Petry adapted to the team's system and his solid play throughout the playoffs.

The signing reinforced Montreal's determination to stress defence and also helped dispel the idea that Montreal is not an attractive market for free agents. Petry described the Canadiens as a first-class organization and said he felt the team was in a position to challenge for the Stanley Cup in the near future.

If he's right, it won't come a moment too soon.

A Note on Sources

The Internet provides a good starting point for any research today but it's important to be aware that the information is only as good as the source.

Wikipedia, the Hockey Hall of Fame features by Kevin Shea (www.hhof.com), Joe Pelletier's website (www.greatesthockeylegends.com), the Canadiens' historical website (ourhistory.canadiens.com), and YouTube all provided background information on players and events.

The Internet Hockey Database website is an indispensible source for statistical information and *Total Hockey: The Official Encyclopedia of the National Hockey League* was particularly helpful in providing statistics for players in the pre-expansion era.

Stu Cowan, my sports editor at the *Montreal Gazette*, provided invaluable help in tracking down stories from the paper's archives. There were times when I had to go the old-fashioned route and I was grateful that the *Gazette* library allowed me to find stories from the *Montreal Star* and *Montreal Gazette* on microfilm. A special thanks to my editor, Adam Motin, and the other folks at Triumph Books, who brought this project to me. I hope readers have as much fun as I had putting it together.

There were several occasions where there were discrepancies in numbers and other facts and I have tried to use what appeared to be the most reliable sources. I regret any errors which are solely my own while standing behind any opinions I express.

Réjean Houle, former player, GM, and current major domo of the Canadiens alumni, was generous with his help, while Murray Wilson, Mario Tremblay, Scotty Bowman, and Geoff

Molson were among those who offered their thoughts on the Canadiens past and present.

I also owe a special debt to Red Fisher, who provided much-needed guidance early in my career and throughout the succeeding 50 years. His insights into the game can be found throughout the book.

Bibliography

Beddoes, Richard, Stan Fischler, and Ira Gitler. *Hockey: The Story of the World's Fastest Sport*, The Macmillan Company, 1969.

Béliveau, Jean, with Chrys Goyens and Allen Turowetz. *My Life in Hockey*, McClelland & Stewart, 1994.

Benedict, Michael, and D'Arcy Jennish, editors. *Maclean's Canada on Ice*, Viking, 1998.

Diamond, Dan, James Duplacey, Ralph Dinger, Ernie Fitzsimmons, Igor Kuperman, and Eric Zweig, editors. *Total Hockey: The Official Encyclopedia of the National Hockey League*, Total Sports, 2000.

Dryden, Ken. *The Game*, Macmillan Canada, 1983.

Dryden, Steve, and The Hockey News. *The Top 100 NHL Players of All Time*, McClelland & Stewart, 1998.

Ferguson, John, with Stan Fischler and Shirley Fischler. *Thunder and Lightning*, Prentice-Hall Canada, 1989.

Fisher, Red. *Hockey, Heroes and Me*, McClelland & Stewart, 1994.

Geoffrion, Bernard, and Stan Fischler. *Boom Boom: The Life and Times of Bernard Geoffrion*, McGraw-Hill Ryerson, 1993.

Goyens, Chrys, and Allen Turowetz. *Lions in Winter*, McGraw-Hill Ryerson, 1994.

Goyens, Chrys, Allen Turowetz, and Jean-Luc Duguay. *The Montreal Forum: Forever Proud*, Les Editions Effix, 1996.

Goyens, Chrys, and Frank Orr. *Maurice Richard: Reluctant Hero*, Team Power Publishing, 2000.

Hornby, Lance. *Hockey's Greatest Moments*, Key Porter Books, 2004.

Hunter, Douglas. *A Breed Apart: An Illustrated History of Goaltenders*, Viking Press, 1995.

Irvin, Dick. *The Habs*, McClelland & Stewart, 1991.

Irvin, Dick. *My 26 Stanley Cups*. McClelland & Stewart, 2011.

Jennish, D'Arcy. *The Montreal Canadiens: 100 Years of Glory*, Doubleday Books, 2008.

Mahovlich, Ted. *The Big M: The Frank Mahovlich Story*, HarperCollins, 1999.

McKinley, Michael. *Etched in Ice: A Tribute to Hockey's Defining Moments*, GreyStone Books, 1998.

McKinley, Michael. *Hockey Hall of Fame Legends*, Viking, 1993.

Pellerin, Jean-Marie. *Maurice Richard: L'Idole d'un Peuple*, Editions Trustar, 1998.

Robinson, Larry, with Kevin Shea. *The Great Defender: My Hockey Odyssey*, Fenn McClelland & Stewart, 2014.

Robinson, Larry, with Chrys Goyens. *Robinson for the Defence*, McClelland & Stewart, 1989.

Selke, Frank, and Gordon H. Green. *Behind the Cheering*, McClelland and Stewart, 1962.

Sports Illustrated. *The Canadiens Century*, Time Inc. Home Entertainment, 2009.

Sports Illustrated. *The Hockey Book*, Time Inc., Home Entertainment, 2010.